MUSLIMS AND THE THIRD WORLD POLITICS

MUSLIMS
AND
THE THIRD WORLD POLITICS

ATTAR CHAND

Forewords by:
Madhavsinh Solanki
Union Minister of External Affairs

Manikrao Gavit
Member of Parliament (Lok Sabha)

S.Y. Khan
General Secretary, Minority Cell

ANMOL PUBLICATIONS
NEW DELHI (INDIA)

ANMOL PUBLICATIONS
4378/4B, Ansari Road,
Daryaganj, New Delhi-110002.

Muslims and the Third World Politics

ISBN 81-7041-625-6

Distributors in J & K
JAY KAY BOOK HOUSE
Residency Road, Jammu-Tawi

PRINTED IN INDIA

Published by J.L.Kumar for Anmol Publications, New Delhi-110002.
Printed at Mehra Offset Press, Delhi.

Dedicated to

– P.N. Haksar, Former Principal Secretary to the Prime Minister of India

– T.N. Kaul, Former Foreign Secretary, Government of India, and Ambassador to America and the Soviet Union

– H.S. Josh., President, Indian Council of World Affairs, New Delhi

For their patriotic services to the Great Indian Nation and its secular inhabitants.

Attar Chand

FOREWORD – 1

GLOBAL PROBLEMS

We seek understanding and cooperation of our partners from developed countries to help us derive full benefits from our recent liberalisation steps and tide over short-run pressures.

Having introduced far-reaching changes in its economic policies, India envisioned sharply increased interlinkages with the world economy.

We also need an international economic environment which is conducive to ensuring the success of such measures.

Developing countries overall external economic environment remains unfavourable. Many face worsening prospects of trade, resources and advanced technology. The alarming debt situation seriously threatened their "economic liability".

There is a need for comprehensive strategy for all categories of affected countries covering all forms of debt.

On multilateral trade, India wants early, successful and balanced outcome of the Uruguay round of general tariff and trade agreement talks.

We are a serious partner in these negotiations, and we have our own interests to safeguard, that is why we have been insisting on specific and time-bound commitments.

The disarmament and development linkage are visible and now the peace dividend needs to be realised at international level.

Introducing non-economic factors like good governance. Observance of human rights, environment and military expenditure into trade was a disturbing trend.

But today these laudable goals should apply to all countries – developed and developing. What is questionable is the linkage of these issues with development assistance of which the recipients are only the developing countries.

Environmental concerns are fast moving to the top of the world's agenda. These problems cannot be isolated from the general issue of development.

We need to forege a global partnership which simultaneously seeks to protect the environment while addressing the development requirements of the developing countries.

The principal sources of emission of pollutants into the environment lie in the developed countries. These countries bear the main responsibility for combating such pollution.

They provide adequate financial resources and environmentally begin technologies on preferential and non-commercial terms.

Otherwise, it will be difficult for the developing countries to adopt environmentally safe and desirable technologies.

The non-aligned movement continued to be relevant though it has to change emphasis from time to time depending on the problems facing the world.

At present, the developing countries are facing major problems in the economic field with rising debt burand NAM has to focus its efforts to find solutions to these issues.

The world is losing interest in the movement. At the recent NAM ministerial level meeting at Accra, Ghana even non-NAM members took it seriously.

September 27, 1991
United Nations
New York

Madhavsinh Solanki
Union Minister of External Affairs
New Delhi.

FOREWORD – 2

RELIEF FOR A MINORITY

If our country had made adequate record of its refugee rehabilitation operations in 1947, it could have been the standard manual for the world including the Kurdish refugees. It is now ironic to recall that the West European nations preferred a Japanese Woman academic for the post of UN High Comissioner for Refugees over an Indian with earlier experience in the field, against the better judgement of UN Secretary General.

Even as western powers grapple with the Kurdish refugee problem, a few hundred casualties take place everyday. The present decision of the Bush administration is likely to have far-reaching consequences in future international relations, since it would constitute a precedent for nations to intervene in the internal affairs of other nations.

While countries like India cannot be a party to American manoeuvrings, they have to uphold the wholesome principle that there should be no outside interference in Iraq's internal affairs. Two countries to which the plea for self-restraint should be particularly addressed are Iran and Turkey because of the contacts they are maintaining with the southern and northern insurgents. If they have humanitarian concerns, these should be addressed through UN agencies or the International Red Cross. It will be entirely appropriate for these neighbours, as well as the rest of the international community, to avoid excessive use of force and to desist from employing horror weapons. I call on the United Nations to immediately help these people. Any delay in help means leaving these people to their death and this is inhuman.

October 2, 1991
New Delhi.

Manikrao V. Gavit
Member of Parliament (Lok Sabha)
New Delhi.

FOREWORD – 3

THE MUSLIM MINORITY

The Muslim minority (Kurds) have no friends except the mountains. They are people who have been exploited by the outside powers. But at no time has their suffering been greater at present.

With some 25 million people spread across the territories of five states, this Muslim minority is the largest nation on earth that has yet to win the right of self-determination. By all the usual creteria, they are a separate and unique people: they have their own language, customs literature and folklore and an awareness of their distinct origin and history. Yet in the states that they inhabit their existence as a nation is, to greater or lesser extent, denied.

In the outside world, the Kurds have failed to insert the idea of their distinct identity into the international consciousness as have, say, the Palestinian Arabs. "They don't speak enough about the Kurds," said the late Kurdish leader Abdul Rahman Qassemlou, "because we have never taken any hostages, never hijacked a plane. But I am proud of this." However noble the sentiment, Qassemlou's explanation only tells half the story. For if it is true that the Muslim minority has no friends, it is also true that Kurds have been their own worst enemies. They have allowed themselves to be used as the cat's paws of competing regional states and of the world powers that in the twentieth century have sought to dominate the affairs of the West Asia and the Gulf region.

The Kurdish movement in Iraq has accepted the help of successive regimes, in Iran, even as those regimes were oppressing their fellow Kurds across the border. The same has happened in reverse. Kurdish rebels in Turkey have been accepted the help of the Iraqi President Saddam Hussein, We, in India want a place for the Kurds under the sky.

September 21, 1991
Bombay.

S.Y. Khan (S.E.M.)
General Secretary, Minority Cell,
Maharashtra Pradesh Congress
Committee, Bombay.

PREFACE

To date, the ethnic conflicts between the muslim minority (the Kurds) and the nation governments have continued without reaching a satisfactory solution for either party. The situation of the Kurds in each of these countries remains as follows.[1]

Turkey

After the military coup of September 1980 in Turkey the Kurdish situation was considerably aggrevated. The Kurds continue to be reduced to 'non-legal existence'. Turkish law does not recognize the existence of these people as a distinct ethnic group. They are known as 'mountain Turks'. Most of the Kurdish leaders are in prison. However the Kurdish Turkish guerrillas have continued to launch attacks on the Turkish civilian population as a political strategy to gain international attention and the Turkish government has intensified its commando operations as a retaliation against them.

Iran

Kurdish resurgence became widespread around the country in response to the Shite domination. During the 1980s the new regime continued to apply to the tribals and other minorities, including the Kurds, discriminatory policies and a strong Persian chauvinism. With the help offered to the Iraqi Kurds, the government of Teheran could control its own Kurds for a while. None the less, the Kurdish resistance is being felt to date and it has been repressed ironically by the same revolutionary guards that are helping the Kurdish Iraqis.

Syria

In the 1980s the Ba'athist Syrian government reduced the repression against their Kurd minority. Relations between the two groups have improved considerably. However, the Syrian government has not officially recognised the existence of the Kurds as a national group and the latter have not accepted the policy of Arab-Syrian nationalism. It is known that the Syrian government is supplying the

Kurd guerrillas of Iraq with weapons through Iran and it has given sanctuary to the Kurdish Turk in the past few years.

Iraq

The government of Iraq is the only one that has offered constitutional autonomy to the Kurdistan region. It has officially recognised the national right of the Kurds through an antonomous law for Kurdistan in 1979. However, this law of autonomy was not accepted by the main Kurdish political organisations because it did not include the whole region of Kurdistan, and most of the local powers were under the control of the central government. In 1984 Baghdad once again reiterated its offer of autonomy for Kurdistan. However, the Kurdish rebels seem to have learned not to believe in the government's promises any longer and with Iranian help continue to implement the separatist movement on the northern front. The Iraqi government has launched strong repressive policies such as demolishing villages and assembling their inhabitants in enclosed camps.

The basic conditions for the development of a separatist movement are present in the Kurdish reality. Mainly, the Kurds are self-conscious of their ethnic identity (bound by language and customs) that distinguish them from other nationalities of the region (primordial factors). An unequal centre-periphery relationship underscores systematic exploitation, discrimination and repression of the Kurds (secondary factors). The formation of a new Kurdish elite (petty bourgeose and an intelligentsia) has permitted the creation of an organisation capable of co-ordinating the movement and linking them to outside groups. However, the four nations in which the Kurds have lived are quite dissimilar and the organisation, as well as length and intensity of Kurdish separatism, have varied accordingly. As we have seen, several characteristics have weakened their movement, especially lack of unity independently and within each of the four countries there has been an internal political disunity. Neither has there been a consensus among the Kurds regarding their demands and their political aspi- rations. Moreover, there have been setbacks to the liberation struggle due to a series of political mistakes committed by the Kurdish leaders.

In spite of this, there have been some positive developments. The Kurds have increased their self-consciousness as an ethnic community and have also moved from a communal organisation to an associational one. All of this has resulted in a measure of maturity that has permitted some degree of unification of the separatist movement. The domestic ethnic conflict. The Kurdish movement has received an instrumental intervention[2] from governments of neighbouring states that considered the ethnic conflict as a good opportunity to promote their foreign interest. Often, the Kurds have mismanaged these foreign connections or have been deceived outright by their erstwhile foreign collaborators to the detriment of the Kurdish cause for self-determination.[3]

An agreement to ceasefire has been signed between Iraqi authorities and Kurdish leaders ending a round of hostilities which broke out last Saturday, a spokesperson for the United Nations High Commissioner for Refugees (UNHCR) said in Geneva, on October 11, 1991. Under delegates in northern Iraqi city of Suleimaniyah told *Kuna* that the ceasefire appeared to be holding.

Sources from Suleimaniyah surgical hospital indicated around 500 minor surgical procedures and 100 serious ones, including 70 women and children. The hospital also reported 45 civilian deaths.

UNHCR was unable to confirm the exact number of Kurdish refugees fleeing the fighting, but initial estimates by the organisation indicated that some 10,000 persons could have fled the regions on Kafri and Kalar and a large concentration of some 20,000 is expected around Sayed Sadik.

Meanwhile, the International Committee of the Red Cross (ICRC) expressed "deep concern" about the consequences of the heavy fighting taking place in Iraqi Kurdistan.

The ICRC "urgently called" on all parties involved to care for the wounded, to respect the lives and the physical and mental integrity of captured persons, and to spare and protect the civilian population.

REFERENCES

1. L.D. Aguado. *The National Liberation of the Kurds in the Middle East.* London, 1990.
2. *See* A. Suhrke *et al.* Ethnic Conflict and International Relations. *Plural Societies* 9(4) Winter 1978, p.3.
3. Aguado. *op. cit.*

ACKNOWLEDGEMENTS

I have always believed in the importance of historical record. For a realistic study of contemporary events, necessarily incurs a long list of thinkers and academies to whome I must express my sincere gratitude. This is one of the most pleasant part of my foremost duties I have to perform. Therefore, the present study could not have reached fruition without the encouragement of my well-wishers, who suggested sundry improvements and provided nourishing guidance and inspiration. I am much obliged to my fellow writers, journalists, academicians and professors whose writings I have consulted and taken notes, in parts or in full, in writing this book of global interest.

My grateful thanks to K. Subrahmanyam (Former Director, IDSA); Air Commodore Jasjit Singh (Director, IDSA); Muhammad Muslin (C.W. Past College of Long Island University); Augustus Richard Norton (International Peace Academy, New York; F.J. Khergamvala (Representative of the Hindu, Madras, in the Arab World); Susheel Raj (Dubai, UAE); Aprajita Sikri (New York); Prof. K.P. Mishra (JNU), V.D. Chopra (Patriot); K.R. Narayanan (Former Ambassador to the US and China and Former Union Minister of Foreign Affairs, New Delhi); Nishi Widge (London); Mohammed Aslam (The Kaleej Times, Dubai); Harish McDonald (Far Eastern Economic Review); Air Commodore Pat Singh (IDSA, New Delhi); Prof. V.P. Dutt (Former Pro-Vice-Chancellor, Delhi University and Members of Parliament); Prof. K.R. Sharma (Delhi University); S.N. Yadav (Secretary, FICCI); Y.P. Srivastava, Secretary, Joint Business Councils, FICCI, New Delhi); M.A. Adelman (Professor Emeritus, the Massachusettes Institute of Technology, USA); Prof. K.R. Singh (JNU); J.P. Sharma (Delhi University); Dr. R.P. Dua, Dr. Harjinder Singh; Dr. Parmanand; Dr. Z.M. Qureshi; Harmohinder Singh (Delhi University); Dr. P.K. Mishra (Sambalpur University, Orissa), Dr. Dharampal (General Secretary, Indian Society for Afro-Asian Studies, New Delhi); and Dr. I.P. Singh (I.F.S. Retd.).

ATTAR CHAND

CONTENTS

1

INTRODUCTION

Conflicts between majorities and minorities, between the nationalities within a country, and between those in different countries, are worldwide phenomena that are causing a resurgence in the study of nationality problems in the social sciences. The problems of ethnic minorities and their inherent potentials for conflict are themselves important factors in the numerous international conflicts that take place against the backdrop of national conflicts. Since national minorities can be used or exploited for or against a country's interests, in multinational states the stability of a country quite often depends on the system of relations woven among its different peoples.

This study, which is concerned specifically with Kurds, belongs in the general classification of works dealing with the analysis and documentation of minority problems. Accordingly, it will be useful first to illuminate the global character of the nationality problem on the basis of a few examples. The definition of a few terms (general terms as well as specifically Arabic terminology) will help to give a better picture of the nuances of the nationality question, with special reference to the West Asian situation.

Nationality problems and conflicts exist today in most countries. Whereas larger ethnic minorities are often able to defend themselves politically and, not infrequently, militarily against oppression, exploitation, and assimilation, the minor rationalities (such as the Indians of South America) are often exterminated, their cultures destroyed, their lands confiscated, and their strength sapped by disease, hunger, persecution, and illiteracy. According to UN estimates, 200 million hunters and gatherers are today faced with annihilation through hunger, disease, and war. And not only do the governments of the native countries contribute to this annihilation, but so also do the multinational concerns and local Christian missions. This is equally true of developed countries – such as the United States, the Soviet Union, Canada, Australia, New Zealand and Third World countries.

For example, in North America, and in most of the South and Central American countries in which the Indian population makes up less than 5 percent of the total population, Indians live on reservations as a national minority, often with restricted rights. In Brazil, for example, according to the "law for Indians," Indians are regarded as legally non-responsible, and are therefore subject to Brazilian guardianship law.

Historically, Indian peoples have been violently exterminated in the Americas when they have stood in the way of the extraction of raw materials, construction of highways, or other projects. It is no different on other continents. For example–

In 1967 the Australian aborigines solemnly obtained their civil rights in their own country – and in addition access to alcohol – under UN pressure. For them, alcohol has become a status symbol of equality with the whites. Since then, more and more of them are to be found hanging about in a drunken stupor on the outskirts of cities. They are losing all points of reference to the world about them, and have proved unable to cope with the other "fifths" of the white man, namely tuberculosis, measles, prostitution, venereal diseases, and money, competitiveness, and greed. Thus the aborigines, invested with their "civil rights", are now threatened by degeneration, the total forgetting of the skills that were necessary for survival, and indeed, a loss of instinct pure and simple. Unable to adapt to that which has never before occurred, to the new, to the intelligible, to the never practiced, these vestigial Stone Age groups are suspended between two worlds, and their creative capacities are stifled and paralyzed. They opt for resignation and so are lost.

The Kurds were dispersed arbitrarily into several countries, where they have been subject to severe persecution and cultural oppression. More than 150,000 Papuans have been killed since 1967 when the Suharto regime took power. The gypsies, who have lived for more than a century in the Netherlands, have neither the right to determine their own lifestyle nor guarantees that they remain permanently in that country. The Maori of New Zealand and the aborigines of Australia had their land violently taken from them on a mass scale. And Germany has its own nationality problem of gypsies and foreign workers; Bonn has yet to make full restitution for the crimes committed against them during the National Socialist (Nazi) era. The litany goes on and on.

In the Soviet Union, the thesis of the "convergence and fusion of the nations under socialism" produced a policy of denationalization, putting the non Russian nationalities under heavy pressure. The principle means used were:

- providing moral, political, material, and economic advantages to the Russified while discriminating against nationality conscious non-Russians;
- the "internationalization" of national cultures through the administratively forced spread of the Russian language; and
- an "international exchange of cadres" and migration of Russians, with "internationalization" usually meaning "Russification".

Just recently, the Soviet nationalities have started to fight openly for their national rights, leading the Soviet Union into a new phase of awakening nationalities consciousness.

In the late seventies, Karoly, a top-level Rumanian Communist Party official of Hungarian origin, wrote to the Bucharest party leadership that the "tendency to force the assimilation of the national minorities living in Rumania is obvious and undeniable." In Hungary, the gypsies have not been recognized as an independent nationality since 1961 and are therefore also subject to the threat of forced assimilation.

Major nationality problems also exist for China's Asian neighbours. In Burma, the Shan and Karens have been carrying on a struggle for autonomy for years. The Burmese government, which has engaged itself militarily against these peoples, has refused them this right. The situation is not much different among the mountain tribes in Thailand, who are often held by opium traders in a state of slave-like depence. The mountain tribes were not granted Thai citizenship until 1974; previously they were regarded as Communists or "aliens", India, the country with the greatest number of ethnic minorities, has deprived its minorities of their means of subsistence by confiscating their land and expelling them, and essentially threatening them with extinction. The resistance of the mountain people in Laos and

Vietnam to resettlement projects is combated by limitary means, including the use of napalm and poison gas. The minorities in the Philippines, i.e., those who do not belong to the dominant Malaysian race, have had their living space constricted and are continually engaged in bloody skirmishes with government troops. And in Indonesia where there are about 30 different ethnic groups, only "Indonesians," no national minorities, exist officially "Bahasa Indonesia" (the Indonesian Language in the schools since independence, and cultural autonomy is suppressed.

These examples are graphic evidence that ethnic minorities are subjected to discrimination, oppression, and persecution in the East and West as well as in third-world countries, and that so far not even the beginning of a solution has been found to the minority problem.

There was only sparse information in the sixties and seventies minorities in China and their actual situation. Official Chinese comments were usually stereotyped: "the working peoples of the different nationalities have come masters of their land and have achieved total political emancipation," or "all the nationalities of China are united as never before". Problems were rately even alluded to in official descriptions. Since very little material was available and the Chinese authorities painted a picture of "unison and harmony", the impression was orchestrated that China was conducting an exemplary nationality policy.

However, since 1978 the Chinese leadership has openly admitted that there were very few changes, if any, in the conditions in minority regions for quite some time and down to the late seventies, and that during the Cultural Revolution there were incidents of violent devastation and severe oppression in minority regions. The consequences were not only chronic economic and cultural backwardness but also a large measure of alienation between the Han (China's largest nationality, generally known as Chinese) and the ethnic minorities.

A closer examination of the term "national minority" shows that the nationality problem is much more complex than is evident from the above description. The term "minority" embraces a group of people who differ in a number of distinctive specific characteristics from the rest of the population of a country whose territory they inhabit. These characteristics may derive from race, language, religion, customs, morals, traditions, dress, social organization, etc. In any case they will be common to all the members of such a group, and make it relatively easy to distinguish them from other groups. Both objective factors, such as the specific relation between the minority and the majority, and subjective in the definition of the term. "Minority" is primarily understood to be a group that does not share the ethnic or national characteristics of a majority of the population. The existence of different categories of minorities creates an additional difficulty in formulating a precise and comprehensive definition. Different groups include:

A basic distinction must be drawn between groups whose territorial habitat is also the hearland of their culture (e.g., Tamils in India, aborigines in Australia, and Marois in New Zealand) and those whose heartland (linguistically, culturally, and usually also politically) is located in another country to which they immigrated (e.g., Germans in the Soviet Union, Chinese in Southest Asia), as well as to groups who were brought forcibly to another place (e.g., Negroes in the United States). Furthermore, it is necessary to distinguish between scoio-economically more developed peoples who have immigrated into areas of less developed peoples, and those who have acquired those areas through conquest and subsequently subjugated or expelled the autochthonous population (e.g., as did Europeans on the North American continent, in South Africa, in Australia, and in New Zealand), and immigration without conquest or subjugation (Chinese and Indians in Southeast Asia, Germans in Rumania).

Most national minorities use a language that is different from that of the majority. But the particularity of language is not crucial to the designation "national minority". For instance, the Negroes in the United States or the Hui in China speak the same language as the majority population. Other groups may speak their own language without considering themselves a separate nationality and thus are only a linguistic, not a national minority (e.g., the Cantonese and the Hakka in China). There are also religious minorities who have been conceded the status of a nationality in certain countries on the basis of their particular cultural – although not necessarily racial or linguistic – development (e.g., the Moslem, nationality group in Yugoslavia and Hui in China).

There are minority groups who inhabit a clear-cut territory (e.g., the Bretons in France, the Naga in India, the Buriats in the Soviet

Union), and groups who live scattered over a vast area (Indians in East Africa; Jews and Rom throughout Europe). There are groups who live in border areas (Hungarians in Yugoslavia, Malaysians in Thailand, Kirgiz in China), and groups whose territory is an enclave within the territory of the majority population (various Indian groups in South America, the Yi and She in China).

Different nationalities represent differing stages of development, although today the tendency is increasingly toward convergence. Minorities that numerically are quite large (such as the Ukrainians in the Soviet Union or the Erytrians in Ethiopia) and whose socio-economic development is at a level with that of the majority are often a politically weightier factor than, say, marginal groups that are still at the "hunter and gatherer" stage and are numerically of minor importance.

The apartheid policy in South Africa, for instance, shows that a numerical minority (the whites) can quite easily constitute a political majority. In English, therefore, the term minority is also construed to mean "non-dominant group". The minority will then be a political minority, although representing the majority of the population.

The complexity of defining minorities, as well as the complexity of the nationality, question in general, should be evident from the above delineations. This is compounded by the context in which the nationality question first arose in a particular country. Thus, (among other categories) there are:

- nationalit states that were formed over the course of history through the incorporation of several major nationalities and that have by and large forged relations of equality among the different nationalities (e.g., Switzerland, Yugoslavia);
- multiethnic states created by the territorial borders drawn by colonial powers without consideration for ethnic boundaries, and in which subgroups of different nationalities live (most of the countries of Africa);
- multiethnic states formed by the territorial expansion of the largest nationality, usually through conquests (Russia and China are examples of this type);
- multiethnic states in which immigrants in modern times have subjugated the autochthonous population and have

thereby become the dominant ethnic group in the state (for example, Australia, North America, South Africa); and

– states that have become multinational states through peaceful immigration (as in Malaysia and Indonesia).

In western social sciences, "national minority" is generally construed to mean an ethnic group that is in principle an integral part of the larger society, but that does not actually "participate to an equal degree in the enjoyment of social goods as do the other members of that society". The term could refer to situations in which "a portion of the state's population is permanently and decisively prevented from participating in the democratizing process and in the exercise of civil rights". Real equality could be achieved only through the abandonment of ethnic distinctiveness, i.e., through assimilation.

Discrimination or hostile tensions between minority and majority are thus declared to be a defining characteristic of a minority. But this definition, which has its origins in the conditions of the modern nation-states of Europe, seems to be correct neither extensionally or intentionally. It describes a national minority in purely negative terms and, moreover, as a group containing an internal contradiction that can only be resolved through the minority concerned abandoning its identity. It assumes a priori that the minority problem is basically insoluble without the elimination of the minority. The logical implication would be that the problem can ultimately be solved only through the assimilation of the minority, through expulsion, or by redrawing borders. A balanced coexistence and the equal participation of ethnic minorities as equals in the democratic process, the right of self-administration in the form of autonomy, and aid in socio-economic development while still promoting the preservation of ethnic identity are thus all declared impossible. The above definition presumes that (a) most (but not all) ethnic minorities in control of the state; and (b) most minorities see themselves as objectively disadvantaged despite equal rights (thus their language cannot become an official language in the state, they are subject to alienation, or their special interests are only conditionally met). However, it does not necessarily follow from (b) that they are in fact discriminated against in every case, and that therefore all minorities are in roughly the same situation.

If we attempt to classify the minority nationalities in West Asia, we find that is a multinational state formed from the territorial expansion of the largest nationality (Muslims) and from the fusion between the Muslims and different peoples over the course of history. The minority nationalities today include autochthonous and immigrant groups, national and religious groups, groups living on a clearly circumscribed territory, as well as groups living dispersed over a large area, groups living in border regions, and groups constituting enclaves within the territory. There were (and still are) major differences as to the level of socio-economic development as well: some of these minorities were still at the level of "primitive society", they were hunters and gatherers, while others were slave-holders, liege-lords, or following feudal structures. The differences required – and continue to require – a nationality policy that takes into account the distinctive features of each minority. This complex composition of Kurdish minority groups thus calls for a more differentiated approach to the minority problem than that which would be adequate for studying countries with a less complex nationality structure.

This book owes its origins to the wish to make my present research on Kurdish Muslim nationality accessible to Arab readers. This is original study on nationality policy of Iraq and other countries. Since the vastness of the project proved to be prohibitive to the production of an Arabic edition, however, the author and publisher agreed instead to publish a volume on some of the current and key problems of the nationality question in West Asia. This meant that most of the material on other nationalities had to be dropped from this edition; it is available to the interested reader in the above mentioned book which, however, is available only in English.

A proposal by western nations to create a United Nations administered 'safe haven' inside Iraq along its borders with Iran and Turkey and Kurds fleeing Baghdad's repression has raked up a major controversy with several diplomats saying that the action could set a dangerous precedent for the future. The council discussed the idea informally on Monday and diplomats said Britain is trying to concretise the idea and is expected to present it to the Council members.

Through the proposal is being vehemently opposed in the Council by several member states, diplomats said a resolution incorporating the idea would surely be carried as western nations could easily muster nine votes needed in the 15-member council for such a resolution to be adopted.

China, the only member who could veto the proposal, is unlikely to vote against and may only abstain.

Coming out of the consultations, diplomats refused to commit themselves saying they were awaiting instructions from their capitals.

In recent days, the United States has been lobbying in capitals before presenting a proposal in the Council. Several questions remained unanswered including how the area would be administered and for how long. Fears are, however, being expressed that if the proposal is accepted, it might in effect mean carving out of a separate territory. For, Kurds once they get settled there are likely to resist any attempt to hand it back to Iraq.

Though it was being explained that the area would be administered by the civilian force, a senior diplomat said that it is mostly likely to be a police force. After all some agency would be needed to maintain order in the area.

UN Secretary Javier Perez De Cuellar told US President George Bush he had received "a very clear rejection" on May 9, 1991 from Baghdad on a US-backed proposal for a UN police force in northern Iraq.

Perez de Cuellar, meeting with the President on a range of post-war issues, and he hasn't made up his own ming on the proposal.

US officials have expressed support for a British proposal for UN police force in help protect displace Kurds in northern Iraq. Now that the last American troops have left southern Iraq.

Meanwhile US troops today completed their pull out from the south of Iraq where a demilitarised zone will be set up under the control of 1,440 United Nations peacekeepers.

Does John Galbraith feel there is any substance to George Bush's "New World Order"?

No I do not, when Mr. Bush talks about the New World Order he is making speeches. Rather than talking about anything very substantial Mr. Bush is somebody who very much considers a speech a substitute for action. I do not see any reality lying behind George Bush's New World Order, frankly. He practiced it a little bit in the

West Asia and not without any great success. We had a war there but Saddam Hussain is still in power. And I read in the paper he still the possibility of a nuclear weapon. The problem of getting a peace conference is still as difficult as ever. I do not see any great brilliant New World Order. There are many things I would like to see as part of the New World Order but I do not see them on Mr. Bush's agenda.[1]

Whatever the nature and content of President Bush's New World Order for the rest of the world, it means Pax Americana for the Gulf. The Americans have made it clear that the USSR, the UN or NAM can play a role only by their courtesy. The Gulf Sheikhdoms are happy with this arrangement Iraq is not of the game and Iran cannot long resist American power in the Gulf. It is trying to build bridges with the US. The only possible counterweight could have been the Soviet Union but it cannot be so due to its weakness at present and in the foreseable future. What will this Pax Americana mean? Militarily, it will mean a US sponsored multinational Arab force with a strong off-shore US presence capable of rapid deployment. Politically, it will imply gradual progress towards democracy allowing the Sheikhs enough time and opportunity for adjustment. In foreign policy, it will result in the strengthening of the Gulf Cooperation Council (GCC) with the addition of Iraq and Iran at an appropriate time with adequate safeguards (arms limitation) against their domination of the other members. Economically, it will mean an oil regime which will keep prices under control and preference for the US and its allies in trade development projects etc. How India should attain its appropriate niche in this framework commensurate with its geopolitical position, economic potential, etc. is an exercise which brooks no delay.[2]

President George Bush has sketched the broad outlines of his much-talked-about New World Order in which, he says, "we must work with others, but we must also be a *leader*".

In the preface to the "National security strategy of the US" released in Washington, on August 14, 1991 he, however, said "the new world order is not a fact – it is an aspiration – and an opportunity".

"We have within our grasp an extraordinary possibility that few generations have enjoyed – to build a new international system in accordance with our own values and ideals, as old patterns and certainties crumble around us", he added.

He hoped that history would record that the Gulf crisis was the crucible of new world order.

President Bush said, "it is up to our generation in America and the world – to bring these extraordinary possibilities in fruition. And in doing this, American leadership is indispensable. That is our challenge".

Mr. Bush said, "in the Gulf we caught a glimmer of a better future a new world community brought together by a growing consensus that force cannot be used to settle disputes and that when that consensus is broken, the world will respond".

"In the Gulf, we saw the United Nations playing the role dreamed of by its founders, with the world's leading nations orchestrating and sanctioning collective action against aggression. But we remain in a period of transition, the old has been swept away, the new not yet fully in place", he added.

Referring to the daunting problems of reforms in Eastern Europe and the Soviet Union, trade disputes, burden-sharing debates among the industrial democracies and turmoil and dangers in the development of the world he said "yet, the Gulf crisis showed what the world community is now capable of and in the very act of meeting that challenge the world community strengthened itself".

Danielle Mitterrand, wife of the French President has always been deeply committed to the cause of human rights. Often the positions adopted by France's First Lady went against the real politik practised by the French State. She had cried out against human rights abuses in Central America, South America and in other African States where France has a "special interest". She has vociferously denounced western supported dictatorships and as the president of a human rights organisation called "France Libertes" waged a ceaseless campaign to help the victims of social ostraction – those suffering from AIDS or other social handicaps.

But the cause for which Mrs. Mitterrand has given herself to heart and sould is that of the Kurdish people. A few years ago, the organisation helped set up the Kurdish institute in Paris.

"This is the only place where their history, their collective memory, their archieves can be stored," Mrs. Mitterrand said in a recent interview. The Kurds are a hunted people. We, the former colonising powers have made promises in the past which we have failed to keep. Through the Kurdish institute we have hoped to promote awareness of the problems of the Kurdish people – a Nation without a State, so I have been writing about them, testifying before international human rights bodies, including the US Congres "human rights committees on how the Kurds have been persecuted over the centuries".

Kendal Nezan, the director of the institute, feels Danielle Mitterrand is one of the few personalities who have understood the agony and the desperation of the Kurdish people.

Asked how many Kurdish refugees had now fled Iraq, Nezan said "approximately two million. This exodus is so huge because the Iraqi Government has systematically razed Kurdish Villages to the ground. The population was interned in camps near large towns. Had they been dispersed in the countryside there might not have been so much panic. But concentrated as they were in camps, the number of victims under Iraqi shelling was very high. When the Iraqi forces began their offensive against the Kurds on March 27, 1991 and when it became clear that the United States would not help them or intervene on their behalf, they just picked up whatever came to hand and began the long march to neighbouring countries".

Asked how he interpreted this reaction on the part of the United States, Kendal Nezan said: certain members of the Allied Forces were not at all happy with the Kurdish and Shiite rebellion in post war Iraq. In particular the Turks. Turgut Ozal promised Turkish cooperation in the Gulf was on condition that the Kurdish question not be raised. On March 27, 1991 our institute held a seminar in the American Senate. Normally, I have always had easy access to the US under secretary for human rights. But this time the US Government absolutely refused to speak to US. They did not wish to displease Turkey.

"And then things in the Middle East are never as they seem on the surface. The Saudis are dead set against the removal of Saddam. The Sunnis are a minority in Iraq. It would not suit King Fahd if a democratic regime is started in Iraq. And since the West cares more about protecting Saudi and Kuwaiti oil than it does about the Kurds, they agreed to allows the Sunni regime to continue to wield power in Baghdad."

Asked about the concept of "humanitarian interference" proposed by France, by which help is sent to a distress or tyrannised people. Mr. Kendal said, that it could act as an antidote to the old concept of sovereignty where a despotic ruler could perpetrate the most horrific crimes against his own people without a murmur from the international community. "But other legal instruments are needed to further change this concept of non-interference in a country's internal affairs. For the moment the French proposal of humanitarian interference was a life save for the United Nations, it has allowed most Western nations and particularly the Americans to soothe their conscience. But the French suggestion does not resolve the problems; the return of the refugees to their homes, and the respect and recognition of their political rights. If the international community stops in midrack, then the French concept will have to come up again and again as an after sales service to massacres committed against an innocent people.[3]

TRAVELLING through the Kurdish areas of Turkey explained why President Tusgut Ozal was making such a big deal of the Kurdish exodus. A fresh influx of a few million additional Kurds was obviously not something the Turkish Government contemplated with any degree of relish. More Kurds meant more problems. Already, the eastern portion of the country was difficult, almost impossible, to administer and any growth in the size of the disaffected Kurdish population could mean civil war here. Consequently, the Turkish government primarily the United States to intervene and ensure that Iraqi Kurds did not spill over in large numbers into Turkey. The United States, on the other hand, had suddenly declared that it did not want to intervene in the internal affairs of *Iraq and too bad the Kurds were getting massacred*. The Turkish Government was indignant at the way of West was trying to wash its hands off the entire matter and leaving Turkey holding the metaphorical baby. It it was stalemate at the level of international diplomacy it was worse at the ground level for the million-off Kurds who were trying to cross into Turkey. Just how had things were was clear once we approached the border. A few miles before the town of Uludere, we learnt from a Gendarmerie outpost that the nearest Kurdish refugee camp could be reached by turning into the next side road, once off the highway, we bumped 12 kilometers over aboninable roads to reach a wide point of the valley where hundreds of trucks, cars and tractors were parked. The camp was deeper into the mountain range and there was no permanent road. Army bulldozers had cut away the mountain side to prepare a temporary mud track wide enough to allow a large truck. The Turkish Army officer in charge checked our IDs and said we would have to trek on foot to the camp site. He would not allow our vehicle. Only a few trucks and tractors towing trailers laden with relief supplies were being allowed up. Soldiers were busy chasing away The hundreds of people milling around the beginning of the track.The only way people could get to the camp site was through this track which marked a natural entry to the higher mountains beyond. For, the valley walls at this point were incredibly steep, barely tolerable for the herds of mountain goat grazing on the hillsides. The Turkish Army had thus turned the camp site into a vast prison camp – no unauthorised person could get in or get out. It was trek into nightmare. A steep climb of about thousand feet brought us to another valley of even higher mountains rising laterally from the one we had left. We walked for about 4 kilometers till we came to another much bigger Army camp. This was still the floor of the valley and it was dotted with camouflage tents. Army trucks and one helipad. From here it was a longer, incredible climb up a steep mountainside. The trailers carrying food were literally being attacked by the hungry Kurds. And there were thousands of them. To control the mobs, soldiers were using their rifle butts mercilessly – at times they even firing in the air to scare the mobs. But nothing can deter the hungry. There old men, children, beautiful young women and in injured – all carrying sackfuls of bread and trekking back to their makeshift camp a couple of thousand feet higher up.[4]

Those scenes have since become famous; on the covers of Time and Newsweek and on the screens of every major TV network. But the sheer horrow of that wretched camp of a few lakh Kurds on the barren mountain-side on the Turkish-Iraqi border was beyond the cameras and the reporters' notebooks. Evening was falling, the air was a freezing cold and the snow on the mountain separating Iraq and Turkey and turned pink as if tinged with blood. Every few minutes rifle shots could be heard across the valley. My white-faced interpreter said that the soldiers were shotting the warn the thousands of *Kurds waiting on the Iraqi side of the border*. The Turkish government was desperately trying to keep the Kurds at bay. They first wanted the United States and other Western countries to commit billions of dollars worth aid and to promise that the Kurds would be returned to Iraq. Until then, the families could freeze. Hundreds were dying on the mountain top, unable to break through the iron screen drawn out by the Turkish soldiers, the refugees told us. I met a Kurd, who lived in the town of Kirkuk. He had left with his wife and children and after trecking for days deeper into the mountains and had crossed across the border along with thousands of others. His youngest daughter died in the crossing; another daughter was lost; two sons and one daughter survived. He took me to see them. His wife could peak English like him. She was a school teacher and he a government engineer. Now they were a faceless family among a thousand other. To get food and water, the husband had trekked down and up the mountainside twice today. He was exhausted but happy. His children had eaten after five days. It suddenly occurred to me that I could have been in his place. It was only that my history and circumstances were different. He was a man without a country, only a little more securely placed than the goats that roam the hill-side. I have brought with me a box of English chocolates and I offered a few to his children. And within seconds I was surrounded by a whole horde of children. There were hundreds of them and clawing for the chololates; my shirt was ripped, my hands clawed by desperate little fingers. When the box vanished from my hands I do not know but I was somehow pulled free by a couple of brawny Kurds. The children were screaming. It was getting dark very rapidly and it was time for the meuzzin's call. But here there was nobody to offer even a requiem. I was among nobody's people.[5]

For the Arab tribes people of the concrete farming villages in the south of the allied security zone, the "safe haven" in northern Iraq has already turned into what President Bush vowed it would never be, a virtual Kurdish enclave. Looting and Kurdish threats of massacre have sent Arabs fleeing with bed-steads, ironmongery and children; a dozen Arab townships are now almost completely deserted. Dust rises from the broad wheat-fields beside the road to Baghdad as herds of sheep, goats and cows are driven sough by Arab shepherds on donkeys and mules. Kurdish leaders are unrepentant about the people they see as Arab colonists. The Arabs were settled there by Saddam Hussain. Now they are leaving. The land is pirs, said Hussain Sinjari, leader of Jalal Talabani's PUK in the security zone. The trouble brewing in the safe haven does not end with the Arab farmers, whose harvest will be reaped by the Kurds. Most senior Iraqi Officials, who were Arabs, have left the security zone, even if the allies, increasingly aware of the dangers, now seem to be pulling back from initial plans to take over completely the north-west provincial capital of Dahuk. As Kurdish guerrillas set up checkpoints all over the zone, allied officers are uncomfortable at being seen to be the protectors of one faction against another. At one point, US military police, backed by a dozen squat fighting vehicles, cruised to the largest Kurdish checkpoint and cleared armed guerrillas from the road. Army attack helicopters buzzed the rebel headquarters and hovered within striking distance as a US colonel strode to the gate for a word with Kurdish leaders. Within a day, the peshmergas returned to the highway. "It's for their own security. We know the people here better than them," said Sinjari.[6]

Sinjari and his security zone counterpart from Mas'ud Barzani's KDP were pouring over an allied map that showed that the coalition security zone had nearly reached its final 75-mile wide by 30-mile deep dimensions – at that stage the intended zone included Dahuk. Far from trying to help the allies out with their wish to leave their effective division of Iraq as soon as possible. Sinjari said the guerrillas wanted the allies to move east to secure the other two-thirds of Iraqi Kurdistan still under fragile guerrilla control. At AEI press time, Barzani was still in Baghdad negotiating with Saddam Hussain for greater Kurdish regional autonomy with intèrnational guarantees for Iraq's 3.5m Kurds, as well as control of the north Iraqi oil town of Kirkuk. After meeting Saddam twice in three days, Barzani told reporters on 12 May such a revitalisation of the 1970 autonomy accords could be signed in a few days. Two other related processes were also under way in the rapid, complex evolution of events in northern Iraq. One was the gradual takeover of refugee camps there by the United Nations and the other the allied attempts to make safe the Iraqi northwest regional capital of Dahuk without actually entering it. US-European Command and senior commander of the relief operation, said in Washington on 10 May that a US presence in the city would be "a tarbaby . . . more than we can handle". But talks arranged by US officers between the Iraqi military, guerrilla leaders and Kurdish clan elders in the camps have so far not produced a compromise. The UN began to establish a presence in Dahuk on 13 May, 1991 sending eight food trucks through under the umbrella of UN envoy Prince Sadruddin Aga Khan's 18 March agreement to set up humanitarian, non-military centres to help displaced Iraqis in several hard hit parts of Iraq. The UN also took over the administration of the Zakho refugee camp from the US military.

On the same day, British Royal Marines came under fire from Iraqi soldiers gaurding one of Saddam Hussain's summer palaces near Dahuk. In the return fire it is thought that one or two Iraqi soldiers were killed. Perhaps to test allied reactions in Dahuk, Iraqi anti-aircraft gunners had already fired twice on a UN navy reconnaissance flight on 7 May and Baghdad later moved special forces troops up to the front line with the security zone. "There are a lot of ways we can provide security for the city without going in . . . I think the ideal here is an Iraqi, a chief negotiator with the Iraqis. But Dahuk and its surrounding area are still almost deserted and bringing it inside the security zone is seen as vital to persuading those refugees remaining on the mountains at the Turkey-Iraq border to return. Reports of numbers conflict, but by MEI press time at least 250,000 people of the 500,000 who fled after Saddam crushed the Kurdish rebellion in March remained in the mountains. Relief workers estimate that of these perhaps 100,000 have no wish to return. Most of those who have returned have gone straight home. Over 20,000 people, three-quarters of them from Dahuk, now live in two camps near Zakho. In the meantime, although few Kurds say they want anything more than greater autonomy. Iraqi central government links with the whole safe haven area steadily weakening. "It's not like previous times. They (Baghdad) can't order me around", said the mayor of Zakho, Abd al-Khaliq Ahmad, sitting at home in his pyjamas and sipping tea three days after returning with his family from a mountain refugee camp in Turkey. He said half his 300 municipal workers, all Kurdish, were now back too and he had a vague offer from the Baghdad government of money for tools. But he seemed to have more faith in the American military. Baghdad's present influence in the security zone is not impressive, just 50 armed police who shelter in the district prefect's office in Zakho to protect General Nashwan Danun, the Iraqi liaison officer with the allies.

A shabby but relaxed group of customs officials still keep the Iraqi flag flying on a small pole at the exit of the Iraqi side of the Turkey-Iraq border crossing at Habur. But they can only helplessly watch as convoy after convoy of allied troops, international relief trucks and reporters' cars violate Iraqi bureaucratic sovereignty. Traffic is also busy on the main road from Zakho to Mosul, despite both Iraqi and allied checkpoints. A few Arabs travel to the security zone to shop, but those travelling towards Zakho are nearly all Kurds, looking for supplies, lost relatives or, for a few, safety in the new safe haven. At Zakho general hospital, the only serious health facility in the zone, half the doctors are still paid by Iraq. Hospital supplies initially did come from Baghdad but now, as is increasingly the case in many spheres, supplies are coming from the West via Turkey. One such effort will be undertaken by the World Food Programme and the relief agency CARE International, which intend to take over the old Iraqi rationing system through food agents in Zakho who even before the Gulf war were feeding over 100,000 people. "It's like taking over their food subsidy system, which was big," said Rowland Broome, representing CARE in northern Iraq. "We'll be in the food business for quite a long time. There's very little purchasing power among the population". Private international agencies are almost embarrassingly keen to help the coalition's wish to demilitarise "Operation Provide Comfort". Non-Governmental Organisations in Zakho hold meetings, under a so far ill-defined UN coordinating mandate day and night along the power-sharing, all-equal model used for relief efforts in Thailand. "Most would leave if the coalition military goes before a proper UN agreement" said one British aid official. "But now it's real race. If you didn't know the agenda sometimes, the way they talk you'd think they were setting up a new state".

Kurdish ethnonationalism in Iran and Iraq, although unique in many respects, represents, dilemmas faced by most multiethnic societies in terms of conflict management in their societies. Historically, autonomy demands by ethnic groups in those societies have elicited complete or near rejection of such demands, followed by a period of varying degrees of repression by the dominant ethnic cultural group. For better or worse, ethnic affirmation has been largely identified with separatist tendencies, disintegration of the political system and the economitant disorder and chaos. This has historically been true in the case of Iranian society which, in addition to the Kurds, comprises several ethnic nationalities.[7]

Granting total autonomy to one ethnic group would necessitate implementation of similar measures with respect to others, hence the first step toward possible disintegration, as many have contended. On the other hand, the enormous cost of perpetual ethnic conflictual relations behaves us to search for a pacific approach to managing such conflicts. Such an approach may entail shifts in jurisdictions, the redistribution of resources, and changes in resource allocation procedures.[8] This approach, of course, would entail a genuine degree of administrative decentralisation and the establishment of a federal system of government with power being shared between the federal and state governments. Perhaps this is easier said than done. But in the absence of another viable alternative, federalism would be the first step towards managing centuries-old ethnic conflicts in the mountainous region.

For, the nation's unity and Integrity have become incompatible with status quo; and the problem in Punjab is but a part of the larger national question of accommodating the democratic rights of the country's *ethnic communities*. The ultranationalists may ridicule the view that India is a multi-national state, but it is an undeniable fact of history that many of its peoples have enjoyed nationhood at one time or another and its village communities enjoyed enviable autonomy until recently. Although India owes its present nationhood to the British Empire, its capacity to sustain itself as a nation will depend upon its surrender of adequate rights to its constituent ethnic communities. Decentralisation and democratisation of the country's political and economic activity, in a multicultural multireligious secular pluralist ethos, are, therefore, inescapable if this country is to survive and develop as a nation. Even while dealing firmly with terrorism and secessionism, the nation must address itself promptly to the task of decentralising and democratising its polity. That, and not the state's counter-terror, is the way to resolve the crises it is facing. Let it be followed up promptly by undertaking the revamping of the political structure. Delay could be disastrous.[9]

In Kurdistan, confusion is a way of life. The areas guerillas control are constantly shifting, with whole cities suddenly coming under their way. The 2 to 3 million Kurds in Iraqi Kurdish region want a secure future, but their leaders cannot bring themselves to sign an autonomy deal with President Saddam Hussein. Children are busy catching up on a lost school year and banks transfer money all over Iraq. But the effective government is the Iraqi Kurdistan. Front, dispensing rough justice in courts that mix Roman law, Islamic sharia, Kurdish traditions and Iraqi practice. Even the currency is not what it seems, with a variety of dinar notes fetching different amounts: Pre-war Iraqi dinars, fakes printed in Turkey and Iran and official high-denomination notes hot off the laser printers in Baghdad are all in circulation. Baghdad's extravagant spending has turned the economy of Kurdistan upside down, with vegetable prices five times what they were before the Gulf war, while petrol prices are still under a penny a litre. Dinars still flow into Kurdistan from Iraqi salary cheques, smuggling, taxes from transit trade between Iraq and Turkey and an unusual Iraqi policy to disarm the Kurds – by buying Kalashnikovs. "These now sell for 1.500 dinars (£ 100). But we've got so many it won't make any difference," said on Kurd, showing off a Soviet model with a 75-bullet circular magazine that made it ideal for "city-centre operations". In fact, the guerillas do little but reminisce about their adventures. Many career around with their commanders in stripped-down Jeeps, spending their evenings in video parlours or propping their rifles against tables in kebab shops such as Shaklawa's "Nights of Kurdistan." Guns are only banned in bars. One leader who came back from exile in Vienna to run a base in Raniyah wandered out in his pyjamas to share a breakfast and confessed he wad tired of having nothing to do but watch Turkish television. "All we have to talk about is weaponry" he said, consoling himself with the fantasy of driving back to his family in Europe in an armoured vehicle. Siamand Banaa, an official of the Kurdistan Democratic Party (KDP), the senior guerilla group, said: "There's a terrible growth in guerilla numbers. There are only 30,000 or so real ones. If there was a real fight these new ones would all run away."[10]

KDP officials resent the multiplication of parties, which, without the responsibility for hundreds of thousands of refugees borne by the KDP, can organise quickly. One group, a federation of tribal leaders, has been dubbed the Conservative Party, though their elegantly pressed baggytrousered suits, cummerbunds and pistols might uneasily of an MP. At the other end of the spectrum the Communist Party, amid the chaos of Kurdistan and the collapse of the ideology, still paints slogans calling for a 35-hour working week. Turkomans and Assyrian Christian minority parties defend their corners too. The great fear of regional states like Turkey and Iran is that the growing self-confidence of this area, twice the size of Lebanon, will act as a symbol of independence to Kurdish minorities in their own countries. Not all guerillas in this region are from Iraq. The Komala group and two factions of the KDP-Iran continue their reportedly fading struggle for Kurdish rights in Iran from bases in the east. The Iraqi KDP says it is increasingly helping the KDP of Iran now that its own relationship with Tehran has soured. There are also Kurdish guerillas from Turkey's powerful Kurdish Workers' (PKK), although raprochement between the KDP and Ankara means that their camps are confined to the border mountains. The KDP and Ankara deny that Turkish aid is linked to repressing the PKK but a scene at the Habur bridge between Turkey and Iraq suggests otherwise. Three Turkish special Team policemen in T-shirts and improbable bandoliers walked up to a group of Iraqi guerillas waiting for the KDP's deputy leader, Nechirvan Barzani. "So Barzani went to Ankara. He made the deal. You stop helping the terrorists. We help you. Got it?", the Turkish soldier declared. "Turkey is big, remember that". The Kurds know that their Indian summer of freedom may be brief. Queueing behind the Turkish border were buses bringing back from camps refugees who want to return home. "The Turks kept us on iron rations and wouldn't let us work or shop in town until we signed," hissed a camp leader, Hussain Sifki. "Our problem is not houses in Kurdistan. It is that there is no political solution for our people." For the moment, Iraqi Kurdistan is rebuilding and is superficially stable. As Banaa said: "We expected a blood-bath here. But there are still the most awful people, Iraqi collaborators, walking around. Where else could everyone be carrying guns and yet everybody feels so safe?[11]

REFERENCES

1. *New Wave*, 14 July, 1991.
2. D.S. Kamtekar. Security of the Gulf and India. *National Herald*, 27 July, 1991.
3. *The Hindustan Times*, 27 April, 1991.
4. Indranie Banerjee. Nobody's People. *The Hindustan Times*, 3 August, 1991.
5. *Ibid.*
6. *Middle East International*, 17 May, 1991; P.16
7. Nader Entessar. The Kurds in Past-Revolutionary Iran and Iraq. *Third World Quarterly*, October, 1984.
8. Martin O. Heisler and B Guy Peters, 'Scarcity and the Management of Political Conflict in Multicultural Polities', *International Political Science Review* 4(3) 1983, p. 329.
9. Devendra Chintan. The Nationality Question. *The Business and Political Observer*, 11 September, 1991.
10. *The Hindustan Times*, 6 October, 1991.
11. *Ibid.*

2

DREAM OF A HOMELAND

"The Kurds," so the proverb goes, "have mountains". They are a national that has been cheated by history, divided by other people's frontiers and exploited in the interests of outside powers. But in no place and an at no time has their suffering been greater than in Iraq. And for the first time the argument is being raised outside the region that a comprehensive settlement in the Middle East must include not only a solution to the Arab-Israeli conflict but also must address the Kurdish question if there is to be lasting peace. With some 25 million people spread across the territories of five states, the Kurds are the largest nation on the earth that has yet to win the right of self-determination. By all the usual criteria, they are a separate and unique people: they have their own language, customs, literature and folklore and an awareness of their distinct origin and history. Yet in the states that they inhabit their existence as nation is, to a greater or lesser extent, denied. In the outside word, the Kurds have failed to insert the idea of their distinct identity into the international consciousness as have, say, the Palestinians. "They don't speak enough about the Kurds," said the late Iranian Kurdish leader Abdul Rahman Qassemlou, "because we have never taken any hostage, hostages, never hijacked a plane. But I am proud of this". However noble the sentiment, Quasselou's explanation only tells half the story. For if it is true that the Kurds have no friends, it is also true that they have been their own worst enemies. They have allowed themselves to be used as the cat's paws of competing regional states and of the world powers that in the twentieth century have sought to dominate the affairs of the Middle East. The Kurdish movement in Iraq has accepted the help of successive regimes in Iran, even as those regimes were oppressing their fellow Kurds across the border. The same has happened in reverse. Kurdish rebels in Turkey have even accepted the help of Saddam Hussein.[1]

Invariably, it is the Kurds who have ended by losing out from these pragmatic alliances and the regional states and outside powers that have gained. In the process, Kurds in any given state have earned the reputation of being potential traitors.[1]

The dramatic success of Kurdish rebels in northern Iraq appears to have brought them closer than ever before to their century-old dream of an autonomous Kurdish homeland. The Kurds, who live in the mountains on the borders of Iraq, Iran, Turkey and Syria, have never had an independent state, apart from a Soviet republic which lasted from 1945-46.[2]

Ironically, they are among the most ancient peoples of the region, living in the mountains long before the arrival of the Arabs in the 7th century and the Turks in the 11th century. There are an estimated 15 million Kurds, two-thirds of them in Turkey and about 3.5 million in Iraq. There are also isolated pockets of Kurds in the Soviet Union.

Throughout history, they have been rugged mountain warriors. Saladin, the chivalrous Islamic leader who battled the crusaders, was a Kurd (born in Tikrit, the home town of *Saddam Hussein*). Less gloriously, Kurdish irregulars joined Turkish troops in the massacre of the Armenians at the start of twentieth century.

Kurdish nationalism was awakened in the 1890s by British and Russian interest in the Gulf. The founding of nation states on the wreckage of the old Ottoman Empire divided Kuridistan – "the land of the Kurds" – among five countries.

They were promised an autonomous Kurdistan after the First World War under the 1920 Treaty of Severes. This pledge, the first of many to be broken, foundered on resurgent nationalism of the Turkish leader Atturk, who saw no reason to give up the south east of his country to the Kurds.

Short-lived armed insurrections broke out, and in 1931-32 and 1944-45 there were serious conflicts in Iraqi Kurdistan. Prospects for Kurdish independence in Iraq were written off when oil was found in the north of the country. It was then unthinkable that such a valuable resource would be handed over.

The late Mustafa Barzani, the most chrismatic leader of modern times, joined the revolt against rule from made a Baghdad in 1931 and was made a majoar-general by the Russians when he joined their brief Republic of Mahabad after World War Second. He later formed the Pesh Merga (those who face death) and was lord of Iraqi Kurdistan by 1972.

The situation was so serious that Saddam made concessions to the Shah of Iran in 1975 in exchange for him cutting off aid to the Pesh Merga. The revolt was then continued by the Iraqi army, but has sputtered on nevertheless. Offers of autonomy from Saddam have proved to be no more than ploys to gain a breathing space for the Iraqi army, which plumbed the depths of brutality by using poisons gas against the Kurdish village of Halabja in 1988. Barzani, who died in Washington in 1979, is succeeded by his son Massoud. If Iraq has been the most military action against the Kurds, it is the Turkey that they have been most repressed. The Ankara government has refused to recognise them as a separate race, calling them "mountain Turks" and pretending that their language (which is related to Persian) is a dialect of Turkish. The blanket ban on the use of Kurdish (even for penning a love poem) has only just been lifted. Their traditional dress—baggy trousers, sash around the waist and coloured turban—has been banned in or near towns and cities. More than 3,000 people have died in south eastern Turkey since 1984 in a revolt led by the Kurdish Workers Party. The Turks have always seen Kurdish nationalism as a threat to their own security. It is a sure bet that President Ozal, now in Washington, will ask President Bush to avoid any encouragement of the Kurdish insurrection in Iraq which could spill across the border.[3]

President George Bush has finally come round to adopting the proposal put forward by British Prime Minister John Major on ensuring security to Kurdish refugees within northern Iraq. The US, British and French air and ground forces will be used to guard a series of refugee camps within Iraqi territory.

U.S. President Bush hopes the camps would be temporary and has clarified that the US has no intention of becoming an occupying power in Iraq or to interfere in Iraq's internal affairs. The administration of these camps would be turned over to the UN as early as possible. This is a total reversal of former US stand against the European Community idea to establish a safe haven for Kurdish refugees in Iraq. Though the term 'haven' will not be used, the idea is identical. This again highlights the fact that the US had no clear assessment about the way of internal situation in Iraq would develop, and thus allowed itself to be manipulated by the Saudis in letting loose Saddam Hussein on his own population. It is now reversing its policy under international and domestic pressure. The cost of this blunder is tens of thousands of Kurdish lives. This reversal in US policy is being effected despite China's opposition to the creation of a safe haven and the Soviet Union's serious reservations on the issue. Presumably, the idea is to enable western allied powers to act on their own without invoking the UN endorsement of their move. In case Iraq complains to the UN on the violation of its sovereignty, that complaint is unlikely to get enough support in the Security Council. The politics behind this move have also to be carefully assessed. While the Saudis could not care less about the Kurdish refugees, Turkey faces a major problem. Already, the Kurdish population within Turkey – the largest Kurdish concentration – is a minority discriminated against and deeply discontented. Turkey needs international assistance to give succour to the refugees. But, if the United Nations High Commission for Refugees is allowed to operate Turkish soil, then Kurds entering Turkey would be formally declared as refugees, thereby becoming eligible to settle down permanently in Turkey is clearly unhappy about such a possibility and had consequently pressed for moving Kurdish refugees back to Iraq.[4]

Secondly, their rehabilitation in the mountainous border terrain of Turkey has been far more difficult than it would have been in the plains of northern Iraq. Then, the US should have discovered by this time that the Saudis are not to be relied upon as sound and balanced advisers, having their own axes to grind. Further, the exaggerated fear of Iranian influence over Iraq – a card played by the Saudis – has also diminished. Lastly, criticism about the victory of Operation Desert Storm having soured, has mounted. If one were to compare this refugee relief operation with others of the post-World War-II era – despite all western media hyperbole about the present relief operation – one cannot escape the feeling of appalling inefficiency of western industrialised nations in handling it. The biggest refugee rehabilitation measured the world has ever seen was carried in the Indian subcontinent in 1947-48. Taking into account the flow of refugees in two directions in western India and mostly in one direction in the East, more than 18 million people were handled. The second largest refugee problem occurred again in India in 1971 following

Pakistani genocide in Bangladesh and ten million people pouring into this country. The third largest was also in the subcontinent, with the inflow of Afghan refugees into Pakistan. The first, two were handled without any external assistance worth the mention. If India had made adequate record of its refugee rehabilitation operations, it could have been the standard manual for the world. It is now ironic to recall that the industrialised nations prefered a Japanese lady academic for the post of UN High Commissioner for Refugees over an Indian with earlier experience in the field against the better judgement of UN Secretary general. Even as western powers grapple with the Kurdish refugee problem, a few hundred gee casualties take place everyday. The present decision of the US is likely to have far-reaching consequences in future international relations, since it would constitute a precedent for nations to intervene in the internal affairs of the other nations. Even as it does not oppose the proposal, India should make it clear that while such interventions may be inescapable in the case of nations with oppressive regimes, they will be impermissible in those democratic nations where there is no refugee problem spilling beyond their borders.[5]

As fierce fighting between Iraqi forces and Kurdish guerillas continues in and around the northern oil town of Kirkuk, Masood Basrani, a senior Kurdish rebel leader has accused the Iraqi government led by President Saddam Hussein of genocide.[6]

According to Masood and Kurdish guerillas fighting the Iraqi Army in northern Iraq, the streets of Kirkuk are litered with the bodies of women, children and young men belonging to the Kurdish community.

Basrani on March 30, 1991 said that the Iraqi Army was carrying out a "pre-mediated, systematic extermination" of the Iraqi people. Basrani appealed to the United Nations and the US forces stationed in the Middle-East to intervene on the side of the Kurds and overthrow Saddam Hussein. However, despite repeated warnings to Baghbad about using extreme measures in quelling the rebellions in northern and southern Iraq, the Bush administration has refused all Kurdish appeals to intervene.

Over 100,000 Kurds and Iraqi soldiers have escaped into the mountains in northern Iraq, the Bonn-based Society for Endangered Nations has announced on March 15, 1991. The refugees are in a desperate situation, completely unprotected from persecution and starvation and need urgent international assistance, the society said in a statement. Saddam Hussein's National Guards have killed tens of thousands of Kurds since the end of the war, it said. The society also called for urgent aid to Kurds who have escaped to Iran and Turkey.

The savage blood-letting now taking place in Iraq stems from the bitter anger of the Kurds, an ethnic minority in the north, and the deprived Shia majority in the south against their Baathist oppressors. Both sides are using the fire-power available to them without any inhibitions but this is only to be expected in a conflict in which losers can expect no mercy. It seems likely that Baghdad will ultimately previal because of two factors; its military superiority reinforced in the south by the division among Shias between those for whom the ethnic Arab bond counts far more than sectarian solidarity and those drawing inspiration from Iran. A pointer to this may be the state made by the senior-most Shia cleric Ayaatollah Al Khoi on Baghdad Television denouncing the insurgency. Teheran claims that he was speaking under duress, a hypothesis that cannot be dismissed out of hand. But the fact that Arab sentiment prevailed during the Iran-Iraq war has also to be kept in mind. Besides, Saddam Hussein is not relying on coercion alone; he is also offering to rewrite the constitution to accommodate pluralism and regional aspirations. In the revamp of the leadership that he was carried out, he has made his top associate, Sa'adoun Hammadi, the Prime Minister, an office that he was himself holding. President Bush may be right in dismissing the changes as cosmetic but not be missed is Saddam Hussein's instinct for survival which makes him willing to bend to avoid being broken. This may work as it has in the past, particularly as the US and its Arab allies have no wish to see Iraq disintegrate because of the destablising impact it would have in a region where many countries are equally heterogeneous. Washington is in fact being quite cynical; it is maintaining enough pressure to thwart Saddam's efforts to retain his badly damaged power structure but is also allowing him enough leeway (including the use of helicopter gunships) to contain insurgency. While countries like India cannot be a party to US manoeuvrings, they have to uphold the wholesome principle that there should be no outside interference in Iraq's internal quarrels. Two countries to which the plea for self-restraint should be particularly addressed are Iran and Turkey because of the contacts they are maintaining with the southern and northern insurgents. If they have humanitarian concerns, these should be addressed through UN agencies or the International Red Cross.[7] It will be entirely appropriate for these neighbours, as well as the rest of the international community, to urge Baghdad to avoid excessive use of force and to desist from employing horror weapons but there is not much more than anyone can do without becoming a party to the dispute.

In a sudden reversal of policy, the United States (US) has changed its attitude towards Saddam Hussein and dumped the Kurdish rebels at a time when they were making major inroads into Iraq. The month-long stalemate in the peace process in the war-torn West Asia and the squabbling over the shifting of Central Command (CENTCOM) head-quarters is reportedly responsible for this policy swerve. Talks between state secretary James Bakers and the Gulf allies, and the Israeli attitude towards the peace plan trigerred an expected deal between the US and Iraq. As per the "deal", the battered Iraqi President, Saddam Hussein, has "agreed" to all the US terms and conditions. Allied troops will leave occupied areas of southern Iraq and Saddam, in return, will act "precisely" in accordance with US wishes in the West Asia. Saddam, therefore, has been given a free hand to crush the uprising of Kurdish and Shi'ite rebels. Saddam's continuance in power is hanging like the Democeles sword over the increasingly independent allied gulf countries, especially Saudi Arabia and Egypt which insisted on a Pan-Arab force, rather than US troops, to maintain peace in the area. Besides, contrary to pre-war agreements with the Saudis, the US move to shift the CENTCOM headquarters to Bahrain has spawned suspicion in Arab ranks. Under-currents of doubt about US intentions surfaced when the Saudis allegedly contacted Moscow upon learning that the US could not be expected to act in their interest but would invariably favour Israel instead. While the decision to let Saddam remain in power was being taken at a high-level White House meeting, the State department, Pentagon and White House were issuing embarrassing and conflicting "official statements' about the US policy towards anti-Saddam rebels. Sources close to policy-makers indicate that US businesses have also played a major role in settling for a pro-Saddam policy. They are said to have pleaded with President George Bush that American firms can bag the contracts for rebuilding Iraq and securing substantial amounts of the oil revenues which are to be controlled by a UN Security Council Commission. The influence of the business lobby can be assessed by the fact that in the midst of a high-level meeting with seven top level meeting with seven top level military and National Security advisers, Bush sent White House spokesman Marlin Fitzwater into the White House press briefing room at the very moment when a few blocks away, the state department and the Pentagon were issuing tough statements against Iraq to the effect that armed helicopter flights by the Iraqis against rebel forces would be considered a threat to cease-fire. To the surprise of Congressional hawks and political pundits, Fitzwater stated that the US did not intend to interfere with Baghdad's attempts to put down the rebellion and would not shoot down the helicopters being used against rebel groups unless they pose a threat to allied forces. Iraq is using helicopters against Kurdish and pro-Iranian Shi'ite rebels in the northern and southern part of the country.[8] The US has also changed its earlier stance that its forces would remain in the occupied zone for an extended period until a formal cease-fire is signed. The idea now is that the deployment in Iraq could last only until a UN observer force is in place. Bush has also diluted the US terms of a cease-fire resolution that is to be offered to the UN Security Council this week. The US originally wanted to ensure the destruction of Iraq's weapons of mass destruction and continue a campaign of political and economic pressure aimed at weakening Saddam's position. The new US policy came after the White House approval of Baghdad's proposal that the Iraqi National Assembly is to meet on April 6, 1991 and institute reforms promised by Saddam. The new "democratic phase" in Iraq will include greater public liberties, increased press freedom and provisions for party pluralism. Accordingly, the Bush administration sent signals to the Arab League that Iraq should be allowed to attend the Cairo meeting today to mark the start of rapprochement. The US also agreed to drop a proposal that Iraq assets be frozen and used to repay those who suffered losses as a results of Iraq's invasion of Kuwait. Instead, compensation is to be drawn primarily from a percentage of Iraqi oil sales. Iraq's annual pre-war oil revenues amounted to $ 200 billion. The new-found amity will certainly help Saddam, who is said to have $ 10 billion hidden in 40 to 50 banks around the world. A few days ago, the US treasury department was said to have been planning to release a list of about 100 individuals and companies around the world that it had identified as being either fronts for or agents of the Iraqi government. The department's move came amid the reports that the Kuwaiti government has hired Wall Street's corporate sleuth, Jules Kroll, to determine Saddam's private assets. Kroll said on a nationally televised CBS show that during his investigations he found that Saddam has systematically skimmed money off Iraqi oil sales and other business deals and had stacked away billions of dollars in more than 40 banks around the globe by using front companies set up by relatives or other cronies, Saddam had allegedly gained an indirect 8.4 per cent stake in the French Company, Hachette, which publishes well-known US magazines—Women's Day, Car and Driver, etc. Kroll is known for his successful investigation of the vast assets of Filipino dictator Ferdinand Marcos, and Haiti's dictator Jean-Claude Duvalier and others.[9]

Chaos threatened to engulf relief operations for Iraqi Kurds on April 11, 1991 as aid workers and Government officials found themselves overwhelmed by the scale of the disaster. Turkey's Health Minister Halil Sivgin warned that any delay in delivering aid would mean leaving people to their deaths. Meanwhile, stock lay undistributed for fear of riots, trucks got struck in the mud, and aid agencies failed to keep track of arriving consignments.

Iran said that it needed 300 million to help the estimated 8,00,000 Kurds, who have streamed across its border with Iraq. "International aid so far has been insignificant, they have just sent a few planes", Teheran's Ambassador to Germany Seyed Hossein Mousavian said in Bonn.

Teheran Radio said that workers with the French relief organisation, Medicines Sans Fronti Aeres, were treating people, including children, who were badly injured after stepping on mines. Several had to have limbs amputated.

The station said the worst areas were round the town of Sardasht, where there were already 1,20,000 refugees and which radio commentators said, "cannot possibly contain this flood of people". Many, the commentators said, "had died before reaching the town and not only from attacks by troops but also from hunder and cold."

On the Turkish-Iraqi border, the sheer size of the relief operation became clear as diplomats compared the scale of the American aid effort alone with the Berlin airlift of 1949. But the magnitude and complexity of the response brought its own problems, said one Western diplomat in the border region.

"There does not appear to be any command and control," said the diplomat. "There is little liaison going on between agencies. There are blockages of transport and communications. The right vehicles are not available".

The problem begin on the bitterly cold mountain sides, where unusually sever weather is hampering the operation and adding to the miserty for hundreds of thousands.

Sivgin said that 70 per cent of the Iraqi refugees were without shelter. He said their water supplies were unhygienic. "I call on the United Nations to immediately help these people," he said. "Any delay in help means leaving these people to their death and this is inhuman".

Yet witnesses said that sometimes available food was not distributed by soldiers for fear of uncontrollable disturbances. On UN official said the desperate scrabblle for food, and scenes of soldiers clubbing refugees, were a result of a failure of organisation.

"Generally, there is self-control among refugees. But this has not been organised because they do not have the administration. It is totally choatic," he said.

Aid workers encourage natural leaders to distribute resources equitably. But in this case the refugees are predominantly townsfolk who lack the traditional village hierarchy.

A Turkish journalist in Cukurca commented that local officials were inefficient. Jobs are given out according to ability and political clout, he said and the poorest, most remote-region of Turkey is not the place for high-fliers.

"Most of the civil servants are basically incompetent or they wouldn't be here," he charged.

Logistical problems continue to be a nightmare, despite the construction of three miles of new road and resurfacing of almost 20 miles. An official of the United Nations High Commissioner for Refugees (UNHCR) said the main bottleneck was in the mountains.

"The weather is really bad. For example, there are something like nine German truks in the mud," she said.

In Ankara and in the regional capital, Diyabakir, there is confusion about how much aid has arrived. The Turkish Red Crescent gave wildly differing figures for aid actually delivered to the border to UN officials and reporters. Officials and journalists complain that embassies are unaware of planeloads of aid arriving from their countries. Yet diplomats are among the most critical of the UN and other agencies, describing coordination as a disaster.

The main UN responsibility has been handed over to the UNHCR, which flew in extra staff to make up a team of around 30. No one was available for comment on whether lines of control were working.

Yet no one blamed any one agency or the Turkish Government. There is general recognition of the overwhelming nature of the emergency.

"Please don't accused us unfairly," said a Foreign Ministry sources. "The Turkish Government is doing its best to do everything it can but the scale of the problem is massive and weather conditions and terrain are impossible." Iraq's Health Minister Shaqwi Sabri Murqus warned that the country faced typhoid, cholera and hepatitis epidemics and appealed for international aid.

Help from relief organisations so far was inadequate to deal with the scale of the potential problem, he said in a statement broadcast on Baghdad Radio. He added that the bombardment of Iraq during the war and the subsequent rebellions had left many of the country's hospitals badly damaged and medical equipment stores wiped out.

Nearly half a million Iraqi Kurds have become homeless, half of them destitutes. Refugees are stranded on Turkish border, some on Iranian border while nearly one hundred thousand are reported to be in Turkish and Iranian refugee camps. Kurds, who are spread over the contiguous mountainous areas of Iraq, Syria, Turkey, Iran and Soviet Union, are struggling for Kurdish homeland for generations. There have been repeated uprisings in Iraq, Iran and Turkey and they have invariably been suppressed with brute force as no country of the region wants a part of its territory to secede, much less allow all the Kurdish populated areas to join and form a new country – Kurdistan. Due to their mutual antagonism, each country tries to incite Kurd rebellion in another country making false promises of autonomy to its own Kurd population. The tragedy of the Iraqi Kurds, in the latest round of rebellion, is that they took American promises of aid to overthrow Saddam Hussein on their face value. They rebelled in their age old tradition only to be suppressed. The blood of Kurds is on George Bush's conscience, a slippery commodity in Bush's New World Order. The UN agencies, besides US and some of its allies, are rushing aid to the refugee camps in Turkey and are airdropping food and blankets for the benefit of those who are stranded in the mountains. This is a poor consolation to Kurds who have been double-crossed by the US specialists in psychological warfare. The UN Security Council was outraged by the plight of Kurd refugees. No such feelings were expressed over the plight of millions of Iraqi population that was ruthlessly bombed along with all the civilian infrastructure in order to establish rule of law in international relations. Iraqi population has no food, no drinking water, no electricity, no medical facilities. But the economic sanctions against Iraq remain in place, though the humiliating peace terms offered by the Security Council have already been accepted by Iraq. It is the Iraqi people who were, and are still being punished for Saddam's miscalculations and misadventure. The only redeeming feature of the protracted exercise in the Security Council is that the Anglo-American plot to dismember Iraq was frustrated by majority of the Council members.

Wherever Americans have militarily intervened in the post-World War-II era, they have not only ruined entire nations, they have also generated millions of refugees whose ultimate destination is the United States. Tens of thousands of Koreans, Vietnamese, Cambodians, Laotians, Chinese and now Afghans and Kurds have no other place to go except the promised land – the United States of America. The US administration has yet another weapon to generate homeless and jobless refugees, namely, the American way of life and magic of the market. This past winter contingency plans were drawn to receive millions of Russian refugees on expectations of magic of market working its way in the Soviet Union. Mercifully the migration did not occur. The Polish President got half of Polish debt cancelled by the US by holding out the threat that millions of Poles would knock at US door if debt was not cancelled and more aid injected in the economy.[10] Magic of market is at work in Eastern Europe and also East Germany. Millions are taking to streets to seek jobs and roof over their heads. The flow of refugees from Eastern Europe, though controlled, continues. In Bush's New World Order the poor are destined to become poorer and the richer.

A US official has threatened to throw Iraqi troops out of northern Iraq if they fail to comply with the coalition forces demand to vacate the refugees' safe haven zones the forces are establishing in the area.

The warning came following the failure of a Military level meeting to secure assurances from the Iraqis to this effect.

"The Iraqi Government," Dayton Maxwell, Deputy Director of the State Department's office of foreign disaster assistance, said, on April 20, 1991 "does have to agree to withdraw. You can call it negotiations. You can call it something else. The Iraqi Government is not going to be happy with this".

The American Three Star General who met the Iraqis on April 20 failed to reach an agreement. Lt. Gen. John M. Shalikashvili, said he would not be meeting with the Military leadership again.

The unresolved issues, he said, would be resolved "through other channels".

Meanwhile, U.S. Commander in the Gulf, General Norman Schewarzkope said that the withdrawal of American troops would have to be delayed unless an agreement was reached.

Maxwell disclosed that the coalition task force of the U.S., French and the British forces plans to take over the Iraqi town of Zakhu and the surrounding villages and return them to their Kurdish residents.

He said tented camps would be built for Kurds who live elsewhere in Iraq.

"The people who live in Zakhu, he said, could go home. The people who live south of Zakhu would go to the camps."

Thousands of Zakhu's former residents now stay in the Turkish mountains of Isikveren, the largest Kurdish refugee camp. At least 150,000 refugees live there in squalid conditions that relief experts say are a breeding ground for infectious diseases.

Across the Turkish Iraqi border region, where an estimated 700,000 Kurds are now living, relief officials say hundreds of refugees are dying daily, most of them infants.

Shalikashvili said that the U.S. Military plans "to make it clear (to the refugees in the Turkish mountains) that we simply cannot provide adequate help where they are. There is no endgame where they are".

However, the General and other senior officials added that the refugees would not agree to come to the safe haven camps in Iraq unless they were sure they would be protected from Iraqi President Saddam Hussein.

"In the short term" said the Polish born American General, "military security is terribly important. It is surely not a long-term solution, other mechanisms must be mount and surely will be".

With the refugee situation on Iraq's borders with Iran and Turkey assuming the proportions of a massive human tragedy. President Bush is beginning to make the painful discovery that waging the war is a lot easier than winning the peace. The mood in the nation was euphoric after the hostilities ended in the Persian Gulf. On a daily basis, the media showed scenes of ecstatic reunions of the returning warriors with their wives and kin. The President was one hand at some of the welcoming ceremonies, beamingly basking in the glory of an unprecedented 92 per cent approval rating. But then, the media also began portraying horrendous scenes of refugees literally dropping by the wayside. Questions began to be asked about the morality of Mr. Bush first inciting the Iraqi people to take matters into their own hands to oust Saddam Hussein, and then standing idly by when some of the Iraqis attempted to do just that and were, as a result, set upon by the Baghdad regime. It did not exactly help the President when the Democrats pounced on his predicament in a bid to repair their own sagging political fortunes. The Gulf war, and the kudos the administration received for the masterly manner in which it had been conducted, left the Democrats confused and without a credible cause or candidate. They were only too happy to fault the Bush Administration first, for ending the war too soon, and secondly, for not anticipating the refugee problem. It is not a coincidence that Bush's approval rating fell by about 20 points after the Kurdish and Shi'ite refugee imbroglio became part of the average American's daily television diet. True, it can be argued that a 92 per cent approval rate is too much of a high to endure, and even a 72 per cent rate is nothing to be ashamed of. But the notion of falling popularity appears to have caused a degree of panic in the White House. President Bush's initial reaction was the time-old strategy of offence being the best defence. Stoutly asserting that his principal aim had been to vacate the dastardly occupation of Kuwait – which the soldiers had accomplished magnificently – Bush said he would now concentrate on bringing the boys home. He would not have a single American serviceman sucked into an internal revolt that had been going on in Iraq for years. With criticism mounting that US efforts to alleviate the suffering of the refugees were to little and too late. Bush's responses clearly assumed a tinge of petulance and stridency that had not been present earlier. It was obvious that an agonising reappraisal was on in the White House.[11]

And sure enough, as with his famous no-new-taxes pledge, Bush has been forced to back-pedal. Defence Secretary Richard Cheney had announced just a few days ago that no US combat forces would be involved in the refugee aid or protection programme. But on Tuesday, Bush unveilied a refugee camps for Kurds well inside Iraq, to persuade them away from the inaccessible mountains down to the plains where the logistics of providing and would be simpler. The camps would be managed by troops from the three countries, who would also guarantee protection to the refugees. The change in policy is drastic and gives the impression that it has been forced on the Administration. As American troops prepare to leave Iraq, a number of essays are being made at analysis-by-hindsight to identify critical decisions that have allegedly tended to dim the bright promise of the decisive military victory. On of the primary themes that run through such analyses is, of course, President Bush's "widely replayed exhortation" to the Iraqi people to rise up against Saddam Hussein. It was this call, it is claimed, that sparked the rebellions in the Shi'ite towns in the south and the Kurdish centres in the north. Kurdish leader Massoud Barzani was reportedly sceptical that the time was ripe for such a revolt and hesitant to commit his forces. But the spontaneous uprisings in response to American encouragement forced his hand. The implication of such scenarios is that the premature rebellion was a waste, since a better-prepared effort at a later date might have had greater chances of success. The second major strategic mistake, according to analysts in retrospect, was the decision to halt the advance of the coalition forces on day too soon. They latch on to the statement of US General Norman Schewarzkopf that key elements of the Iraqi Republican Guard were trapped with their tanks and artillery in the south and could have been eliminated in another 24 hours. Instead, they were allowed to make good their escape to Baghdad, and became the decisive factor in turning the tide of battle against the lightly armed Shi'ite and Kurdish rebels. Some of the analysts suggest that a humanitarian concern about excessive casualties might have caused an early end to the war. That is, however, difficult to square with the highly successful allied bombing strategy. Despite dramatic television footage of "smart" bombs entering target buildings precisely through the skylight, it is now known that a very large number of bombs missed their targets, sometimes by wide margins. The result was death and destruction on an unprecedented scale. The massive air attack did not quite succeed in its stated aim of destroying Saddam Hussein's command and control systems which had back-up arrangements. But the air raids did achieve the near total destruction of the Iraqi electric power grid. That, in turn, has made the water pumping stations and sewage facilities inoperable for a long time to come.[12]

A United Nations team found the effects of the bombing on the civilian economy "near apocalyptic". A senior UN official also found that the Iraqi people had been "pushed back to the pre-industrial age." When talking about humanitarian concerns and morality, it might be well to ask whether such lasting civilian damage was really necessary to the war effort. Now that the US Administration has finally decided to move in for aiding the refugees, a question that is often raised is: why did Mr. Bush wait so long to act and seem to indecisive in contrast to his bold leadership in the early phases of the war? To understand that dilemma, one has to appreciate a dichotomy in the American character – it afternates between idealism and pragmatism. Idealism demands that something be done to alleviate the suffering of the refugees and pragmatism militates against involvement in Iraq's internal affairs. It is understandable if Mr. Bush feels that he is damned if he does and damned if he doesn't. The sad truth is that the Iraqi mess has no solution that does not bring about a new set of problems. For instance, if the allied troops had continued their advance and had completely annihilated the Republican Guards, southern Iraq would probably be in the hands of the Shi'ite rebels and effectively under the control of Iran. And that would hardly have been a desired US Policy goal. Or, suppose the US had made it clear that the Iraqis could not use their helicopter gunships against the rebels. The Kurds then might well have succeeded in establishing in independent Kurdistan. And that, in turn, would in all likelihood have led to a Kurdish uprising in Turkey, a long time usually. It is a no-win situation.[13]

The history of the Kurds, reported to be negotiating with Baghdad on autonomy in their mountaining homeland has been one of broken promises, failed deals and repression by the governments of the region.

The Kurds, numbering 15 to 20 million, are a non-Arab, Sunni Muslim people, speaking a language akin to Persian and living in a mountainous area stradding the borders of Iraq, Turkey, Iran, the Soviet Union and Syria.

They were mentioned by the ancient Greek historian Xenophon as long ago as 400 BC. Saladin, the Islamic leader who fought the Christian crusaders in the 12th century, was a Kurd.

But for all their history they have been subjugated by stronger neighbours. Turkey, Iraq and Iran haves firmly resisted in independent Kurdish state.

Kurdish nationalism stirred in the 1890s when the Turkish Ottoman empire was on its last legs. The 1920 Treaty of Sevres, after World War First promised them independence.

But three years later the Turkish leader Mustapha Kemal Ataturk tore up the treaty. For the Kurds, one of the history's losers, it was a story that was to be repeated again and again.

They fared worse in Iraq, then under British mandate from the League of Nations, where revolts were put down in 1919, 1923 and 1932.

In Iran, the Kurds succeeded in establishing a Soviet backed Republic of Mahabad in 1946. But Reza Shah soon crushed it.

Under Mustafa Barzani, the Iraqi Kurds waged an intermittent struggle against Baghdad after World War Second. Finally in 1970 an agreement was reached allowing for linguistic rights and self-rule in Kurdish areas. But it broke down over distribution of oil revenues and the exclusion of oil-producing Kirkuk area from Kurdistan. By 1974 it was open war again and some 130,000 Kurds took refugee in Iran. The rebellion collapsed the following year after Iran withdrew aid in return for border concessions from Iraq in the Shatt Al-Arab waterway. The Iran-Iraq war, which broke out in 1980 and lasted eight years, gave the Kurds another chance to exploit regional hostilities for their own benefit. The revolutionary turmoil in Iran allowed them to establish a no-go area for government troops but they were unable to hold onto it for long.

The United Nations has consistently refused to take even a look at the Kurdish national question. Under existing assumptions, UN should not interfere in the international affairs of its member-States—the same argument that stood in the way of alleviating the suffering of Bangladesh at its birth. A senior figure in the UN system. Madam Sadako Ogata, UN High Commissioner for Refugees, has expressed her fear that "the danger of genocide is a real one." The Pope did not use the world war 'genocide' but he pointed to it when he said that "the very survival of the whole (Kurdish) community is in danger". The UN General Assembly unanimously adopted more than 40 years ago the Convention on the Prevention and Punishment of the Crime of Genocide. This international law makes not only genocide after it is completed but also conspiracy or incitement to commit it and even attempts at it or complicity in it punishable. Surprisingly, the Kurdus—except for a small group in Turkey—are not agitating or fighting for irredentism and sovereignty. They have accepted the impossibility of putting the boundaries of the States existing in West Asia in a melting pot and bringing out a new order with a State for the Kurds in it. The Kurds say they will be satisfied with autonomy for their areas inside the existing national boundaries. They are justified in insisting upon genuine autonomy and not the kind as in Iraq, where Kurdistan does not include vital Kurdish territories like oil-producing Kirkuk, and is the target nevertheless of aggressive Arabization. In Turkey the Kurds were not permitted to use even their own language. It is only out of a fear or Kurdish resurgence in the aftermath of the Gulf war that Turkey has started talking about amending its laws and allowing the Kurds to study in their own language at school. The new world order promised by President Bush does not have a place worth talking about for the Kurds or the palestinians. The idea today goes no further than relief operations to help the Iraqi Kurdish refugees not to die. It is to be seen if the latest Kurdish autonomy agreement with the Iraqi authorities will work out, or whether they will once again be betrayed.[14]

When the Somali President Siad Barre was forced to flee in February 1991 and the country was laid open for violent anarchy, the American and Soviet ambassadors in Mogadishu were evacuated in the same helicopter. Chances are that a similar exercise is due to any time now in the country next door, Ethiopia, where the rebel forces are closing in on yet another dictator in Addis Ababa. It is indeed, a curious climax to the super powers' role in the Horn of Africa, where for two decades they alternately propped up dictators and rebel groups in both the countries in pursuit of their conflicting Cold War interests. It is also symbolic of the manner in which the superpowers disentangle themselves from the crises they themselves precipitate. There are several such countries whose post-Cold War dividend has been in the form of civil wars and strife that ensued the sudden political vacuum caused by abrupt superpowers' abandonment of the client regimes and rebels. While the superpowers' policy towards the Kurdish question is not in the same league, undoubtedly, a great deal of blame for the plight of the Kurds can be apportioned to them, particularly the US. If the consequences were not so tragic, comical would have been the world word to describe President Bush's disclaimer about his support to the Kurds' fight to liberate themselves from the yoke of President Saddam Hussein's tyranny. Having repeatedly enticed the dissident forces within Iraq to overthrow the Baghdad regime, there is no plausible way President Bush can hide under the finer text of not having pledged to break up Iraq, particularly when the main target of his enticement has been historically fighting to carve out an independent state. This is not to suggest that the US has an easy task in formulating policy responses towards the Kurdish question. Being the largest displaced ethnic community in the world of nearly 25 million—more than the (Armenians and Palestinians), inhabiting a region spanning across Iraq, Turkey, Iran and the Soviet Union, the issue of Kurdish self-determination is fairly sensitive and not amenable to easy solution. Understandably, the entire world community including the Third World chose to ignore the issue all these years. But knowing very well that enticement of the Iraqi sub-national forces to rebellion would stir the hornet's nest of Kurdish question, it is exceptionable that the US has not addressed itself to the likely consequences. But more than that, having achieved its war objectives against Iraq with unexpected ease, the US, in pursuit of undiluted self-interest, has tacitly given a carte blanche to Iraq to deal with the Kurds by turning a Nelson's eye on their resistance.[15]

For, any tactical or strategic victory of the Iraqi Kurds is likely to act as a catalyst to Kurdish nationalism in the adjoining countries, particularly Turkey which has the second largest concentration of Kurds and where their systematic repression rivals that in Iraq. Though the US is sensitive to the interest of Turkey, its NATO partner, a greater reasons for American perfidy lies in its strategic interests in West Asia itself. A dismembered Iraq can radically alter the equilibrium of power in a manner that would not be either conducive to peace in the region, or, in the absence of threat from powerful Iraq, irrespective of the status of Mr. Saddam Hussein, make allowance for the region's dependence on the US for security. Washington's studied deference to the principle of sovereignty, which is also being interpreted as Presidents Bush's Bay of Pigs, appears ludicrous in the light of the inhuman suffering of multitudes of fleeing people into inhospitable terrain and con- ditions – a tragedy that would have been averted if only the US has made it clear from the very outset that its call for internal rebellion would not automatically mean aiding or abetting Kurdish self-determination. The US administration's pathetic groping for a proper response to the British Premier John Major's UN mandated "safe haven" formula is predicted on the apprehension that a Kurdish enclave within the Iraqi territory would sooner or later raise the question of its legal status, and as a consequence compel the parties to create a Kurdish state since it will be impossible by then to remerge the enclave into Iraq. No wonder, China and the Soviet Union, whose dubious attitudes towards the Kurdish question have a much longer history, have opposed the proposal. Whatever may be the compulsion, the safe-haven formula would amount to violation of Iraqi sovereignty which has no sanction of the international community. But at the same time, the civilised world cannot afford to ignore the plight and rights of these international orphans. By pitting the sacrosanct concept of sovereignty which is a cardinal factor in the orderly functioning of the international system, against an equally civilised and democratic issue of human rights, the Kurdish crisis has come to be global dilemma. Unfortunately, it is only the Americans and West Europeans who are attempting to grapple with the issue. The Third World nations have betrayed their complicity in the Kurdish tragedy through their discreet silence. Their involvement has been at best negative in so far as some of them have opposed the British proposal without coming up with an alternative solution. It is ironical that all those countries that supported President Hussein during the Gulf war and decried the so-called brutal bombardment of Iraq who should be so unconcerned about Iraqi repression, the causalties of which outnumber those of the war by at least one to ten. Humanitarian considerations apart, it is necessary that nations friendly to Iraq must exercise pressure on its President to deal with the Kurds humanely and democratically, and thereby prevent the western nations from taking any measures that may set dangerous precedents for future interventions. Already, France is toying with a proposal for the amendment of the UN charter to include the UN's "duty of interference" in areas of particularly outrageous abuse of human and minority rights. The Third World will little justification to oppose such a provision amenable for misuse unless it acts to avert the deepening of the Kurdish tragedy.[16]

Congressman Stephen J. Solarz has compared the atrocities against the fleeing Kurds by the Iraqi forces to the brutalities inflicted by Pakistan upon the Bengalis 20 years ago during 1971.

Solarz, who is the Chairman of the House Foreign Affairs Asia Sub-committee, said in a letter to President George Bush that alleviating the misery of the Kurds and Shias was not "just a moral and humanitarian question" but also a strategic one with repercussions for "peace and stability in the region".

He said "it was imperative that the US recognise that with the continued flow of hundreds of thousands of fleeing Kurds and Shias across the border into Turkey and Iran, these countries may fell obligated to do what New Delhi did in 1971, after millions of Bengalis had fled to India to escape the brutalities inflicted upon them by Pakistan Solarz said there was a possibility that both Turkey and Iran could send troops into Iraq to remove the Government there in order, to bring the refugee crisis to an end."

While acknowledging that a UN resolution demanding Saddam Hussein's ouster "would be unprecedented", Solarz said that "the principle of non-intervention in the internal affairs of other countries is not an absolute".

"It cannot, for instances", he said, "be allowed to serve as a rationalisation for paralysis when a Government that clearly lacks legitimacy is engaged in a campaign of mass murder against its own people".

Solarz said that in any case, the situation was no longer "just an internal Iraqi affairs, since the presence and policies of the Baathist regime are now generating millions of refugees, which has created a continuing threat to the peace and stability of the region as a whole".

Solarz noted that given Washington's interest in preserving the territorial integrity of Iraq, "it would be far better for the regime to be removed by a UN force committed to preserving the unity of Iraq than by Turkey or Iran, which he warned, "may decide to linger on long after Saddam is gone".

He reiterated that it was morally and politically unacceptable for the international community to simply standby and allow Saddam to continue transforming Iraq into a killing field.

While praising current efforts to help the millions of refugees who have fled "Saddam's brutality", Solarz observed that "parachuting blankets and food into the mountains of Iraq, is not a long-term solution".

Kurds have, of course, taken part in the war. They make up 20 per cent of President Saddam Hussein's armed forces and Kurds were among the bedraggled conscripts who surrendered so willingly to the allied forces. Others opted to flee to the mountains and to the peshmerga before the ground war began. The Kurds in Iraq seek autonomy within the borders of the present state rather than aspiring to the distant dream of independence for a Greater Kurdistan. In Turkey, the militant Kurdish Workers' Party (PKK), seeks outright independence and has shown it is ready to use terror tactics to further its aims. However, just the claim to statehood, there is a pragmatic recognition among most Kurds that the time is not yet right. In the current state of international relations, the idea of a new state that would control most of the oil resources of Iraq, Syria and Turkey and the headwaters of the Tigris and the Euphrates is geopolitically unthinkable. The competing interests of both regional and world powers would see to it that such a state never came into being. But if lesser demands for autonomy are also stifled, the Kurdish leadership may not be able restrain a younger generation of Kurds from following the PKK's lead and turning to terrorism. Among the claims now being put forward by the Kurdish leadership are a right to representation in any post-war

Middle East conference and observer status at the UN, a privilege long accorded to the less numerous Palestinians. It is a concept that would offend Turkey, Iran and the Arab states, but one that whatever friends the Kurds have outside the mountains believe should not be ignored.[17]

REFERENCES

1. Harvey Morris. Kurds. *The Independent* (Bombay), 6 March, 1991.
2. *The Independent*, 27 March, 1991.
3. *Ibid.*
4. K. Subrahmanyam. US Stance on Refugees. *The Business and Political Observer*, 18 April, 1991.
5. *Ibid.*
6. *The Hindustan Times*, 31 March, 1991.
7. *The Times of India*, 30 March, 1991.
8. Vinod Ghildiyal. Iraq. *The Sunday Observer*, 31 March, 1991.
9. *Ibid.*
10. *New Wave*, 14 April, 1991.
11. *The Hindustan Times*, 20 April, 1991.
12. *Ibid.*
13. *Ibid.*
14. Punyapriya Dasgupta. Iraqi Kurds. *The Hindustan Times*, 2 May, 1991.
15. Sunil Adam. Bush's Bay of Pigs. *The Business and Political Observer*, 18 April, 1991.
16. *Ibid.*
17. Harvey Morris. Kurds. *The Independent*, 6 March, 1991.

3

THE SAGA OF FREEDOM

One out of four Iraqis is a Kurd. To go by the official estimate of the Iraqi population of 17 million people, there are thus about four million Kurds. That is to say, a virtual four million opposed to the regime of President Saddam Hussein, and what an opposition. Since 1962, the Kurds at Baghdad, fighting for their cultural rights and, of roucrs, also for their national rights, the right to autonomy. During the heydays of the Kurds resistance. General Barzani used to be the unquestioned chief of an army of 100,000 men (60,000 Peshmergas and 40,000 militamen). On three occasions, the Peshmergas ("those who go ahead of death") played a role in provoking the fall of the Baghdad Government in 1963 (that of Gen. Kassem), in 1966 (that of Marashall Aref) and in 1968 that of Gen. Aref). In March 1970, they forced the Baathist regime (when Saddam Hussein was its vice-president) to sign an agreement conceding them autonomy within the framework of the Iraqi Republic. That was a big victory for the Kurd National Movement. For the first time, since the Sevres Treaty of 1920, the nationalist aspirations of a fraction of the Kurds were recognised by a Government of the region, and lot not just by some far-away big powers . . . Alas, later on Saddam Hussein, took the substance away from an agreement which he had thrust upon the Iraqi Army. And hostilities started again in 1974. A year later, Hussein was driven to the wall; this short war cost him $ 4 billion, about 10,000 soldiers killed and wounded and any army that had lost a lot of ammunition. When the Shah of Iran stopped aid to the Kurds, Mr. Hussein encashed upon it by giving up the "historic rights" of Iraq over the half of Shatt-al-Arab. Afterwards, it was the famous Algiers accord (March 6, 1975) which Hussein, who signs agreements only to denounce them later, repeated in September 1980 before invading Iran, only to recognize it again in August 1990, after having invaded Kuwait. This historic recollection helps one to understand that, though the Kurds are only a minority in Iraq, no Government can reasonably hope to remain in power without satisfying their aspirations. Whereas no one, not even Khomeini, had ever succeeded in mobilising the majority of the Iraqis – its 60 per cent Shi'ites – against the dictators of Baghdad, the Kurds constitute a frightful force, fairly well-structured. It is hence difficult to understand why the Western Governments, which seek to wage a "just" a war against. Hussein, are not making use of the Kurds: by launching these terrible warriors on Hussein, they would have spared an appreciable number of lives of the American French and British soldiers; and at the same time, they would have made amends for a historic injustice by enabling the Kurds at last to snatch from the future Baghdad Government, the recognition of their nationalist rights. . . Paradoxically, this scheme, which makes sense to quite a good number of journalists and political analysts, does not attract the attention of the "decision-takers" – the diplomats and politicians. "Do you think that John Major knows who the Kurds are?" asks a diplomat of Her Majesty "who, for his part, is well informed about the Middle-East" . . . perhaps, it is a spicy aside tinged with British humour. But, in fact, the American, French, British and Soviet diplomats and Government experts do not right now consider the Kurds as an important factor in the Iraqi equation. They recall that, after the death of Gen. Barzani in exile in United States in 1979, the Iraqi Kurd Movement split into about half a dozen organisations of relative importance, more or less pledged to Teheran or Damascus. Besides, these organisations differed on their ultimate objectives: autonomy, or self-determination. And, none of the war-chiefs who succeeded Gen. Barzani had the stature of a statesman. "We would very much like to take into consideration the interests of the Kurds, but with whom?", asked a diplomatic adviser of Gorbachev to one of his Kurd visitors.[1]

These experts also feel, not without reason that after the Iraqi army's crushing down the Kurd resistance (in which Iraq massively used chemical weapons from March to September 1988), the famous Peshmergas are found more on the Kurd refugee camps in Turkey or in Iran than on the snow-clad peaks of Iraqi Kurdistan: the scorched – each policy of the Baghdad regime, attained such an intensity – all the villages and towns found in a 30-kilometer deep strip all along the border were razed, the entire population deported and all the fruit trees felled – that any effort to put the rebels there, is next to impossible . . . And of course, the use of chemical weapons had somewhat killed the spirit of the Peshmergas: Hoshyar Zibari, the European representative of the Democratic Party of Kurdistan (PDK) wonders what can be achieved by an honest fighter armed with his traditional Kalashnikov against an adversary who did not hesitate to gas to death about 5,000 Kurds at Halabja in March 1988 . . . and who will not hesitate to begin again. That is why the Western experts are rather sceptical when a Kurd leader says that he has at his disposal about 3,000 men who are ready to attack. Hussein as soon he gives them the order. Refusing their own weakness, the Kurd leaders say that he has at his disposal about 3,000 men who are ready to attack Hussein as soon he gives them the order. Refusing to admit their own weakness, the Kurd leaders say that the silence of big powers can be attributed to a veto by Turkey. Alarmed by the progress of the separatist agitation of the Kurdistan Workers' Party (PKK) among the Kurd population of Turkey, the President, Mr. Turgut Ozal, is believed to have a put a condition for his involvement with the allied forces against Iraq; the Iraqi Kurds will not have any role to play and they should not be "rewarded" by being granted autonomy in the post-war Iraq, an idea that seems to be taking shape in the minds of various chancelleries. To cut short his allies questioning him on the most garish aspects of the repression of Kurds in Turkey, Ozal intends to legalise the use of Kurdish language, though in a very restrictive manner: Kurdish will continue to be banned in public places (offices, meetings, etc.); and if the folk cassettes are authorised, the publication of books in Kurdish will remain prohibited. On this issue, perhaps. Ozal could find a desperate support from . . .Teheran: Since Iran is also confronted by the problem of a minority of about five to six million Kurds in border provinces with Iraq, it can but view with concern the creation of an autonomous Kurd state on the other side of the border. The Iraqi leaders have reaffirmed on many occasions their attachment to the "established borders of the region" and to "integrity" of Iraq. But the most important veto, and about which much less is said, is that of Saudi Arabia finding it difficult to accept a regime in Baghdad that is really democratic – and hence Shi'ite – the Saudis would rather favour the setting up of a "provisional military Government" formed by retired generals like Gen. Ibrahim Daoud or Gen. Abdul Ghani Al-Raoui who have the advant- age of being Sunnites, and Arab rationalist or ex-Baathist, though they may be totally discredited in Iraq. The Kurds know that they have nothing to expect from these generals.

After having seen in the invasion of Kuwait, a "historic opportunity" to be rid of Hussein, the Kurds are wondering with bitterness whether the big powers are once again going to impose a solution that does not take into account their interests. But the situation on the spot – where the population in the big Kurd towns are more openly showing their opposition to Hussein – may probably bring round the Allies, especially the Americans in the first place, to bear in mind and not "forget" the 25 million Kurds without whom there could not be any durable stability in the Middle-East.[2]

Kurdistan's history is one of great sacrifices. During its short time of freedom during March 1991, one of the most characteristic sights in the cities and towns was that of people clustering around notice boards covered with blurred photo-copied posters. These were of the shaheed – the martyrs – the men and women in the Peshmerga, the Kurdish guerrilla forces, who have given their lives for Kurdistan, some dying in combat, some in Iraqi prisons. Many of the death go back 15 to 20 years, and in few cases even earlier. The small posters show an indistinct picture, sometimes a posed affair with a gun, more often a portrait from an identity card, and then details of name, parents, birth date, death date. Occasionally, there is a brief account of achievements in battle. People read them again and again. You had to put yourself in their shoes to understand why. It was impossible in Saddam's Iraq to mourn, to show grief, to make public the bravery of a Kurdish fighter. It was dangerous even to mention their names. This was a country without war memorials. For a few weeks, then, before Saddam's armies rolled back the revolution, it was possible for a people to celebrate their heroes and weep openly for those who died.

The first Kurdish guerrilla we met, on the Syrian border, brought out from his pack a small plastic box that contained new color prints of Mollah Mustapha Barzani, the old nationalist leader, of his son, of his younger son Massoud, who now leads the Kurdish Democratic Party, and of Margaret, a Kurdish Christian women fighter killed in 1975. Saint Margaret, they call her. And of Leila, another women – fighter, executed in 1974 after being arrested in Baghdad. A nation's icons in a grey plastic box. They were passed around the group of Syrian Kurds with reverence. Halabja, the town that Saddam Hussein gassed, is for all Kurds a symbol of their harsh destiny. Again, it was never possible to speak in public of that tragedy, never possible for a people to express its sense of anger and of violation. For three weeks, the cinemas of Arbil showed amateur videos of Halabja six times daily. As the images passed across the screen – the crumpled bundles that had been men, women, children and animals, lying in the streets of the stricken town – whole cinemas full of people wept. Finally, they could weep, they could share grief. At Halabja a few days ago there came a moment when the Kurdish revolution reached full tide and began to ebb. It is strange and sad that it should happen in such a place. We drove to Halabja on March, across the broad green expanse of the Shahrazuk plain, which stretches east from Sulaimaniyah toward Iran; amid convoys of joyful traffic. These were not yet refugees, these people in trucks and tractor-drawn trailers, stoves, mattresses and agricultural tools piled crazily high, with the small dark heads of children perched on top peering over the tailgates.[3]

They were going home to Halabja. In a place that had come to be a synonym for death, a new life was beginning. Halabja, where 5,000 people died in the poison-gas attack on March 17, 1988, was once a thriving market and trading two town on the border with Iran. Not a soul had lived there since the Iran-Iraq war ended in June, 1988, and Saddam Hussein cleared the entire area – town and surrounding villages alikes of all human habitations. Elsewhere in Kurdistan a few villages survived the Iraqi campaign of forced relocation, but in Halabja district there was nothing. The place today resembles a ruined Flanders town in the First World War. On the outskirts, the roads are mere paths through foot-high mounds of rubble. Towards the centre the shattered mosque and school can still be recognised and there are a few streets of half intact buildings. Broken glass and rubble are everywhere. Part of the town was destroyed by the Iranians, part by Iraqi bombing after it fell into Iranian and Kurdish rebel hands. Much of the rest has since been systematically demolished by the Iraqi army. From the relocation camps in which they had festered for the last three years the people of Halabja were coming back in their hundreds and thousands. They had not seen it since the black days of 1988. Since it was absolutely forbidden to enter this area – not even for one day a year to visit the graves of ancestors. In this wonderful high plains country, which has some of the best soil in the Middle-East, there was no cultivation after the clearances until the

UN embargo forced the Baghdad government to alter its policy. Even then the previous inhabitants were not allowed back: instead the land was ploughed by feudal chiefs loyal to the government. Of the once 1,200 villages in Sulaimniyah provinces, only a handful of "show" villages remain – for the benefit of visiting foreigners and journalists, the Kurds say. The others were all bulldozed in the "anfal" campaign, the name coming from a verse in the Koran in which Mohammed gave his followers the right to take the crops, property, and women of the Jewish communities then opposing Islam in Arabia. Hence, the weirdly empty countryside. When we visited, there were already 5,000 people back in Halabja, which was a town of 70,000 in the old days, as well as many in the surrounding land. It already bustled. Fallen in the dust at the entrance to town was a metal triumphal arch on which was written, "A salute of love and loyalty to the Great Leader." This is the same great leader who ordered the gas attack, described the ensuing international protest as a "storm in a tea cup" and then tried to destroy the town forever. It was the last day of Kurdistan that George Bush – they were still calling him "Hajji Bush", was still regarded as a great man. John Major also rated a Hajji – the Muslim honorific for those who have made the pilgrimage to Mecca. "Even Margaret Thatcher is a Hajji" roared the tea shop owner.[4]

But only 90 miles away the fight for Kirkuk was over and the Peshmerga, the Kurdish guerrillas, had failed to hold Saddam's army. Already the first refugees from the fighting were beginning to reach Halabja – a place with no resources or medical capacity, that had only been reoccupied for a week. The refugees in Halabja constituted a grim counter-point to the busy work of the returning families, filling the air with the sound of hammering and the clater of cooking pots. Halabja had begun its new life but Moloch a was coming down the road. A family from Tuz Kurmatu, a town south of Kirkuk where the fighting has been severe, had walked two days and two nights to reach Halabja. "It is near the Iran", the father said, "and the we think we may have to go there if the army follows us here." We went to Kurdistan to see a joyful revolution. We saw instead its sudden and tragic collapse, its abandonment by the West, and the iron tread of Saddam's army inexorably crushing down the hopes and the aspirations of the Kurdish people. But there was little sign of this even a week ago, and certainly little sign that the Kurds themselves feared such an outcome. In every town, crowded around the headquarters of the main local political party, the Kurdish Democratic Party in some, the Patriotic Union of Kurdistan in others, was an exciled and happy crowd. The local English speakers would literally run to met us when they heard that Western journalists were in town. "A dream come true", they would shout. "This is poetry—the most beautiful poetry there is," one man cried out in Dohuk. Another said, "I wish from the roots of my hair to kiss George Bush. To kiss him, yes, to kiss him". Our arrival was seen as yet another proof that the revolution was safe. Western journalists today, people seemed to think, Western ambassadors tomorrow. In the distance an Iraqi helicopters was rocketing Kurdish troops, at that stage, 10 days ago, the helicopters were not seen as a real threat. People watched with interest and without fear. In reach place the local military commander was a figure of almost mystical importance. Although people by now knew his real name, they continued to refer to him by his *non de guerre*. He would appear, usually weary looking and taciturn, only to be besieged by scores of people needing a decision which only he could authorise. It was a typical little scene of the revolution—the commander taking out his notebook and scribbing an order on a page, tearing it out and handing it over to the supplicant. But his preoccupations were with civil administration. The assumption was that the war was all over bar the shouting, that the expected government counter-attack at Kirkuk would be held, while Mosul would fall into Kurdish hands through negotiations. Meanwhile, the big problems were to get enough food, fuel and medicine into the country and to set up a civil administration. Committees with representatives of all seven political parties in the Kurdistan Front were established even in threatened places like Kirkuk.

That was the whole feeling. There would be a little more fighting, and some of its might be pretty tough, but the real problems were political and administrative. Large efforts were made to restore electricity and water to the towns and cities which had been without either since the American bombing during the war for Kuwait. In Sulaimaniyah, in the eastern part of Iraqi Kurdistan, engineers managed to restore both water and electricity shortly after the revolution. Then they began to work on the damaged turbines at the big Dukan dam to the north, and to repair the transmission tored lines so that electricity could be restored in April, the biggest city in Kurdish hands.[5]

Iraqi opposition groups meeting in West Beirut conceded on March 13, 1991 that Saddam Hussein's Republican Guard was steadily smothering the rebellion inside Iraq, regaining control of Karbala, Najaf and Basra. The most convincing evidence came from Abdul Aziz al-Hakim – the brother of Ayatollah Mohammed Bakr al- Hakim, who is leading the revolt in Basra – who acknowledged that Karbala and Najaf were no longer "in the hands of revolutionaries".[6]

An Iraqi Communist Party delegate, Kazen Habib, said that the Iraqi uprising was now facing "serious uprising was now facing serious difficulties" and lacked organisation and co-ordination.

The vagueness of the information available to the Iraqi opposition only served to emphasise how remote their contact was with the uprising. Most have not been to Iraq for many years, which is why they chose representatives to travel there on March 13, 1991 resistance leaders.

Only Kurdish delegates were able to encourage the conference with claims that their own guerrillas were still capturing villages north of Kirkuk.

In a message read to the conference, Ayatollah Hakim himself said the revolt was "not an organised act". President Saddam's dictatorship, he said, "cannot be confronted by popular revolution, but only by accurate and organised underground acts".

Abdul Aziz al-Hakim had flown to Beruit from Tehran in a private aircraft to give his brother's message.

As the resistance inside Iraq is crushed, so Iraqi opposition groups here have been issuing ever-longer statements on the need to overthrow President Saddam and establish a parliamentary constitution.

Pressure for such a democracy was expressed on Wednesday by the Iraqi al-Dawaa party, widely regarded as the most influential opposition group inside the country.

Abu Bilal al-Adib, the party's principal delegate from Tehran, promised to abide by a parliamentary constitution under which it would stand in a general election. Coming from a group which – despite its denials – is believe to have tried to kill the emir of Kuwait and to have blow up the American and French embassies there in 1933, this desire for democracy is little short of extraordinary.

Al-Adib said on March 13, 1991 that several of the 17 men later imprisoned for the embassy attacks had once been members of Dawaa, but that the party, which is controlled by a secret Majlis el Shura of around 12 members, was interested only in the collapse of Saddam Hussein's regime. President Saddam Hussein banned the party on 31 March 1980, since when thousands of its members have been tortured and executed, including the Dawaa founder, Ayatollah Mohammed Bakr Sadr, who was hanged in Najaf.

In Washington, the United States government said that the Iraqi rebellion – or rebellions – might be developing into a continuing guerrilla war, rather than a set-piece insurrection easily quelled by the Iraqi military.

Richard Boucher, the state department spokesman, said: "Cities and towns where urest has been suppressed by government forces often revert entirely or partly to control by dissident elements once heavier forces depart to deal with the unrest elsewhere".

Boucher said that was especially so around the Shia holy cities of Najaf and Karbala in southern Iraq, where government forces appeared to have gained greater control on Monday but were again "dealing with considerable unrest" on Wednesday. He also said that "dissident activity" in the Kurdish town in north Iraq was continuing at "high-levels".

In Riyadh, as the fact of president Saddam Hussein's survival becomes more evident, some voices are complaining that the American-led Gulf war coalition left the job half-finished. The suspicion has grown that the US, remembering the humilitations it suffered at the hands of a Shia Muslim regime in Iran, does not want anything similar in Baghdad. Washington appears to have decided that a weakened president Saddam would serve its interests best, critics say.

A Tehran radio broadcast, monitored in Nicosia, reported as refugees as claiming that Iraq is carrying out napalm attacks on rebels in Basra and that victims began arriving in Iran on Monday.

Iran's official Islamic Republic News Agency, also monitored, quoted an unidentified spokesman of the Patriotic Union of Kurdistan as saying Iraq threatened to kill 5,000 Kurdish hostages, mostly women and children, who had allegedly been rounded up and taken to Kirkuk.[7]

One of the puzzles in the American policy towards Iraq is the unpublicised US decision to permit Saddam Hussein to use his helicopters to suppress the uprising of the Shias in the south and the Kurds in the north. On February 15, 1991 shortly before the start of the ground offensive, president Bush called for the "Iraqi military and Iraqi people to take matters into their own hands to force Saddam Hussein to step aside".

He further declared, "we have no argument with the people of Iraq. Our differences are with Iraq's brutal dictator." The Iraqi military did not rise against Saddam Hussein but the Iraqi people, both Shias in the south and Kurds in the north, did. As these uprisings were gathering momentum, on March 26, 1991 Washington announced that it would not prevent Iraq from using its helicopters. Using Napalm and phosphorous bombs from the helicopters the Iraqi ruler was able to crush the popular uprising. A plausible explanation for this reversal of policy in Iraq by the United States has been given by Laurie Mylroie in The Asian Wall Street Journal of April 11, 1991. Earlier Laurie Mylroie had written a book along with Ms Judith Miller on "Saddam Hussein and the crisis in the Gulf".

In that book the authors had described Saddam Hussein's relations with other Gulf Arab States and his actual threats to them in the last three years. In this article Mylroie attributes the change in US policy to pressure from the Saudi rulers who were more terrified about the emergence of either Shia influence backed by Iran or democracy in Iraq. The continuance of Saddam Hussein was presumably preferred to either Shia influence or democracy.[8]

Tracing the developments leading to this denouement the author refers to a Saudi attempt to stage a military coup in Iraq using the good offices of one Salah Omar Ali Al-Takriti, hailing from Saddam Hussein's native town. The Saudi preference was for an Iraqi general to replace Saddam Hussein. Presumably the Saudis and the US intelligence community failed to assess properly the hold Saddam Hussein had on the military apparatus. Salah al-Takriti failed in his efforts to trigger off a coup. It would also appear that Saudis who were coordinating this activity were so abysmally poor in their intelligence they suggested names of generals who were dead ten years ago as candidates who could help to take over from Saddam Hussein. The above who version tends to be confirmed by an interview in the CNN on 12th of April by Fariade Hiwaizi, a member of British-Kurdish Friends Society. In the course of the interview he said that abandoning of Kurds might be partly because of racist considerations. Kurds are not Arabs and the Arab Muslims did not protest when Saddam Hussein used chemical weapons against the kurds at Halabja in 1988 when the Kurds rose against him. So much for Muslim sympathy for fellow Muslims. The US administration appears to have decided to go along with Saudi leadership and allow Saddam Hussein to re-establish himself. While the US Congress and US Administration talk of human rights in various parts of the world in Iraq the US evidently decided to play the role of Pilate and wash its hands off the matter of the killing of Kurds. The US even succeeded in watering down the UN resolution from "condemnation" of Saddam Hussein to one of "deploring" his action. Iraqi has 59.5 per cent Shia Arabs, 18 per cent Sunni Arabs, 18 per cent Christians. Saudi interest is in perpetuating the minority rule of 18 per cent Sunni Arabs over the Kurds and majority Shias. The Iraqi Kurdish population is estimated at around 3.25 million. Of these nearly a million are now likely to become refugees in Turkey. Another 900,000 are stated to have entered Iran and its is expected the refugee influx might go up to 1.5 million. If this were to happen then this even will be the most spectacular depopulation of an area in proportionate terms – nearly 77 per cent originally resident in the territory. In the US record of support to human rights this will rank along with their stands on Bangladesh and Cambodia. In all the three cases the United States has chosen to support by omission or commission a genocidal regime. One aspect that stands out in all these developments is the total failure of the United States to assess the situation in West Asia correctly and consequently their being manipulated by West Asian despots. The Shah of Iran was able to do it in the seventies, then Saddam Hussein did it and now the Saudis. What a great victory for human rights and democracy: What a beginning for the new international order.[9]

After acting with exemplary resolution to oust Iraqi forces from Kuwait, the Americans have now ruled out offering the kind of help to the Iraqi insurgent which could have helped them overthrow president Saddam Hussein. Faced with armed Kurdish guerrillas in the north and religious-led Shi'ite Muslims in the south, Saddam's regime last week seemed close to collapse. But, thanks to incaction from the American forces in southern Iraq, he appears to have got the better of the Shi'ite uprising. The Washington decision, announced on Tuesday, not to down Iraqi helicopters striking against the rebels is now likely to tip the balance against the Kurds. The Iraqi armed forces should be well placed to drive the Kurds out of their prize capture, the oil city of Kirkuk, and back into their mountain strongholds. For the Kurds, it is clear that the allies prefer to deal with the devil they know – Saddam – now that his horns have been blunted by his Kuwait flasco, rather than the unknown quantity of the 23-party opposition alliance.[10]

"Bush's policy has been contradictory", said Hoshiar Zebari, representative of the Iraqi Kurdistan Front in London. "He called for the Iraqi people to overthrow Saddam and now they are voting with their lives, yet the Americans stand back and do nothing." The opposition is bitterly disappointed. It was widely believed that, under the terms of the ceasefire with Iraq, the use of helicopters in attacks was a ceasefire violation. After a week of dithering, the White House spokesman, Marlin Fitzwater, on Tuesday set out the administration's view: "Any understanding with the Iraqis on helicopters was an oral discussion, nothing in writing". It is clear that the speed and extent of the twin rebellions caught the allies by surprise. But the impression given is of tacit support for the status quo. For all their brave talks of wanting Saddam gone, the allies clearly see the rebels as too great a risk. The Iraqi Kurds, a 3.5 million minority who have been in more or less constant revolt against rule from Baghdad for two generations, are still far from admitting defeat. But there is no talk now of joining up with the Shi'ites to over-throw Saddam. They intend to hold on to their positions.[11]

Allied officials explain their refusal to help the opposition on the grounds that they have no UN mandate: the UN requires them to restore "international peace and security" in the region, not to install a friendly government in Baghdad. But the real reason is that the opposition – a broad array of Kurdish rebels, Islamic fundamentalists, communists and Western-educated liberals – is fatally flawed for the task that Washington needs carried out. Since all its members come from outside a Saddam's entourage, western officials believe they do not have the trigger to remove the dictator. Secondly, the opposition's interests are so divergent that they would be likely to tear the country apart. If the Shi'ites controlled the south, it is argued, they would be dependent on Iranian help and thus increase Tehran's already considerable influence in tahe Gulf, to the consternation of the Arab states. A Kurdish homeland in the north of Iraq would encourage Kurds in Turkey to follow suit, thus upsetting the Ankara government, which has proved a loyal ally. The West's last hope of removing Saddam now lies with the Iraqi army. Despite the hammering it took at the hands of the allies, it remains stronger and better equipped than the allies had believed. This loci has not escaped Saddam. Given a breathing space by the allies, he has sought to consolidate his power by appointing Saddoun Hammadi, a Shi'ite. Whether he succeeds in extricating himself from the mess he created depends now more and more on the men who surround him in Baghdad and less on the rebels.[12]

The civil war in southern Iraq has come to the Americans in the form of thousands of desperate, frightened people running from the fighting and from Saddam Hussein's repression of the south for its uprising against his regime. The sheer numbers of the refugees are straining the US military's ability to deal with them and enforce a ceasefire at the same time. Most of the Iraqis fleeing into US-controlled areas are civilians. Almost everyone brings now-familiar stories of atrocities carried out by troops loyal to president Saddam Hussein against their families and neighbours. "The burnt my family alive". "The soldiers raped nurses in Nasiriyah hospital and cut off their breasts before killing them". "They bombed my house and I am now alone". Some refugees have been injured in the fighting or have been shot by troops while trying to flee. Other refugees are soldiers-turned-rebels whose forces have been crushed and who now have nowhere else to turn. Some are deserts from the Iraqi army and Republican Guard who could no longer carry out orders for attacks against their own people. They vome on foot, or in cars piled high with their possessions. Some have a driven or walked for days. Others are passengers packed densely into the back of lorries. All come pleading for food, medical care and shelter. Above all, they are seeking protection. "Please help me", one man asked foreign journalists after failing to gain the attention off US officers. "I must have political asylum. I hate Saddam. If I stay in Iraq I will die."[13]

The refugees choke US check-points set up along the Nasiriyah highway which runs parallel to the demarcation line agreed at the end of the Gulf war. Until late last week, the Americans provided no facilities for the refugees and were turning back soldiers who wished to surrender. Now, after quiet pressure from the International Red Cross, the Americans have set up refugee camps, mobile medical hospitals and POW holding areas in the flat stretches of desert that straddle the highway. They also opened a refugee camp and food distribution centre in the Iraqi border town of Safwan. The establishment of these facilities has served only to attract even greater numbers of refugees. At the same time, the Americans have started to take POWs again, but not at all checkpoints. Some US positions are geared up to control civilian traffic, while others have a defensive role and cannot afford to be tied down with prisoners and refugees. But even those with a non-defensive mission are felling the strain. "We just don't have the logistics to keep talking these, people", one US officer said, complaining to a colleague after US counter-intelligence officials ordered his checkpoints to continue accepting the surrender of Iraqi soldiers. All vehicles are stopped and searched at gunpoint for arms and contraband such as drugs and medicine. The lengthy searches lead to long queues and put a great deal of strain on US soldiers, who must keep alert for a possible terrorist attack. Units are rotated every few days because of the stress. Although the US says it is not helping the rebels, in some places, such as the checkpoints around Suq ash Shuyukh. Iraqis moving north of US positions with guns are allowed to keep their weapons. If they move south across the US line of control they must surrender their arms. The cache collected at Suq ash Shuyukh on March 25, 1991 was a pitiful arsenal of old AK-47s, a few hand grendades and assorted ammunition.[14]

The Iraqi refugee tragedy, June's (1990) disastrous earthquake, and serious floods in the southeast have shifted international attention away from Iran's political evolution, now at a turning point. But Tehran's Gulf war neutrality, its offer of sanctuary to hundreds of thousands of mainly Kurdish Iraqis and its readiness to accept help from abroad are further signs the bad-tempered isolationism of the past 12 years is coming to an end. Many Iranians are confident that the dominance of anti-western Islamic radicals will be broken in elections to the single-chamber Majlis (parliament) due to just one year. In the meantime, in the shabby capital and in western towns not reconstructed since the 1980-88 war with Iraq, changes are in the air, while in foreign policy, fence-mending is underway in all directions. Not that Iran is about to abandon its militant brand of Islamic fundamentalism, but regional cooperation, reconstruction, and economic and social developments all now seem more important than women's head scarves.

February 1991 budget encouraged the private sector, set realistic foreign exchange rates, allocated large sums for post-war reconstruction and accepted the need of billions of dollars' worth of foreign credits. The first World Bank loan of $ 200 million to Iran since the 1979 Islamic revolution was approved recently. The resumption of diplomatic relations with Saudi Arabia last month will permit 100,000 Iranians to go on the Haj (Muslim pilgrimage) this year and opens the door for Gulf security—mainly meaning containment of Iraq without the further need for foreign troops. Iran's economy is more than ever dependent on oil revenues, giving it another reason for wooing the Saudis.

"Tehran will expect a reduction in Saudi oil production in order to bring world prices up to a reasonable level", said an editorial in the English-language Tehran Times on April 15, 1991.

Foreign Minister Al Akbar Velayati goes to Riyadh on Saturday for talks expected to cover all these issues.

Rajai Khorosani, chairman of the Majlis's foreign affairs committee, this week called for full ambassadorial relations with Egypt, long-described for making peace with Israel.

Iran forget ties with Britain last September and improved them this month with the release of British businessman Roger Cooper after more than five years in jail for alleged spying. Current overtures to the European Community could also result in formal relations with the 12-nation Ec.

The new atmosphere has brought a surge of western businessmen to Tehran in search of lucrative contracts for the first time in a decade.

Iran is developing the island of Qesham in the Strait of Hormuz, opposite the Sultanate of Oman, as a free trade and industrial zone.

The Iranian Government has eccused the Iraqi Army of violating border agreement in their relentless pursual of Kurdish refugees. Tehran radio said on April 16, 1991 that Iraqi tanks inside Iraqi Kurdistan opened fire upon Kurdish refugees inside Iran, killing many "men, women and children."

On its part, the Iraqi Government accused Iran of sending a detachment of heavily armed troops inside-Iraqi territory on a sabotage mission. Before retreating back inside Iranian territory, the troops killed a number of Iraqi servicemen.

However, there are no independent conformations of these violations of border agreements in the region marked-off by the United States Army as the "de-militarised zone".

Meanwhile, as relief operations get underway, the United Nations High Commissioner for Refugees, Madam Delgata, who yesterday visited refugee camps on border areas, said that the present scale of relief and food supplies reaching refugees were not enough. Delgata said that the intensity of food and relief supplies had to be increased if the majority the refugees were to benefit.

The United States has already indicated that its operations will "double" in the next few days with the use of heavy-lift helicopters which are able to reach stranded Kurdish people in the high mountain passes in between Iraq and Turkey. However, a spokesman for the British "Save the children Fund", a relief organisation active in the region, said today that refugees not staying at the larger camps on the mountain slopes might be neglected of the food drops and airlifts being carried out by the united States, British and French airforces. There are thousands of refugees in between the larger camps and the Turkish and Iranian border camps. A United Nations assessment said that over half a million Kurdish refugees were waiting on the borders of Iran.

The United States' State Department in Washington today revealed the grim detail that up to one thousand Kurdish refugees were dying a day due to exposure and diseases.

There is a growing tendency in the western media and the intelligentsia to put the blame on President Saddam Hussein for the Kurdish refugee problem. But none has tried to look into problem in a wider historical perspective. The Kurdish problem is not the baby of the "Mother of all Battles". It dates back even to the periods of the Ottoman empire, World War First and the subsequent western 'rule' over the region. A century ago the Kurds have been a pastoral and nomadic race, a loose collection of shifting tribes. Until World War First, national frontiers were of no significance to them. The demarcation and closing of international frontiers after the war put a stop to their periodic migrations which hit some tribes hard economically and so made for their discontent. In some instance, these artificial barriers were formed and frontiers cut arbitrarily through the territory of certain tribes, thus splitting them. They, however, failed to capitalize on the political situation after the war. The fresh map of the Middle East drawn up did not include a separate Kurdish nation. Despite the fact that there was a Kurdish advocate in U.S. President Woodrow Wilson, who mentioned the statehood for the Kurds in his project for the League of Nations. But the British imperialists, who were in control and who decided to appropriate the oil fields of 'Kurdistan,' would have none of it. The Anglo-Iraqi declaration of December 1922 was devised to obtain international confirmation of the inclusion of the area within the Iraqi frontiers to "secure for the British the right to exploit the fields of Kurdistan". During this period the Kurdish insurrections in Turkey and Iran were put down firmly. Iran even declared that it has no "Kurdish problem," Turkey went one step further in refusing to admit that they had any Kurds at all. Turkey, Iran and Iraq joined hands in signing a treaty in 1937, clearly aimed against the Kurdish movements which were in their infancy then. Mustafa Kemal's "secularism" and Reza Shah's "iron hand" proved too much for any uprisings of the Kurds. They were deprived of their language, education and even their mosques. The Iraqi regime, though weak was backed by its patrons in subduing the Kurds. But by then the Kurdish nationalism had taken its roots in all these regions.

It even flourished to the extent that the Kurds established a small temporary Kurdish Republic, during the Soviet presence in Iran, soon after World War Second.[15]

With the Soviet's heart with the Kurdish people, an East-West power struggle started in the region. The communists of the region sympathised with the Kurds and supported the Kurdish uprisings to a large extent. The Kurds even established a party of their own, the Kurdish Democratic Party (KDP), a party inspired by Marxist-Leninist ideas. From then it was the flag bearer of the Kurds in its various struggles. The following decade found many ups and downs in the Kurdish struggle till 1961, when a major Kurdish revolt broke out, though confined to Iraq. The Kurds, led by the Barazainis started a major assault on the Iraqi forces and inflicted defeats on many fronts. Turkey and Iran made sure that these revolts did not spread to their territories and called them the Iraqi Kurdish revolts. The Iraqi victory came on the diplomatic table by the signing of the Friendship Treaty with the Soviet Union in 1972. The Soviet leaders who had until then shown considerable understanding of the Kurdish people's struggles believed that the Treaty was justifiable not just in terms of immediate self interests but also because of Baghdad's struggle against the western oil companies. During 1970-75, the Iraqi Baath chose different accomplices and foreign allies. To achieves its ends in the light of the changing political situations. President Saddam launched a major offensive when he was assured of the co-operation of the Iraqi Communist Party (ICP) and substantial Soviet military aid. The US military aid started flowing to the Kurds through Iran, their ally in the region. But neither the Shah nor President Nixon desired a victory for their clients. They hoped to ensure that the insurgents world be capable of sustaining a level of hostility just enough to sap the resources of Iraq. The Kurds were thus made a "card" in the international power game. The Algiers Agreement of 1975 was pushed through President Saddam's throat, of course, with Mr. Kissinger's blessings. Iraq agreed to settle the border dispute, along the Shatt-Al-Arab, with Iran in return to Iran stopping aid to Kurdish rebels. Thus, the war came to an end following some international horse-trading at the expense of the Kurds. The events in the region took a turn with the failure of American "two pillar policy" in the region after the Iranian Revolution of 1979. The US alienated itself from Iran and started supporting President Saddam even during the eight year war. Iran as before started aiding Kurdish revolt along with the war which forced President Saddam to fight a two pronged war, against the Iranian forces across the border as well as the Kurdish rebels within the country. But neither the US nor the Soviet Union or any other big powers tried to stop him then. They wanted the war to be prolonged at any cost and kept mum when thousands of Kurds were killed during the war. But later they started accusing President Saddam of using chemical weapons and causing the genocide of his own people. But none of these powers expected, even in their wildest of dreams, Iraq to turn against them and fight a war. Thanks to the supper power collaboration they could defeat him in the war. But the 'allies' tried to liquidate him through other means – by instigating rebellion. Here lies the hypocrisy of the US policies. On the one hand they support and give aid to the rebels and speaks of "non-interference" in internal matters, on the other. But who is to be blamed for all this? No, certainly not the Kurds. But one cannot blame President Saddam also. It is the legacy of the various rulers of the region and the western powers who thwarted all the Kurdish nationalist movements.[16]

There cannot be any doubt that history has given the Kurds a raw deal; though they constitute a fairly large national group, they are a people without a state. In the period immediately following the First World War, there was an attempt to set up a Kurdish state but the Treaty of Severes put an end to that and the Kurds remained a people who constituted a permanent minority in Iran. Iraq, Syria and Turkey, with the last having the largest number. A people in permanent revolt against the established order, which has only favoured their oppression, the Kurds have been the pawns on the diplomatic chessboard of West Asia; Kurdish revolts have been aided, abetted and financed by rival powers to suit their political interests; the Shah of Iran and the American Central Intelligence Agency financed and gave military assistance to the Kurds in their revolt against the Baathist regime in Iraq in the early seventies; and the 1974 agreement under which Saddam Hussein accepted the Iranian terms was the direct result of the Kurdish uprising which had brought Iraq almost to its knees. Having secured his objective, the Shah coolly abandoned the Kurds and the Iraqi government was able to wreak vengeance. Betrayal is part of Kurdish history. They have been tools in the hands of others to destabilise neighbouring regimes, but Turkey, Iran and Iraq are united in their desire to deny statehood to the Kurds. A Kurdish state could undermine the balance of power system in West Asia. Strangely enough, it is Iraq which has given the most generous deal to the Kurds: in Iran, they have been savagely suppressed; in Turkey, till very recently, the very existence of the Kurds was denied, they were referred to as mountain Turks and semi-permanent emergency existed in the areas where they are in a majority. They could not identify themselves as Kurds, speak the Kurdish language or have cultural organisations. It is only now under Ozal that things have begun to change. The United States and the West European countries, which have become increasingly concerned about human rights in Iraq, never thought of putting pressure on Ankara; Turkey, after all, was the guardian of the Southern Flank of NATO and strategic considerations took precedence over human rights.[17]

REFERENCES

1. Chris Kotschera. Kurds. *The Hindu*, 24 March, 1991.
2. *Ibid.*
3. Martin Woolacott. Kurds' Saga of Freedom Struggle. *The Hindustan Times*, 6 April, 1991.
4. *Ibid.*
5. *Ibid.*
6. *The Independent*, 17 March, 1991.
7. *Ibid.*
8. K. Subrahmanyam. A Puzzling Reversal of US Policy. *The Business and Political Observer*, 17 April, 199.
9. *Ibid.*
10. *The Independent*, 30 March, 1991.
11. *Ibid.*
12. *Ibid.*
13. *The Independent*, 31 March, 1991.
14. *Ibid.*
15. Ajith Chaly. Who to Blame for Kurdish Crisis? *The Business and Political Observer*, 23 April, 1991.
16. *Ibid.*
17. K.M. Panikkar. Kurds. *Patriot*, 13 April, 1991.

4

SEPARATISM – A NEW DANGER

United by common ethnic, cultural, linguistic and religious characteristics, the Kurds were artificially divided in 1923 among four different national states: Turkey, Iraq, Iran and Syria. Since then there has been continuous armed struggle between the military forces of the different countries and the militant Kurds, the former fighting to preserve the integrity of the state and the latter searching for the unification of their communal group within one territory.*

The Kurds are an ancient Middle Eastern people with a history stretching back 3,000 years. They speak a variety of dialects of an Indo-European language and belong to the Muslim religion of the Sunni sect. They claim a distinct ethnic identity, separate from the Iranians, Turks, Arabs and others.[1]

The Kurds live in a territory known as the Kurdistan whose 500,000 sq. km includes the vast mountainous area that adjoins Turkey, Iran, Iraq and Syria (see Fig. 10.1). It is considered a region of strategic importance because it is located in the so-called 'Heart of the Middle East' with its enormous wealth in natural resources, mainly oil deposits and mineral resources.[2] Estimates of Kurdish population area extremely variable with the four governments concerned tending to minimise their numbers. However, they are said to be the fourth most numerous people in the Middle East with about 20 million people.[3] Their probable distribution among the different countries is shown in Table 10.1. Except in Syria where they constitute less than 10 percent of the population, the Kurds account for a quarter to a third in the countries where they reside. There are also Kurds located in the Soviet Union, but they are not discussed here because

---

*L.D. Aguado. The National Liberation Movement of the Kurds in the Middle East. In *Secessionist Movements in comparative perspective*. Ed. by Ralph R. Premdas London, 1990.

their situation is very different from that of the other countries.[4] There is also a Kurdish refugee population living in Lebanon, around 70,000, and in several countries of West Europe, around 380,000.[5]

The traditional social organisation of the Kurds was tribal and semi-nomadic, but this is disappearing as a result of the direct control of their internal affairs by their respective governments. Kurdish society is rural and is based on agriculture (wheat, rice, fruits, cotton and tobacco) and cattle-raising. In general terms the territory of the Kurdistan is economically underdeveloped.[6]

The Kurdistan territory has never been politically distinct, always forming part of different Empires in thé Middle East from 650 BC until the beginning of the twentieth century (1915).[7] In 1639 the Kurds were partitioned between the Ottoman and Persian Empires and remained there for almost five centuries. During this period, they enjoyed a certain degree of autonomy that allowed them to maintain their distinctive ethnic characteristics. At the beginning of the nineteenth century, however, the Sultans transformed the Empire into a centralized military state provoking a series of Kurdish insurrections intended to strengthen their identity and maintain their territorial autonomy. However, in these uprisings the Kurdian tribesmen did not yet think in terms of a sovereign state.[8]

Table 1

The Kurd Population in the Middle East: 1984

Country	*Total population of the country (1982)*	*Total population of the Kurds in each country (1984)*		*Percentage of total Kurd population*
		No.	*%*	
Turkey	44,736,957	10,000.000	22.4	50.5
Iran	40,240,000	6,000.000	14.9	30.3
Iraq	13,530,000	3,000.000	22.2	15.2
Syria	9,660.000	800.000	8.3	4.0
		19,800.000		100.0

Source: Christiane Moore, *Les Kurdes aujourd hui:*

During the period of European contact with the Ottoman Empire, numerous ethno-nationalist movements emerged (Greeks, Slavs, Arabs, Kurds, etc.).[9] With the eruption of World War I and the break-up of the Ottoman Empire, the Middle East came under the control of the League of Nations, which was in charge of demarcating the boundaries of the new states. Under the principle of self-determination, the Peace Conference of 1918 stipulated that the non-Turkish nationalities of the Ottoman Empire would be 'assured an absolute unmolested opportunity of autonomous development' and specifically decided to give the Kurds the right to create their own independent state – the Kurdistan state.[10] The Serve Treaty created Kurdistan as well as the three Arab States of Hedjaz (Saudi Arabia), Syria and Iraq, a Turkish state and an Armenian state.[11] However, the treaty was not ratified by the Turkish National Assembly which disapproved of the delimitation of boundaries made for their own territory.[12] In 1923, a new treaty was signed (Lausanne Treaty) revoking the right of self-determination for the Kurds and Armenian people and ratified the creation of Saudi-Arabia, Iraq, Syria and Turkey. Since then, the Kurdish territory remains divided between Turkey, Iran, Iraq and Syria.[13] The Kurds then became a minority in each of these countries.

After World War First the new countries of the Middle East were created without any geographic, ethnic or religious cohesion; they were under direct or indirect Western control for almost twenty-five years. The European powers pressured the new Middle Eastern governments to guarantee the protection of their minorities. However, in the face of modernisation and strong nationalistic centralised governments, security and unity were sought by the homogenisation of their people even though the majority of these countries were ethnically heterogeneous.[14] Arab nationalism deteriorated into authoritarianism. Its main objective was the achievement of uniformity and the destruction of diversity offered by minorities.

Under the Persian nationalism of Riza Shah, unification policy was executed by destroying the minority tribal systems.[15] Most of these countries applied different degrees of assimilationist policies – 'Turquafication, Arabisation of Persianisation' – that sought to destroy minority identities. They prohibited the use of the written and oral Kurdish language, their costumes and traditions, and their organisations and celebrations.[16]

The governments applied discriminatory policies that marginalized the people of Kurdistan. The Kurdish region and population were less developed economically, had a higher illiteracy and infant mortality rate and received a lower than average proportion of each government's budget. Political representation was also limited.[17] Another type of policy applied was the transfer of population in order to alter the ethnic balance of the region. Thousands of Kurds were removed by the majority groups. In addition, the governments concerned created several settlements in Kurdistan of people belonging to the ethnic majority.[18] There has also been massive deportation beyond the national borders. They were settled mainly in Syria and Lebanon, primarily by the Turkish government.

Twentieth-century Kurdish separatism began in all four states at the close of the World War First. The divided Kurds have not forgotten the historical (Serve Treaty). Since then the Kurdish people have undertaken a long struggle for national liberation. Although Kurdish nationalist aspirations and separatist agitation manifested themselves in each nation, the centres of gravity of these national liberation movements have been displaced from one country to another in different historical periods. We can distinguish three periods. The first centre of gravity was in Turkish Kurdistan from 1925 to 1938. The Turkish leaders promised the creation of the Federal State of Turks and Kurds if the Kurds collaborated in the struggle for Turkish independence. When the Turks got their independence and these promises were not fulfilled, the Kurds launched a series of armed struggles with the aim of secession. The second phase was located in Iranian Kurdistan from 1945 to 1946. This period of struggle was unique since it resulted in an independent Kurdish State. The Kurdish Republic of Mahabad led by qazi Mohammed had an existence of less than a year, when it was eliminated as the Allies left Iran in 1946. The third centre of gravity was located in Iraqi Kurdistan from 1961 to 1975. These struggles were divided into five different internal wars that were interrupted by the changes of government that occurred in Iraq. Mullah Mustafa, after signing the Treaty of Algeria in 1975 between Tehran and Baghdad, *subdued by force all demonstrations of discontent* in each of these countries.[19]

In general terms, the Kurdish liberation movements have had two main political phases. The first phase, from the nineteenth century up to World War II, was characterised by traditional tribal revolts and a coherent religious system. However, there was a great deal of disunity among the tribes and as much energy was spent fighting among themselves as with their traditional enemies – the Christian Assyrians and Armenians, and the Muslim Azerbaijanis and Turkomen.[20] This fissiparous feature of Kurdish political behaviour played a decisive role in undermining the destiny of Kurds.

When the new states were created in the Middle East in 1923, there were several Kurdish political organizations with different views of their destiny. One, a radical militant youth group, was aiming for the independence of the Kurdish provinces. The other, led by the President of the Kurdish Association and member of the Ottoman state, Abdul Padyr, defended the incorporation of the Kurds in the new Turkish Republic. This division weakened the Kurdish movement and allowed the Allies to decide the Kurds' future without them being able to raise a unified protest. This period was the most opportune moment for the liberation of Kurdistan and the establishment of an independent state. Nonetheless, this opportunity was missed by the Kurds because of their political disunity. Once the Kurdish territory was divided, the uprisings that followed took traditional tribal lines, leaving them isolated and fragmented. Tribal loyalty seemed much stronger than an embracing national identity. The second phase of the liberation movement started after World War II and it was characterised by more unity. There was the growth of a Kurdish town population, a new bourgeois class and an intelligentsia had appeared in whom tribal loyalties were weaker and national political ideas stronger. The penetration of socialist ideologies permitted the creation of 'revolutionary' and progressive cadres and the growth of a Kurdish national spirit, partly in reaction against pan-Arabism. The principal new Kurdish political force was the Kurdish democratic Party (KDP) born during the Mahabad Republic and spread to other Kurdish regions, swallowing older Kurdish organizations. The KDP fought for the rights of the Kurdish people inside each of the countries where they lived. From the 1940s to the 1970s it was the only significant political party that existed in Kurdistan. This party forged an alliance with some of the left parties that existed in these countries. Even though the KDP had the same nominal title in each of these countries, their objectives and programmes were different. The KDP in Turkey and Syria, created in 1965 and 1957 respectively, were trying

in Turkey and Syria, created in 1965 and 1957 respectively, were trying to win their national rights in relation to their language and culture. The KDP in Iran (1945) wanted the creation of a federation, like Yugoslavia, where minorities would enjoy a certain degree of autonomy and the Kurd language would be recognized as official. The KDP in Iraq (1946) wanted to liberate Iraq from imperialism, but looked for autonomy of their territory inside an Arab-Kurd State.[21]

The political organisation of the Kurds was modified after 1975, following the defeat of the Kurdish Democratic Party in Iraq. Since then there has been in each of these countries a fragmentation of political parties, each having its own ideology and specific political programme. They differed in aim and composition and often competed for membership. Sometimes this factionalism resulted in open conflicts. Each group maintained its own links with other non-Kurdish political organisations within the country and with other Kurdish political organisations in and outside their own country. Most of them had foreign representation as well. Today there were nine Kurdish political parties in Turkey, the main ones being the Kurdish Workers party and the Kurdish Socialist Party. In Iran there are three Kurdish political parties; the most important is the Kurdish Democratic Party. In Syria there are seven such political parties, with the Kurdish Democratic Party being the most outstanding. In Iraq there are eight, of which the principal ones are the Kurdish Patriotic Union and the Kurdish Democratic Party. All these organisations are committed to obtaining a certain degree of autonomy in their territory within the boundaries of their countries. However, these diverse political organisations of the Kurds have detracted from their revolutionary struggle. To begin with, their skills in battle were exploited historically by European governments for mercenary activities. An example of this situation is the collaboration of the Kurdish leader with the Turkish government during the 1920s in the Armenian genocide. This fact has enormously weakened the prestige of the Kurdish people. Kurdish tribes have also were struggling for their liberation. Secondly, the Kurdish political organisations inside each of these countries have maintained the tribal structural division, which led to a proliferation of the political parties that were never successfully able to mobilize support for autonomy. Thirdly, there has not been an unified liberation movement of the Kurds that includes the different Kurdish communities of the Middle East in one common and consistent struggle against Iran, Iraq, Turkey and Syria for a Kurdistan settlement. This lack of unity can be explained partly by the national border division that makes collaboration and co-ordination very difficult. Fourthly, political parties of the Kurds have practically given up the claim to self-determination, even though they are conscious of the existence of a linguistic and cultural national unity in 'Kurdistan'. Today there is only one foreign Kurdish party, the Yekbun, established in 1978 in Sweden, that is struggling for a united liberation movement for the whole of Kurdistan through secession. Fifthly, the Kurdish political organisations that had obtained external help were not able to comprehend that often such help came with strings attached. Consequently, these groups were usually manipulated by the foreign countries. Once this was done, they became victims of movements on which they had come to depend economically and militarily. In the Middle East, there have been many struggles among the different governments for supremacy in the region. A common political strategy used to weaken the neighbouring countries was a contribution to the national liberation movements of the frontier country. This inevitably embroiled the Kurds in a variety of causes which have served as well as backfied on them. The Kurds, for instance, have been both an ally and a foe of the Iranians under the Shah. Most recently, since 1980, with the outbreak of the Iran-Iraq war, once again the new Iranian regime is collaborating with the Kurds of Iraq. They have succeeded in uniting two of the main Kurd political parties (the Kurdish Democratic Party and the Kurdish Patriotic Union) opposed to the Iraqi government. They have continued to supply the rebels with military equipment and the Iranian Revolutionary Guards have participated with the Kurdish guerrillas in attacking Iraqi oil installations (Kirkuk). This new co-operation has helped the Kurdish separatist movement to obtain a certain degree of success. It is said that by June of 1987 they doubled the area under their control (800 square miles). The Iranian government has stated that the Kurds have become 'one of the most important instruments of pressure on Iraq'. It is left to be seen if the Kurdish Organisations will once again be out-manoeuvred by their erstwhile allies.[22]

REFERENCES

1. Emmanuel Sivans, 'The Kurds: Another perspective'. In Case Studies on *Human Rights and Fundamental Freedoms*. The Hague, 1975, vol. 2. p. 140.
2. Martin Short, *The Kurds*, London, 1981, p. 5.
3. Christiane Moore, *Les Kurdes aujourd' hui Paris*, 1984, p. 21

4. The Kurds in the Soviet Union are not located in the border area of the Kurdistan territory. The Soviet Kurds do not have a specific Kurdish territory—there are several Kurdish communities in the Transcaucasian Republic and Central Asia—spread between Armenia.
Georgia and Azerbaijan. They are recognised as one of the nationalities of the Soviet Union, and are allowed to preserve their national and cultural identity through native schools, universities, publications, etc. Communication with Kurds living in other countries is infrequent (See Martin Short, *The Kurds*, London, 1981 9.13).
5. Moore, *Op.cit.* p. 21.
6. Gerard Chaliand *ed.* 'People Without a Country: The Kurds and Kurdistan', London, 1980, pp. 79-80; see also J. Nagel, 'The Conditions of Ethnic Separatism', *Ethnicity*, vol. 17 (1980).
7. C.J. Edmond, *Kurds, Turks and Arabs*, London, 1947, p. 6.
8. Sivans, *The Kurds*, p. 141.
9. A.H. Hourani, Minorities in the Arab World, London, 1947, pp. 30-1.
10. Short, *The Kurds*, p. 6
11. Chaliand, *Op. cit.*, pp. 66-7.
12. The new Turkish regime under the leadership of Mustafa Kemal Ataturk considered the Serve Treaty inadequate to protect their interests. The Turkish territory was reduced to a Protectorate, occupied by British, French, Italian and Greek forces and their original territory was enormously reduced. That is why they rejected the guarantees offered to the non-Turkish nationalities of the Empire (Short, *The Kurds*, p .6).
13. L.M. Von Taubinger, 'Suffering and Struggle of the Kurds', Case Studies on Human Rights and Fundamental Freedom, The Hague, 1975. p. 245.
14. In Turkey there are Kurds, Arabs, Circassians, Greeks, Armenians, Georgians, Lazes, Jews, Zaza; in Iran there are Armenians, Azerbaijanis, Lurs, Gashgui, Bakhtiari, Arabs, Baluchi, Shah Savans, Afshars, Dard, Turkomens, Assyrians and Kurds; in Iraq there are Armenians, Turks, Turomens, Yazidis, Assyrians, Persians and Kurds; and in Syria there are Armenians, Assyrians, Yezidis, Alawites, Oruzes, Ismailis and Kurds (Eric Fischer', *Minorities and Minority Problems*. New York, 1980).
15. Richard Tapper, ed., *The Conflict of Tribe and State in Iran and Afghanistan* New York, 1983, p. 21.
16. In Turkey the use of the Kurdish language has been prohibited since 1924. The words Kurd and Kurdistan were eliminated from the Turkish vocabulary. The government suppressed from the libraries all books that mention the words Kurd or Kurdistan. The education of the Kurds continues to be implemented in the Turkish language. In 1966 the Justice Party prohibited the first socialist Kurdish magazine and all the recording of Kurdish music as well as broadcasting radio station in Kurd language (*ibid.*, p. 114). After the destruction of the Mahabad Republic in 1946, the Kurdish language was prohibited for thirty years. The Persian language has been the only language for education and there are no schools for Kurds with an education imparted in the Kurdish language. During the Shah's dictatorship freedom of expression and the press were suppressed; the Shah closed all

Kurdish printers and publicly burned all books written in Kurdis, *ibid*, pp. 161-2.

17. Nagel, '*The Conditions of Ethnic Separatism*', p. 288
18. In 1932, the Turkish government enacted a deportation law for its Kurdish population. This law had the objective of dispersing the Kurds through the regions of Anatolia and sending Turkish immigrants to Kurdistan (*ibid*., p. 101). The same policy was applied in 1958 by General Abdual Kassem in Iraq. Hundreds of thousands of Kurds were transferred from the oil region known as Kirkuk to the desert region of Dianiya and Nisiriya. A number of Iraqi Arabs were settled in this oil region (Short, *The Kurds*, p. 16). The government of Syria inaugurated in 1962 a project known as the 'Arab Belt' that had the objective of expelling all the Kurdish population established in Djazira, bordering on Turkey, and to repopulate it progressively by an Arab population (Von Taubinger, 'Suffering and Struggle of *The Kurds*' p. 248).
19. Aguado. *op. cit.*
20. Nagel. "*The Conditions of Ethnic Separation*"; p. 286.
21. Moore. *Les Kurdes*.
22. Aguado. *op. cit.*

5

THE SAFETY ZONES

Havalo called a Kurd from newly liberated northern Iraq to his cousins over the Hazy river border with Turkey, the increasingly anxious home to half the Kurds of the Middle East. "That means 'friends', I think", said Cemal Ozalp, a Kurd from the Turkish river side hamlet of Ovakoy, eyeing the Iraqi Kurd waving a white handkerchief.[1]

None of the small group on the Turkish side had the courage to call back. And when a rumour spread that a Turkish soldier was coming over from the border post, everyone beat a hasty retreat. Decades of harsh repression of Kurdish nationalism in Turkey are not easily cast aside. In Ankara, president Turgut Ozal has recognised the danger posed to Turkey by the new order in the Middle East, especially that of an independent Kurdish State. After talks with president Bush in Washington this weekend, Ozal again vowed that Turkey would never allow one to appear.

Ozal is attempting to outflank Kurdish radicals and win over Turkey's own Kurds, about one in five of the population, by offering to relegalise the Kurdish language, to free political prisoners and to close his eyes to Kurdish autonomy in Iraq.

But even these modest reforms have upset domestic balances. They remain blocked by the establishment, including an increasingly anxious army raised on the firm, unifying Turkish nationalist cult of Mustafa Kamal Ataturk.

"This is a dangerous game," said Kenan Evren, the retired armed forces chief and former president. "It starts with asking for social rights and ends with independence. The Western states want to revive Severes (a 1920 treaty which granted an independent Kurdish state)."

But Hashemi, mayor of Cizre, one of the most nationalist Kurdish towns in Turkey, said that there was no turning back now. "The arrow has left the bow, but it is not clear how far it will go," said Hashemi. "I don't think it can get to independence. The important things is that Ozal is breaking taboos, he has been very brave. People are happy, there's excitement and the people support him."

Ironically, liberalisation is not welcomed by the PKK, the Kurdish Workers' Party already suffering military reverses in a bloody separatist rebellion. Abdullah "Apo" Ocalan, the PKK leader, met reporters in Damascus last week to say that he was ready for a cease-fire and talks if reforms of the kind offered by Ozal became reality.

Ocalan said he personally wanted a united, independent Kurdistan, as do most of his Kurdish racial supporters in Turkey. Trying to square the circle in a gesture for the 'Turks, he added that "one shouldn't mix up independence with a separate state. We are not separatists." The PKK's occasional terrorist tactics and austere ideological mix of Kurdishness, Marxism and Islam have brought conflict in the past with northern Iraqi groups like those of Masoud Barzani.[2] Western diplomats have even maintained that the PKK is now in alliance with Saddam Hussein. But Kurdish sources say there are signs of PKK rapprochement with the anti-Baghdad rebels and that it has recently been fighting with Kurdish rebels in northern Iraq.

Saddam Hussein's attempt, the ruthless suppression of US-incited Kurd rebellion, has created conditions for to another Anglo-American plan to militarily intervene in northern Iraq, this time in the guise of humanitarian aid to Kurd refugees. The aerial destruction of Iraq was done to restore law in international affairs. Having accepted all the humiliating terms dictated by the US, Saddam hoped that the international community would wash its hands of Iraq's internal affairs. That was not to be. The British plan to dismember Iraq is now being implemented. Thousands of American troops have entered Iraq from the Turkish border to build camps for Kurd refugees. Since the UN has not sanctioned American military support to refugees, one of the numerous security council resolution is being twisted to justify Anglo-American intervention. Of all the permanent Security Council members only China has come out against the American action. Non one would oppose humanitarian aid to Kurd refugees who have been uprooted from their soil by Saddam's troops. But this job could have been done under the UN refugee organisation if the motive behind it would have been humanitarian. The Anglo-American intention, however, is to use the Kurd refugees as a shield to tigthen up the screw on Iraq and eventually get Saddam killed or overthrown. Anything short of Saddam's physical elimination would not satisfy the Anglo-American ambition to impose their will on the Arabs. The British, with their age old experience in dividing countries, creating new frontiers and igniting ethnic conflicts, know how to guide the Americans to re-establish the Anglo-Saxon hegemony in the world. Kurd refugees are only a pretext for the greater design in Asia. The Kurd demand for a Kurdish state comprising parts of Iraq, Syria, Turkey and Iran is not new, though non of the countries where Kurds reside is prepared to grant the Kurd demand. They use the Kurds to settle scores with each other and forget them the moment they have come to term with each other. After a long struggle the Kurds had got a promise from Baghdad in 1970 that they would have autonomy within Iraq. Four years later, the Kurds were manipulated to start insurrection with Iranian, Israeli and American help. In 1975 the Shah of Iran and Iraq settled their territorial dispute and the Kurds were left high and dry. Even so, it took nearly 12 years for Baghdad to reestablish its authority throughout the Kurdish areas. During the Iraq-Iran war Kurds were used as a pawn by Iran. Once the war came to an end in 1988, Saddam ruthlessly suppressed the Kurds. The Christian conscience of the West was not pricked by the Iraqi use of poison gas to subdue to the Kurds. Instead, the US was providing assistance to Saddam to defeat the Iranians.[3]

The latest phase of Kurd rebellion was incited by the US and its allies in the region. It has rendered tens of thousands of Kurds homeless. They believed American rhetoric and made an all-out effort to have a homeland of their own. They have lost everything. Though Saddam has promised to rehabilitate the refugees and allow them to have autonomy as agreed in 1974, it is doubtful if Kurd refugees would agree to return home. If the UN does not intervene, Americans will be tempted to fight to the last Kurd to remove Saddam and dismember Iraq. In any case the US is creating a dangerous precedent.

The man who once talked of successfully waging the mother of all battles has not only suffered an ignominious military defeat, but is locked in a grim struggle for his very political survival. It is not surprising that the rebel campaign to oust President Saddam Hussein has originated in southern and northern Iraq. These regions are largely populated by Shi'ites and Kurds—communities which between them constitute over 70 per cent of the country's population. The government in Baghdad is largely a Sunni dominated show. The Shiites and the Kurds therefore left out of the political process. In fact, the Kurds have been battling the nation's Baathist regime almost ceaselessly for the past two decades. It is but natural that they have now significantly stepped up their campaign since Saddam's domestic standing has never been lower. Besides, the Shiite and Kurdish areas are relatively far from Baghdad. It is, no doubt, easier to launch an anti-government movement in these regions than in the capital. This isn't too to suggest that public anger has not manifested itself in Baghdad. Moreover, southern Iraq has been particularly devastated by the Gulf war. Many of the southerners, whose economic lives have been shattered, naturally feel resentful towards the nation's rulers.[4]

Though the coalition forces headed by the US have suspended their hostilities for nearly three weeks now, the people of Iraq have not had peace. They are perhaps suffering today from as many casualties as they did during the war with the US and its allies and their plight is now worse than ever before. The communication and transportation infrastructures have been wrecked and power, water and fuel are not readily available. The cumulative impact of months-old economic sanctions is being felt. The environmental contamination is taking its toll along with shortage of food and medicines. Tragically enough, those who demonstrated in the streets all over the world in support of Mr. Saddam Hussein, the tyrant and aggressor, are not marching and shouting today to bring succor to the unfortunate Iraqi masses. Those who waxed eloquent about the Ummah and agitated on peripheral issues in the name of Islamic solidarity are deafeningly silent while the shrines in Karbala and Najaf are behind damaged and the sufferings of the Iraqi people are being prolonged. Even as leaders of nations, peace protagonists and fellow members of Ummah are inactive, the envoy in Iraq Marti Attisari is a rushing to UN headquarters with an alarming report on state of affairs in Iraq. One hopes the secretary general will act promptly and persuade the Security Council to life the sanctions against Iraq. Indian should already have acted in this respect in the Security Council. It is time to mobilise the support of nine non-permanent members of the Security Council for rehabilitation measures in Iraq. The US and its allies may favour a limited lifting of sanctions. It is necessary to make sure that sanctions in respect of equipment and materials to repair the infrastructure are fully withdrawn along with those on food and medicines.

Only arms and ammunition should be prohibited. The fear of Iraq clandestinely arming itself in a short term should be disabused. The Iraqis do not have the wherewithal for the purpose.[5]

Supply of food and medicines to the populations in areas under the control of the Kurds and other opposition groups should be explored in consultations with authorities who are in occupation of the territory through the agency of international Red Cross and local Red Crescent societies as has been done in Ethiopia and Sudan. Iraq is food importing country. Since its infrastructure has been crippled severely and its gross domestic product is likely to drop down precipitously because of the destruction of oil and petrochemical industries, Iraq would require prolonged assistance including food assistance – before it can stand on its feed even in respect of meeting the bare essential needs of its population. Even at this stage an alternative leadership to Mr. Saddam Hussein is not easily identifiable. The various oppositions groups that met in Beirut could not agree on anything more than basic principles. The fighting against Mr. Saddam Hussein's forces is not co-ordinated. In the north the Kurds claim to have captured the oil town of Kirkuk (yet to be confirmed by the Americans) and brought most of Kurdistan under their control. In the south the Shiite opposition is waging a not too easy war with Iraqi government forces. The neighbours of Iraq do not seem to have an agreed policy towards the future dispensation in that country. The Turkish government have had discussions with Iraqi Kurds a development without precedent. Presumably this was a damage limiting operation to contain Kurdish demand for autonomy to Iraqi Kurdistan and to stem its outflow into Turkey where nearly half of all Kurds reside.[6]

Demonstrators in the northern Iraq oil city of Mosul stormed two prisons and released 4,000 political prisoners on March 14, 1991 according to Kurdish leaders.

Kurdish forces have surrounded Mosul, according to an opposition leader in London, who said the commanding general of loyalist forces in the far-north providential town of Agra had already surrendered to the rebels.[7]

The Kurds said their forces have suffered few casualties in the fighting because there is little resistance in many areas.

The reports indicate the Kurdish rebels are saving their strength for a major push on Kirkuk and Dohuk, Traditional hotbeds of Kurdish resistance.

Kurdish rebels have begun organising a new system of democratic government in the liberated territories of northern Iraq. Celebrations of victory over Saddam Hussein's regime are well underway in Kirkuk, Zakho, Arbil and other liberated towns, reporters of the Turkish daily Milliyet said in their first report from northern Iraq. On March 25, 1991. Kurdish rebels are in control of the 300 km long Turkish-Iraqi border in the north. The exclusive report includes photographs showing that Saddam Hussein's troops used napalm bombs to quell the rebellion.[8]

It is the Kurds themselves who have been the victims rather than the perpetrators of treachery. When in Vienna in 1989, Qassemlou tried to negotiate a peaceful settlement of the Kurdish question in Iran, he was murdered by the emissaries from Tehran who had been sent to meet him. The modern history of the Kurdish revolt dates from 1908, when the Young Turk took power in the Ottoman Empire in a military coup and granted limited national rights to minorities such as the Kurds, the Arabs and the Albanians. But the new pan-national mood in the empire was swiftly overtaken by the Turkish ultra-nationalism of those who had taken power. It was a process that was to lead to the disintegration of the empire, the fate of which was finally sealed by defeat in the first World War. Kurds fought on both sides in the war alongside Ottoman and Russian forces. By Kurdish accounts some 700,000 were massacred by the Turks. It was the post-war-settlement, dominated by the imperial concerns of the victorious European powers, Britain and France, which was to seal the fate of the Kurds and led to their present plight. In 1918, President Woodrow Wilson set out his Fourteen Point Declaration before the US Congress, which included a promise to the Kurds of "an absolute unmolested opportunity of autonomous development". At the Treaty of Severes in 1920, the allied powers agreed that the Kurdish provinces should be allowed to break away from Turkey if a majority of the population so desired. The population of the Mosul Governate (northern Iraq), by now occupied by the British, was to be allowed to join the new independent state of Kurdistan. The League of Nations was mandated to test the will of the Kurdish people and to judge whether it was capable of independence. The treaty was never ratified; the colonial powers had quite different plans for the future of the region. The British devoted the rich oil reserves of the Mosul region and in November 1920, three months after Sevres, annexed the region to the new state of Iraq to be governed by an Arab King, Faisal, the Sharif of Mecca. The Kurds rose up under Sheikh Mahmoud, who declared himself King of Kurdistan, in the first of a series of abortive revolts against the authority of Baghdad. In ensuring years, the British mandate powers discovered the virtues of air power in taming the rebellious Kurds. The RAF bombed and destroyed Kurdish villages and developed the use of time-delayed bombs that would explode after fleeing villagers had returned to their homes.[9]

The fate of the Kurds in the twentieth century has been to be in conflict with the more powerful rival forces of Arab, Turkish and Iranian nationalism. Iraq proclaims itself as – and is widely accepted to be – an Arab state, and yet of its 17 million inhabitants at least 3.5 million are Kurds and a further half million are Turkomans. In Turkey, the very existence of a distinct Kurdish community has been denied, although Kurds account for some 12 million of the 57 million population. In Iran, Kurdish guerrillas under the leadership of Qassemlou rose in support of the 1979 revolution against the Shah of Iran, only to be brutally suppressed by the regime of the Ayatollahs.

Describing the situation of the Kurds of Iraq, Hoshyar, Zebari, the European representative of the Kurdish Democratic Party, has said: "A Kurd has no land, according to the official Baathist ideology, because the land does not belong to him, even if he had lived on its from ancient times, but to the Arab Nation, including of course Iraq."

The period of the Iran-Iraq war, in which the Kurdish Peshmerga renewed their intermittent revolt against Baghdad, saw a systematic attempt to annihilate Kurdish separatism through killings, deportations and the forced Arabisation of Kurdish lands. By 1988, more than 5,000 Kurdish villages had been destroyed along with their cattle and crops and their surviving populations relocated in strategic hamlets. In one operation along, 8,000 members of one tribe were rounded up, taken tribe away and never seen again. Eighties rebellion followed a nine-year revolt in the Sixties under the leadership of Mulla Mustafa Barzani. The Kurds won a measure of autonomy from Baghdad under a 1970 agreement broken by Vevgeny Primakov, now Mikhail Gorbachev's Middle East adviser. But the deal broke down by 1974 and the war resumed, with the Kurds accepting backing from the Shah of Iran and indirectly from the CIA. This aid was suspended in 1975 when Saddam Hussein signed a treaty with the Shah on regulating the Iran-Iraq border at the Shatt-Al-Arab. Barzani's revolt collapsed and he died in exile in the United States. The war was the result of cynical manipulation by Washington and Tehran to undermine the Soviet-backed regime in Baghdad. According to a CIA memorandum of 1974; "Both Iran and the US hope to benefit from an unresolvable situation in which Iraq is intrinsically weakened by the Kurds' refusal to give up their semi-autonomy. Neither Iran nor the US would like to see the situation resolved one way or the other. This experience helps to explain why the Kurds, whose Peshmerga guerrillas are the only armed opposition force in Iraq, stayed out of the Gulf war. They had no desire to be seen once more as agents of the Americans against their Arab fellow citizens. Baghdad had also made it clear that there would be no sympathy for Kurds if the Peshmerga joined the allied struggle against Saddam Hussein.[10]

Kurdish leaders inside Iraq have held their first direct contacts with Iraqi army commanders since the start of the uprising sweeping the north and south of the country, and are hopeful that the army will joint in the fight to topple Saddam Hussein. A senior opposition source, who described the contacts as one of the most dramatic developments in the uprising, also said the rebellion had now passed from the spontaneous stage to an "organised system of command structure and communications", both within the north itself and between in north and south. The rebels were "very close" to taking the oil city of Kirkuk, demonstrations were spreading around Baghdad, and at least 30 cities were said to be under rebel control.[11]

In a setback for the rebels, however, the Republican Guard attacked the Shia holy city of Karbala on Sunday and killed 500 fighters, according to Ayatollah Taki al-Modaresi of Tehran, speaking in Beirut. "The Republican Guard, backed by tanks, stormed the city . . . which was liberated five days ago," he said. If the report is true, the action will only exacerbate Shia anger. An Iraqi opposition source said the Kurdish commander-in-chief, Massoud Barzani, had conveyed to Iraqi army commanders in the north that "if you want to get rid of Saddam, we will support you entirely". He said the Kurdish leadership was expecting a "positive response"; the rebels were therefore seeking not to target the army in the uprising, but concentrating on Baath party establishments and security force installation. Five thousand army troops had already surrendered to the rebels. Opposition sources said the uprising was swiftly moving westwards and Kurdish fighters had already taken control of several towns near Arbil; the north-western city of Suleimanyah remained firmly under rebel control for the third day. Kurdish sources said Barzani had issued an appeal to the International Red Cross to send a fact-finding mission to Iraq to assess casualties and the needs of the population. Opposition sources said they had reliable reports that president Saddam had not yet deployed chemical weapons against the rebels, but were convinced he would do so unless the allied powers deterred him. The United States, adamant that it does not "intend to get involved" in Iraq's internal affairs, has been reluctant to take a public stand even on the question of how it would react in the event of a chemical attack against the Iraqi people. Yet at the weekend James Baker, the secretary of state, said he had warned Iraqi officials against the use of such weapons. Opposition spokesmen said his statement came after they had repeatedly put to the state department and Senate committees the question: "How would the United States react were Saddam to use chemical weapons against his own people"? They said they were still waiting for a reply.[12]

The latest claims of rebel advances came as the leaders of the united Iraqi opposition gathered in Beirut for a conference they hope will lead to the formation of, at least, a parliament in exile. A spokesman for the opposition's joint action committee said on arrival in Beirut that its members parties would never work with Saddam Hussein. "He is a criminal and we will never share power with him . . . the minimum we ask is for Saddam to step down, stand trial, his system to be dismantled and for free general elections," said Muwafaq Rubal, a leading member of the committee. Rubal's remarks amounted to a rejection of a call on Sunday by president Ali Akbar Hashemi Rafsanjani of Iran for president Saddam and the opposition to co-operate. "It is necessary that the government and all groups inside Iraq co-operate to calm down Iraq's internal situation," he was quoted by Tehran Radio as saying . . . An Iranian source said Teheran, worried about a possible dismemberment of Iraq and the installing of a Saudi-backed government, was hoping to get president Saddam to work with the opposition by "getting through to him that if he allows Iraq to be destroyed from within, he will go down in history as a swine."[13]

Iraqi exiles say president Saddam Hussein's forces are cracking down mercilessly on a two-week-old rebellion, leaving bodies pilling up in holy cities where civilians fled for safety.

A Bush administration official said, forces loyal to Saddam were using "very brutal and very bloody" tactics to quell the unrest that erupted after his army's rout in the Gulf war. The official said there was no evidence to suggest that Saddam's loyalists were using chemical weapons against rebels either in Kurdish strongholds in the north or in the southern Shi'ite heartland. Jalal Talabani, one of Saddam's leading Kurdish opponents, said in Beirut that Saddam's troops had taken 5,000 women and children hostage and said they would kill them if attacked. Iraqis living in London appealed to Bush in an open letter to intervene to end what it said was an attempt by Saddam to annihilate his 17 million people. The appeal was made on behalf of Iraqis everywhere. It quoted witnesses as saying that as Iraqi troops tried to put down popular uprisings, "piles or remains beyond recognition are accumulating in (the holy Shi'ite Moslem cities of) Najaf and Karbala, and hundreds of women, children and elderly people were dying daily." The open letter to Bush was sent from the London office of the Supreme Council of the Islamic Revolution in Iraq (SCIRI), the Iraqi Shi'ite group co-ordinating the revolt in the south of the country. A senior US official said the Kurds appeared to be faring well but Saddam had gone to great lengths to quell unrest from Shi'ites. Saddam and most of his administration are Sunni Muslims. Washington has said it will not intervene in the internal affairs of Iraq but has made no secret that it would be happy to see Saddam overthrown. It has warned him against using chemical weapons to quell the unrest.[14]

Despite US promises of a Middle East settlement, the region's future is far from assured. America now wishes to extricate itself from the Gulf. But what will it leave behind? Already, Kuwait is in turmoil, its inhabitants demanding a democracy in which its emir – returning recently to a distinctly cool reception – has very little interest. The city's largest non-Kuwaiti community, as many as 2,40,000 Palestinians, are now under threat. Thousands of gunmen are at large in the city but the Americans, remembering their harsh experience in Lebanon, are refusing to take responsibility for what happens in the streets of the capital. Iraq is now in bloody insurrection. Regional powers are preparing to carve up the nation whose territorial integrity Washington claimed it would preserve. Having won his war in the Gulf, Bush is now facing the prospect of something not unlike defeat: the setting up of a Shia Islamic republic in the South of the country. It was to avoid just that, after all, the Americans tacitly supported Saddam during his war with Iran, and that Saudi Arabia and Kuwait paid for that war. Little wonder that Bush is now warning Iran against annexing Iraqi territory. The Americans – and the British and the French – are still celebrating their victory. But the consequences of war in the Middle East rarely tally with the military outcome. It would be satisfying, for example, if Saddam Hussein could be overthrown and replaced by an Iraqi democracy. But democracy would almost certainly lead to fragmentation and, at least in the south, to an Islamic republic. Elsewhere in the Middle East – in Algeria, for instance, and perhaps in Egypt – democracy could produce the very fundamentalist regimes which the Americans least wish to see created. The "New World Order" has a hollow ring; it will not include democracy for the Arab nations. In their desire to extricate themselves from the Gulf, the Americans are trying to fill the vacuum there with a cocktail of conservative Arab states (the Gulf Cooperation Council), one semi-conservative state (Egypt) and a radical nation (Syria). Washington had hoped that Syria would also be able to bring the Iraqi opposition together to form a coherent alternative to Saddam. But the two most powerful groups within the opposition – the Shias and the Kurds – have no loyalty to the new pro-US alliance.[15]

While Britain's contacts with the Kurds and other Iraqi opposition parties grow ever more intense, the US administration is holding to its dogged refusal to talk to any of them. Given that the Kurds are seizing control of large parts of Iraq, that they have traditionally held a pivotal role in Iraqi politics, and that they will play a crucial role in a future provisional government formed by the Iraqi opposition, that policy seems remarkably short-sighted. British diplomats said recently that they hoped to "elevate further" their contacts with the Iraqi opposition – which has hitherto reached the junior minister level—to the possibility of meetings with Douglas Hurd himself. At the same time, an Iraqi opposition delegation returned from a three-week visit to the US having failed to obtain an audience with even a low-level official at the state department. The group was led by the eminently sensible and well-informed European representative of the Kurdish Democratic Party, Hoshyar Zebari, who has been an important participant in the British Foreign Office; the latter body had the foresight to initiate those contacts before the end of last year. During the Gulf war, the US excuse for avoiding talks with the Kurds was, in the words of one Iraqi opposition source, "the price Washington paid for keeping Turkey out of the Gulf crisis." Turkey, with a large Kurdish population, feared a strengthening of Iraqi Kurdistan which is could not control; yet now the Turks are holding talks with Iraqi Kurdish groups, and "that excuse by Washington isn't there anymore."[16]

Indeed, Jalal Talabani, one of the Kurdish leaders who has met Turkish officials in the past few days, said Ankara had promised it "would do its best to make the Kurdish cause known, would be a voice for Iraqi Kurds in Europe and America and would support setting up direct political relations between the Kurdish movement in Iraq and the US administration." A leading Kurdish source recently cautiously welcomed that possibility, but admitted he favoured the "stranger and more reliable" bridge which the British Foreign office had already erected in acting as the only conduct to Washington. As an Iraqi opposition figure said: "It is clear, with the loss of the Turkish veto excuse, that the overall policy of the Americans is that they simply do not want, for their own reasons, to deal with any part of the Iraqi opposition. Their aim is what they take to be stability to Iraq, not democracy." In the better-the devil-you-know tradition of geopolitics, that stability means the continued rule of an enfeebled Saddam Hussein. The administration, in response to challenges on the Kurdish question, has fought back with a non-argument, whether deliberate or ill-informed: that it is loath to deal with Kurds who seek little less than an independent state. In fact, the Kurds of the United Iraqi opposition stress that they are after autonomy within Iraq, and that coalition with other groups, including the Shias, is the only way to hold Iraq together. The Shia role recalls another significant point about Washington's pusillanimous attitude; in the words of the one US analyst with close contacts to the state department: "The wolf is at the door; but the US is so burnt by seeing a dictator like the shah of Iran followed by another offensive regime it simply cannot get involved in this one; it is afriad of Shia fundamentalists, and it is afraid of chaos; the state department Arabists don't want to talk to the Kurds either, because they are not Arabs; it is a bankrupt policy." In the meantime, president Bush is issuing statements of concern that Iran is "grabbing territory" in Iraq; his warning followed dubious claims to that effect by the Iranian opposition Mujahedin who, as opposed to the Iraqi opposition, do have direct contacts with the United States administration. The Iraqi opposition acknowledge their weakness was in emphasising European base, and are planning to set up offices in the US as soon as possible. At the same time, Britain is responding at the UN to appeals by the Iraqi opposition for protection for the Iraqi people; it wants to add a demand for the destruction of Iraq's chemical and biological weapons to UN Security Council resolutions, and wants to maintain sanctions against Iraq as a lever. The conclusion of that move rests, again, on a verdict by the United States.[17]

In the grip of cold and hunger, Iraqi refugees along the Turkish border on April 12, 1991 said they would go home if the United Nations assured them of protection from Saddam Hussein's army.

"If the United Nations will protect us in northern Iraq, we prefer to go back instead of waiting for death here", said Ismet Abin, a lawyer from the northern Iraqi town of Dahuk.

"It's hard to believe, but if we get a guarantee from the UN, America and Britain, we would rather go back", said Salih Afman, a Peshmerga guerrilla in rain-soaked Khaki uniform.

Britain has asked the other four permanent Security Council members to consult on a new UN resolution which would safeguard refugees in case Iraq failed to co-operate with relief efforts or resumed military attacks on Kurds.

US President George Bush said he was in full agreement with the European Community and UN Secretary-General Javier Perez de Cuellar on the idea of creating a haven in northern Iraq under UN supervision.

Cuellar has said that such a zone could not work without the agreement of the Iraqi government. Washington has warned Iraq not to use force north of the 36th Parallel, an area which takes in most of Iraqi Kurdistan, but Kurdish guerrillas said Iraqi troops had attacked rebel-held areas on April 11 in apparent defiance of the US warning.

Iran too has said that it would like to see the orderly repatriation of hundreds of thousands of Kurds who have flooded across its frontier with Iraq.

Refugees on the Turkish border said they were desperate to get away. "We can't stand it any longer," said Abdul Ahmed, a teacher from Dahuk, who was trying to force his way into a tiny grocery shop packed with refugees buying food with Iraqi dinars.

Wretched conditions at this border camp have already driven about 500 refugees, mainly Christians and some Kurds, to return to Iraq. Dozens of babies and old people are dying daily in the camp, which has little food, medical care, sanitation or clean water.

More than 30 bodies wrapped in blankets and towels lay on a dusty carpet inside the local mosque, now a makeshift mortuary. "We have no place left at the cemetery to bury the dead", said a harassed official.

Meanwhile, reports from New York talked of a step-up in international efforts to reach aid to an estimated 1.7 million refugees, in view of a major humanitarian disaster being imminent.

The World Food Aid Programme, an arm of the United Nations, announced that it had secured pledges for sufficient emergency food aid to meet the requirement of refugees in Turkey and Iran for upto 30 days. But logistics in reaching aid to the needy could pose a serious problem due to the difficult terrain.

The Red Cross Committee has sent out an appeal for $ 742 million international aid for the Kurdish refugees.

In other developments, a top Iraqi diplomat—despite his suspicion that the United States continued to have some secret agenda against his war-beleaguered country—stated at the United Nations that Baghdad's main goals now were to rebuild and mend ties in the Arab World and the region.

Speaking to mediamen after the pronouncement of a formal ceasefire in the Gulf, Iraq's envoy to the UN Abdul Amir al-Anbari said that in a way, the war was not over.

"I hope that what you call permanent ceasefire would not be permanent, because what I would like to see is a permanent end of hostilities. Yet, intentionally and in violation of previous resolutions, the United States has termed it as a formal ceasefire, which implies that the state of war continues. I hope it would, some time sooner rather than later, eventually come to an end", he said.

"But I assume that the US is still having some secret agenda to impose on Iraq. Only time will tell," he added.

On the Kurdish issue, Mr. Al-Anbari said, "Don't forget that it is almost nine months since the US and its coalition partners imposed a total seige on Iraq."

Meanwhile, reports from Seoul quoted South Korean foreign ministry as announcing an aid of $ 300,000 for the Kurdish refugees.

The money will be given to the UN High Commissioner for Refugees and the UN Disaster Relief Coordinator, after the details are discussed between the government and the UN agencies, Chung said.

A four-man Kurdish delegation reached Baghdad on April 21, 1991, at the request of Iraqi President Saddam Hussein to discuss the plight of the millions of Kurdish refugees, a spokesman for the Kurdish Democratic Party (KDP).

Jalal Talabani, Secretary-General of the Patriotic Union of Kurdistan, Mactcheervan Barazani, member of the KDP, Sami Abdul-Rahman, Secretary-General of the Kurdish socialist party in Iraq, were in Baghdad.

"They are thereupon the request of Saddam Hussein", the spokesman, Falak el-Deen Kaka'i, said. Efforts were being made to arrange a meeting between the Kurdish leaders and the President, he added.

Kaka'i said the visit had been prepared at meetings between representatives of the Kurdish groups concerned and an Iraqi Government delegation.

In addition to discussing the plight of the Kurdish refugees, the four-man delegation would ask that the 1970 treaty that gives the Kurds autonomy in Iraq be implemented. "But the delegation is going to insist that any new deal that is going to be struck should be sponsored by the United Nations", Kaka'i said.

Earlier Kaka'i said the talks in Baghdad should not only focus on the refugees but should also address the "political problem of the

Kurds". He was referring to the Kurds' long struggle with the Iraqi Central Governments to gain autonomy.

"I think that some progress could be made during the discussions because the situation of the Kurds is bad and the situation of the Iraqi regime is bad as well", Kaka'i said.

Kaka'i said attempts to start a dialogue with Saddam were mainly spurred by the pathetic situation of an estimated two million Kurdish refugees huddled along the Turkish and Iranian borders or fleeing toward those nations.

Kurdish leader Jalal Talabani had said that the rebels had reached an agreement in principle with Iraqi President Saddam Hussein which could end their revolt.

Details of the agreement needed to be negotiated and further talks would be held soon, said Talabani, who led a Kurdish delegation in talks with Saddam on April 25, 1991.

He said all Kurds who had fled after the revolt was crushed were being told to return to their homes in Iraqi Kurdistan, in the north of the country.

Talabani, leader of the Patriotic Union of Kurdistan (PUK) one of the major Kurdish opposition groups, said the talks centred on four issues: normalization of relations, democracy in Iraq, Kurdish rights and national unity.

He said they discussed free elections for a national assembly, freedom of the press and freedom to assemble.

"We have not reached a state of details on the agreement. It was only in principle," Talabani said.

Talabani said all eight Kurdish rebel groups in Iraq agreed with the decision to meet with Mr. Saddam and reach a peaceful settlement to the fighting that has sent more than a million Kurds into refuge since the end of the Gulf war.

The Kurdish leader said the agreement basically would honour the framework of a 1970 accord between the Kurds and the government.

He said the talks were possible because of a military stalemate.

Meanwhile, the UN Iraq-Kuwait Observation Mission (UNIKOM) became operational yesterday when it officially took over three observation posts in the demilitarised zone.

A Unofficial said aerial reconnaissance of the entire zone was carried out on Tuesday as part of the engineering survey as preparations were being made for deployment of the peace-keeping force whose total strength stood at ten. It will ultimately have a strength of 1440 with 300 observers and support staff including five infantry companies.

The mandate of UNIKOM is to monitor the demilitarised zone between which runs 10 km into Iraq and five km into Kuwait. The civil administration will be run by Iraq and Kuwait in their respective territories.

Infantry units from the UN interim force in Lebanon and the UN peace-keeping force in Cyprus were travelling overland and are expected in the area shortly.

According to reports from Tokyo, Japan is to provide $ 100 million in emergency financial aid to UN operations helping Kurdish and other Iraqi refugees.

Japan has so far provided $ 10 million to the UN disaster relief organisation in emergency relief funds for some 1.6 million refugees who have fled Iraq.

Japan also decided yesterday to send a flotilla of six mine sweepers and two auxilliary vessels to the Persian Gulf, in what will be the armed forces first overseas mission since the end of World War II.

Japanese Prime Minister Toshiki Kaifu's cabinet approved the measure despite strong criticism from opposition parties.

The harshness of their fate made the Kurds envious sometimes of even the Palestinians. Both these peoples are victims of the mainly-British imperialist game, after the First World War, of dictating who in West Asia should live where, who should and who should not have a sovereign State. The Palestinians were dispossessed of their homeland but they have succeeded in at least keeping the world informed of their plight, claim and ongoing struggle. The Kurds, longer-time sufferers of various inequities, failed to catch the world's eyes or ears. Their current tragic flight from Iraqi Kurdistan across difficult terrain and weather, to save themselves from Saddam Hussein, has earned the Kurds, for the first time, some attention from outside. By all tests of modern political theory, the Kurds could have claimed a state by self-determination. They are a distinctively identifiable people, have a language and culture of their own, inhabit a geographically coherent area, would not be assimilated by others and are numerous enough for an independent sovereign polity. The Arabs succeeded in carving out several sovereign States from the ruins of the Ottoman empire; the Kurds, with the same historical qualifications, failed to secure any. Some 20 million Kurds have been living distributed over five States: Turkey, Iran, Iraq, Syria and the Soviet Union. Population-wise, the Kurds could have created a State stronger than any of those existing today in West Asia except Turkey and Iran. The Kurdish home is a wide belt of territory taking in much of southeastern Turkey, North -eastern Iraq, north-western Iran and bits of Syria and the Soviet Union. This is the core area from which Salauddin Ayubi (Saladin to the West), a Kurd and Islam's most famous warrior after Prophet Mohammed, struck out to create a West Asian empire some eight centuries ago. The victorious Allies of the First World War had, for a brief while, a vague intention of allowing the Kurds some scope for political advancement, not for any love for them but to make the punishment of Turkey as severe as possible. The Treaty of Sevres in 1920 stipulated "local autonomy where the Kurdish element is preponderate", in Turkey and present-day Iraq. It also hinted at the possibility of a fully independent Kurdish State later. This was not a plan for a comprehensive Kurdish State; Iranian Kurdistan was out of the picture altogether and the Kurdish areas west of the Euphrates were excluded because France had to be given its pound of West Asian flesh under a secret agreement. The Kurds did not get any State nor even autonomy anywhere. Kemal Ataturk stepped into the Turkish scene, trore up the Treaty of Sevres and made any assertion of Kurdish identity punishable by death. Kemalist Turkey gave the Kurds a new name: Mountain Turks. The British also remembered that they must keep for themselves the Kurdish oil of Mosul. Out of this design emerged Iraq as a new State, with the British ruling it under a League of Nations mandate.[18]

The Kurds were expendable in the game of nations. Mustafa Barzani, the legendary leader of the Iraqi Kurds' fight for autonomy, knocked on all doors he could see. The doors opened one by one. He spent years in the Soviet Union, returned home and accepted aid from the Shah of Iran and thanks to him became a client of the CIA. He was betrayed by all. Moscow's Treaty of Friendship with the Iraqi Government was, in effect, switching sides in the Kurdish context. The Shah forgot Mustafa Barzani as soon as Saddam Hussein, in his anxiety to isolate the Kurds, signed the Algiers agreement conceding the midstream of the Shatt al Arab as the Iraq-Iran boundary. Barzani, who had nursed more faith in the Americans than in the Shah, sent an urgent appeal to Washington as the Iraqis reopened their campaign against the Kurds. Henry Kissinger, the master of real-politic, did not even care to reply and advised surprised CIA officials to remember that "secret service operations are not missionary work". Mustafa Barzani died in the USA in 1979 but others, including his son, Massoud Barzani, have carried on the struggle, unaided by others, Fighting has become a Kurdish tradition. They fought in the past in Turkey, the Sultan, the Young Turks Kemal Ataturk and his successors; in Iran the Shah as well as Ayatollah Khomeini's Islamic revolutionaries, and in Iraq, the British, the monarchy installed and manipulated by them, Abdul Karin Kaseem, the Aref brothers and finally the Baathists led by Saddam Hussein. They thought that with Saddam badly mauled in the Gulf war, the time had come for them to settle scores finally with Baghdad. And despite their past experience, they chose to believe that the call of President Bush to the Iraqi people "to take matters in their hands" carried a pledge to assist those who might fight Saddam. President Bush had not probably foreseen that the battered Saddam, would be able to use his iron first again on his own people. He is trying to satisfy critics by providing safe havens for Iraqi Kurds struggling to survive on the inhospitable border with Turkey or Iran and escape what may turn out to be nothing short of genocide.[19]

As Iraqi troops and armour advance into parts of northern Iraq after pounding Kurdish guerrilla positions for four days, Masoud Barzani, a Kurdish leader appealed to the United States and the United Nations once again to save his people from total destruction.

Barzani said that more than three million Kurds had fled northern Iraq and thousands were killed, in the wake of the relentless onslaught of the Iraqi army.

However, even as the Bush administration, as well as the UN rejected the appeal, Government troops backed by helicopter gun-ships, artillery and tanks rolled into Kirkuk, Mosul, and other smaller towns, once occupied by the guerrillas.

Barzani on April 2, 1991 stopped short of admitting absolute defeat of his separatist groups, and instead warned the Western and

Arab world of the impending annihilation of the Kurdish race in northern Iraq, if the army was allowed to pursue the fleeing civilians and rebels into the countryside.

Barzani said that though nearly all guerrilla positions had been over-run by the army, pockets of resistance were engaging the Government troops in the town of Safwan.

In southern Iraq, after heavy shelling by both air and land on Shia rebel dominated positions, Iraqi Government forces, which consist of mostly Republican Guard units, have begun to move forward across the Euphrates river.

Western journalists, just returned from conducted tours, both from the Iraqi side as well as areas held by the US-led coalition forces have reported direct shelling and heavy machine gun fire into the market places of the towns of Karbala and Al-Najaf.

President George Bush said in Washington on April 17, 1991 the US military would set up safety zones in northern Iraq for hundreds of thousands of Kurdish refugees. He warned Iraqi leader Saddam Hussein not to interfere.

George Bush announced a "greatly expanded and more ambitious relief effort" to help Kurds who fled to the mountains on the Iraq. Turkish border after Saddam Hussein's forces crushed their rebellion and who are now in desperate need of food, warm clothing and medicine.

The President made the announcement in the face of criticism that he has done too little and too late for Kurds who said they rose up against Saddam at Bush's urging, only to find he would not commit US forces to help them fight.

Bush also for the first time raised the prospect of exile for Saddam if he would leave power. He said he wanted Saddam out of power "so badly" that he might be willing to consider allowing his "to live a happy live forevermore" in exile.

Bush made the decision to expand the relief effort after telephone conversations with British Prime Minister John Major, French President Francois Mitterrand, UN Secretary General Javier Perez de Cuellar, Turkish President Turgut Ozal and German Chancellor Helmut Kohl.

John Major had been trying to convince George Bush that a protective zone was the best approach to providing security for the Kurds, British officials in London reported, on April 17, 1991. They believed they had the president on board.

However China has expressed its opposition to the creation of 'safe havens' under United Nations auspices for Kurdish refugees in Iraq.

Iraq will never accept that its people be partitioned, Iraqi Deputy Premier Tarek Aziz said, stressing that the Kurdish issue was merely meant to destabilize and weaken Iraq.

Aziz, who toured the five Maghreban countries recently told the Moroccan daily Al Ittihad al Ichtirakit on April 30, 1991 that Iraq was ready to allow the Kurds have an autonomous government.

This autonomy should be part of practical forms of democracy in the context of the unity of the state, the homeland and the society and not a form of division and prelude to the country's partitioning, the Iraqi official said.

He said the principles Iraqi leaders agreed upon and that are explained in the new constitutions would enable the country to adopt the multiparty system and convert the revolutionary institutions that ran the country for two decades into constitutional institutions.

Aziz said his country wanted to have normal relations with all Arab countries based on the Arab League charter, the joint defence convention and economic cooperation.

The myth of the unity will disappear among the majority of nations of the Third World in the nineties. Be it the Arab World, India, Africa, even China, state unity is most often a fictious label affixed to an incredible diversity of peoples and cultures. All these nations have probably so far tolerated the burden of state and national unity only because they hoped for economic progress. This progress was either not forthcoming or else interrupted. Therefore we must expect that every such nation, each tribe, each province will try to regain independence, hoping this will be better. I believe Iraq will explode, not only under the effects of the international crisis it has provoked but also because Iraq is a mosaic of peoples held prisoner by a totalitarian government. Among these victims the first to seek independence will probably be the Kurds, threatening to bring in its wake the secession of some parts of Turkey and Iran in order to create, a state of Kurdistan. Such events might affect the entire Arab world. The same applies to China. One can expect that Tibet will continue demanding independence, but there may also be upheavals among the Chinese Muslims who will turn to Ulan Bator and not towards Beijing. Finally it may happen that under the pressure of demands for autonomy in the coastal and southern Chinese provinces this empire will collapse after the death of Deng Xiaoping – for the second time in its history.[20]

On the whole, a good many states may disappear, and many nations may re-emerge, their existence having been forgotten outside these states. However peoples have a long memory: the richest lesson of the nineties will certainly be that during this period many forgotten civilisations will surface again, having preserved intact their language, their religion and their myth.

Iraq's Kurdish population was sinking still further into a state of physical and psychological despair on April 6, 1991 as President Saddam Hussein claimed to have crushed their insurrection and appealed to them to return to their homes and live in peace. The appeal came as a Kurdish Democratic Party spokesman in Damascus acknowledged that the rebels had lost control of their last stronghold, Sulaymaniyah, but were still holding out in mountains and a few villages. He also accused Iraq of dropping phosphorus bombs on fleeing civilians. Baghdad Radio said leaders of the Kurdish revolt had spread false rumours that the Government would victimise people living in the area. "Citizens in the cities and the areas where law and order have been re-established need not worry about their lives, property and legal rights", it added. The statement, issued after a meeting of Iraqi leaders chaired by Saddam, Hussein said only those involved in "crimes of murder, war, rape and theft, or (who) raised arms against the State and law" would be held accountable. Most of the country's 3.5 million Kurds have joined long, ragged processions into the mountains or towards Turkey, Syria and Iran.

REFERENCES

1. *The Independent*, 29 March, 1991.
2. *Ibid.*
3. *New Wave*, 28 April, 1991.
4. Jal Taraforevala. The War is Not Over, Yet. *The Independent,* 26 March, 1991.

5. K. Subrahmanyam. Focus on Iraq. *The Business and Political Observer,* 21 March, 1991.
6. *Ibid.*
7. *The Independent,* 15 March, 1991.
8. *The Independent,* 26 March, 1991.
9. Harvey Morris. Kurds. *The Independent* (Bombay), 6 March, 1991.
10. *Ibid.*
11. Kurds Seek Iraqi Army Support. *The Independent,* 14 March, 1991.
12. *Ibid.*
13. *Ibid.*
14. *Ibid.*
15. *The Independent,* 19 March, 1991.
16. *Ibid.*
17. *Ibid.*
18. Punyapriya Dasgupta. The Plight of Iraqi Kurds. *The Hindustan Times,* 2 May, 1991.
19. *Ibid.*
20. Guy Sorman. The Nineties. *Review of International Affairs,* 5 January, 1991.

6

THE TRAGEDY AND NEW WORLD ORDER

World attention is now focused on the Kurdish people and the impending large-scale refugee influxes into Iran and Turkey. Already, Turkey has received some 100,000 refugees. Hundreds of thousands more are massed on the Turkish border, and Ankara is reluctant to admit them unless international aid on an adequate scale is pledged. The European Economic Community is meeting to consider the problem. France and Britain have expressed their concern. On the Iranian side, a million Kurdish refugees have assembled to move into Iran which is not placing any impediments for the refugees to cross over. Both in Turkey and in Iran the Kurdish refugees will move into areas already inhabited by the Kurds. Half of the 25 million Kurds live in Turkey and the rest and split between Iraqi and Iranian Kurdish areas. The Kurdish people are not Arabs nor Iranians but a separate subnational group. Their ambition to have a separate Kurdistan at the end of the World War I was thwarted by the British and the French with the arbitrary marking of the borders of Iraq, Syria and Turkey. The Kurds have been agitating for autonomy since then. They were regularly bombed by the Royal Air Force based in Baghdad in the late twenties and early thirties. Subsequently, successive Iraqi regimes have been keeping down the Kurds who have been waging a long struggle first under the leadership of the Marxist leader Mustafa Barzani (the 'Red Mullah' as he was then known), and subsequently, that of his son Masoud Barzani, the present leader of the Peshmergas as their insurgent force is known. The Kurds are politically organised under the Kurdish Democratic Party and a break-away faction based in Syria called the Kurdish Workers' Party. A smaller third armed resistance group calls itself Patriotic Union of Kurdistan.[1]

The Kurds have been pawns in the international game and in the seventies the CIA and the Shah of Iran extended some support to the Kurds. It was by playing the Kurdish card that the Shah compelled Saddam Hussein to sign the Algiers agreement of 1975 in which Iraq renounced the British claims for the entire water spread of Shatt Al Arab river and accepted the midline of the river principle to demarcate the border. In 1980, Saddam Hussein launched his attack on Iran to reverse the agreement in favour of Iraq. After the Algiers agreement, the Kurds were let down by the Americans and the Shah. Towards the end of Iraq-Iran war in 1988, Saddam Hussein came down on the Kurds with massive violence and used chemical weapons against them in the town of Halabja which led to thousands of casualties and exodus of 50,000 Kurdish refugees into Turkey. Since Turkey does not favour the demand of Turkish Kurds for autonomy and till a few months back did not even extend to them the right to use their language, they have kept the Iraqi Kurdish refugees in isolated camps away from the Turkish Kurds. President Bush has a moral responsibility for the present situation since he repeatedly called for the overthrow of Saddam Hussein by the Iraqis. His own Commander, General Schwarzkopf had somewhat different views about allowing Saddam Hussein to keep and operate such a large portion of the remnant Iraqi armed forces against the local population – especially the helicopters, tanks and artillery. Bush's open call for uprising against Saddam Hussein along with the latter's crushing defeat raised the hopes of large sections of the Kurdish population that the time had come for them to assert their right for autonomy. At this stage, President Bush decided to keep off from attempting to influence the outcome of the Iraqi civil war which in effect meant permitting Saddam Hussein to crush both the Shias in the south and the Kurds in the north. The Iraq Republican Guard which never offered battle to the coalition forces are now displaying their prowers in destroying poorly armed Shias and Kurds who have risen against Saddam Hussein. The Ummah, as usual, is keeping eloquently silent when Muslims are being slaughtered by fellow believers. The US, which came down heavily on the Soviet leadership for the deaths in Lithuania, is content to see the large-scale killings of Kurds without any humanitarian action on its part. The Kurdish issue has again highlighted the major differences between Iran on one side and the US and other Arab regimes on the other. It also raises an interesting question on the sincerity of Washington's espousal of human rights. France and Turkey are moving the UN on the issue. However, efforts to intervene in the domestic jurisdiction of nations in the name of human rights should be resisted.[2]

Increasingly, the full ramifications of Iraqi invasion of Kuwait are coming to light. It has not only brought about the complete collapse of the international order but, as is becoming more and more apparent each day, threatens in the Third World to erode nation-State sovereignty. According to the American scheme of things, the US is fast assuming the responsibility of deciding what a Third World State should not do within its own national boundaries. In its latest dictate the US has asked Iraq not to fly its military aircraft north of the 36th parallel, an east-west line about 30 miles south of the Iraqi city of Mosul in an attempt to guarantee a safe haven for Kurdish rebels in northern Iraq. This amounts to flagrant violation of the non-interference code and national sovereignty–hitherto regarded as sacrosanct principles of international law applicable also to Third World countries. This is not to imply that the plight of the Kurds does not deserve attention. Some 25 million people spread across territories of five states, the Kurds have long been struggling for their rights. Iraqi Kurds, like Iraqi Shias, were first incited by the victorious US leaders to rebel against President Saddam Hussein, and when the rebellion broke out and was brutally suppressed by the Iraqi military, President Bush allowed the rebels to be brutally punished. When the rebellion failed to overthrow Mr. Hussein US decision takers suddenly awoke the plight of Kurds and Shias fleeing their country. The obvious intent behind Washington's encouragement was the hope that by helping to remove Saddam Hussein, the Kurdish rebels might bring US war aim in Iraq to its logical end. Yet, by not sending American troops to back the Kurdish struggle, the US succeeded merely in making it more vulnerable to attacks by Iraqi forces. The US refused to intervene pleading that it had "no desire to see Iraq splinter into its many constituent parts". Such statements of America's pious intentions, however, did not help camouflage its self-serving scheme in the region. Obviously, such restraint on the part of the US was prompted by the realisation that with several other heterogeneous states in the region, any assertion by the Iraqi Kurds of their autonomy could have a dangerous destabilising effect in the region. It might well prompt a Kurdish rebellion in Turkey, a prized NATO ally of the US or even give an unnecessary fillip to the struggle of Shitte rebels in southern Iraq, facilitating hereby the setting up of a pro-Teheran Islamic regime in Baghdad – developments which would not suit US neostrategic interests in the region. Although humanitarian considerations seem to have belatedly compelled to US to take notice of the sad plight of the Kurdish refugees, the 'safe haven'solution that the US has sought to guarantee is not only extremely partisan but amounts to a gross violation of Iraqi national sovereignty.[3] The US must realise that the best hope for Kurds, and other ethnic minorities like them elsewhere, is the gradual spread of democracy. Already, not only has Turkey softened its stand towards its Kurdish, population but even Iraq offered amnesty to its Kurdish rebels. Above all, the US must realise that it cannot right a wrong by perpetrating another wrong.

Moscow is opposed to setting up "safe havens" for Kurds in northern Iraq, a Foreign Ministry spokesman said on April 12, 1991.

Safe areas for Kurdish refugees have been proposed by Britain.

Foreign Ministry spokesman Vitaly Churkin said they would imply "the abolition of Iraqi sovereignty over part of its territory without the agreement of the Baghdad Government, contradict UN Statutes and set an absolutely unwanted precedent."

The spokesman added that Moscow's position on the Kurdish issue was unchanged and that the Soviet Union was alarmed at recent developments in Iraq's Kurdish settlement area.

Soviet observers were ready to take up positions on the Iraqi-Kuwaiti border in compliance with UN Security Council Resolution No. 687, Mr. Churkin said, adding that observers were waiting for the green light from UN Secretary-General Javier Perez de Cuellar.

France and Britian on April 27 proposed complementary UN security guarantees to lure hundreds of thousands of Kurdish refugees back to their homes from campus in northern Iraq, Turkey and Iran.

France called for a meeting of the five permanent United Nations security council members to study the situation in Iraq after the tentative accord between Baghdad and Kurdish leaders providing for Kurdish autonomy in Iraq.

The Kurds have demanded more security before they return home, French foreign minister Roland Dumas said. The UN must be involved in returning the Kurds, he added.

Britain proposed sending UN police force to Kurdish cities to assure the Kurds that they can safely return home. Such a force would replace the US and other allied troops now providing protection for the Kurdish refugees in northern Iraq.

Dumas and British foreign secretary Douglas Hurd proposed their ideas at an informal EC foreign ministers meeting in this resort town on the Luxembourg-French border.

The five permanent UN Security Council members are the United States, the Soviet Union, China, France and Britain.

Dumas said they should assure the Kurds that they can return home in safety from the mountain camps in northern Iraq, Turkey and Iran to which they fled after their post-Gulf war revolt against Iraqi president Saddam Hussein was crushed.

This could be done, he said, by monitoring Saddam's complicance with the Kurdish autonomy accord.

I have always wondered what makes the men of conscience who throw up their hands in horror at the altrocities committed against the Kurds in Iraq tick. It is not the first time that men of goodwill in the West with large bank balances and fat paunches, have expressed their pain and anguish at massacres in distinct distant lands; the Bulgarian atrocities and the Armenian massacres had evoked the same kind of response. I am not in favour of atrocities any where, and I do believe that history has given Kurds a raw deal. They have been betrayed so often that betrayal has become part of their way of life; they expect their friends and allied to betray them. They are a brave people who, ignoring all odds, have repeatedly risen in revolt against their oppressors; their quest for freedom has been unceasing. If the Kurds, divided between five countries, are able to win a measure of freedom, then it is as event to be welcomed by all. No, it is not the Kurdish liberation movement that I am opposed to: it is nations, for the moment I am willing to include Turkey among them, in condemning Iraq. It is well to remember that these same countries thought nothing of bombing Iraq. If not exactly back to the stone age, at least to the pre-industrial age; and whose soldiers and airmen, not to speak of the newspaper, expressed delight and glee at what they called the "Turkey shoot", bombing a defeated army incapable and unwilling to fight, retreating pell-mell. And the treatment of the refugees by the Turkish soldiers, according to Western reporters, is hardly any better than that of the Iraqis. I fail to see any difference between the coalition forces' treatment of Iraqis and the Iraqi government's treatment of the Kurds; both, according to me are inhumane beyond measure. It can indeed be argued that the coalition forces were waging war on Iraq and in a modern war, the civilians are as much involved as the frontline soldiers; they too get killed, maimed and injured. The idea is to inflict the maximum casualties on the opponent at minimum cost to oneself. That was the objective and the Americans are delighted at the success scored by their hi-tech weapons.[4]

Though not a pacifist, I am opposed to wars. I believe it is an outmoded way of settling disputes; a recognition that in the final analysis it is only force that matters. But once you accept the use of force to settle disputes, you cannot deny the Iraqi government the right to resort to force. It is well to remember that the government in Baghdad faced an extremely difficult situation; the economy is on the verge of collapse; military defeat and American incitement led to serious rebellions in the North and the South, the rebellions have so far not been suppressed, and if the government had not responded ruthlessly, its authority would have collapsed and there would have been absolute chaos. One can hardly dispute the Iraqi government's right to cruch a rebellion in that country; the British government with its methods of barbarism in Northern Ireland should be the last go question an independent sovereign state's right to deal with revolts and rebellions. It can, of course, be said that the government used excessive force, that the civilians rather than the Peshmergas were the major victims of the bombings and bombardments. That is true enough. But if one reads the reports on the Kurdish rebellion, one is forced to come to the conclusion that it is a mass uprising, an entire people is involved and that is what makes the problem so painful. The Iraqi government needed a quick solution to the problem, it resorted to the same methods that the coalition forces had used against it, an excessive use of force. The disproportion in strength between the government forces and the rebels is not much greater than that between the coalition and Iraq and a repetition of the 'Turkey shoot' took place. Saddam Hussein is a clone of Mr. George Bush and it is hardly befitting that the American President should condemn someone who expresses his admiration by imitating him. Yes, I fail to understand the moral posturings of these Western politicians, their sudden concern for the Kurds, their equally sudden abhorrence for man's bestiality towards man. They are politicians, certainly not in the humanitarian business; I suspect their so-called generous impulses, because it serves merely as a facade for the pursuit of political interests; they will merely exploit the generous impulses of the people.[5]

I don't trust the generous impulses of Western politicians. They are not really interested in providing humanitarian assistance to the Kurds. That could have been done under the UN umbrella by the private organisations; military intervention on the scale that is taking place in Iraq, has a much more sinister purpose. It seems that the West in anxious to establish the principle of the right to intervene in the internal affairs of independent countries in the Third World and the Gulf war and its aftermath has provided it with the opportunity.[6]

In April 1991 Britain's Prime Minister John Major made his surprise proposal to establish in Iraq "an enclave under UN protection which could provide shelter and housing for the Kurds until it is safe to return to their homes".

It was President Bush who took the world by surprise by putting the vital US stamp on the concept of encampments, capable of providing temporary food and shelter within a safe environment for at least 300,000 or more refugees.

John Major had been uncertain of the American response until the vital telephone conversation with President Bush that produced the outcome he wanted: the Americans had accepted the need to police the proposed camps with US, British and France forces.

Without a uniformed presence to reassure them, the Iraqi refugees would never be persuaded to come down from the mountains, the British had been arguing, uncertain to the last moment whether President Bush would be prepared to take the risk of such a commitment.

It was a success John Major desperately needed. Even his most diehard critics have not suggested he was prompted by electoral considerations when he launched his campaign to bolster Britain's humanitarian aid to the Kurdish refugees with "safe havens". Like everyone else – including Opposition leader Neil Kinnock's office – he was appalled by the scenes of misery reported over Easter.

But the Prime Minister's successful gamble came at a domestically opportune moment, when Labour is resurgent and the

Cabinet is beset by poll tax local government revenue problems and rumblings about "dithering" on left and right. The fact that former British Premier Margaret Thatcher went public first with a "something must be done" statement wrongly created the impression she had goaded White hall into action.

Recently, Tory MPs could be found professing horror when John Major diffidently admitted during a television interview with Brian Walden that he "would rather end up with egg all over my face having tried and failed than not having put forward solutions to this problem." Nor what Thatcher would have said, noted some.

Until recently, even Britain had assumed it would be enough to establish a massive presence of aid workers in Iraq to provide a safety shield, and that the deployment of forces could be avoided. But the media reporting from the borders with Iran and Turkey brought it home to the Government that the refugees were so consumed with fear of Saddam Hussein that only a uniformed presence at clearly defined sites might induce them to turn back.

Moreover, it was depressingly obvious that the UN aid agencies and the voluntary bodies could not get their act together quickly enough and that experienced army personnel were essential to set up the aid infrastructure.

Prime Minister John Major's original proposal had taken its cue form Turkey's President Ozal, who saw that the half million and more Kurds on the cruel mountain border between Iraq and Turkey would have to be helped down, either to Turkey or back to Iraq. He did not want any more Kurds in Turkey and urged the US and its Allies to create an infrastructure of camps in Northern Iraq.

President Saddam Hussein of Iraq should be brought to trial for crimes against humanity, including his invasions of Iran and Kuwait and his repression of the Kurds and others in Iraq, according to European Community Foreign Ministers.

The Luxembourg President of the EC Council of Ministers, Jacques Poos, will discuss how this could happen when he meets the Secretary-General of the United Nations, Javier Perez de Cuellar, in Strasbourg.

The resolution to seek the indictment and trial of the Iraqi leader was proposed on April 15, 1991 by the German Foreign

Minister, Hans Dietrich Genscher. "This man must be made personally responsible for his crimes against humanity. He could be tried either in Iraq, or in another country," he declared.[7]

The Italian Foreign Minister, Giani de Michaelis, said that President Saddam should be changed under the 1948 Geneva Convention against genocide. "What Saddam Hussein is doing against the Kurds clearly is genocide and he should be brought to an international tribunal to answer for these and other action", said de Michelis.

Although responsibility for bringing the Iraqi leader to trial is to be passed for study by the United Nations, the ED EC Ministers saw their decision as a political declaration. "It is a clear signal that the European Community believes it is essential now for President Saddam Hussein to stand down from power", one diplomat observed.

Commenting on the decision, the British Minister of State at the Foreign Office, Tristan Garel-Jones, said that it might not be out of the question to try President Saddam in absentia. "We will ask the UN Secretary-General to see just how this matter can be brought forward", he added.

The resolution reflects the growing frustration of EC Governments with the apartment success of the Iraqi leader in holding on to power in spite of catastrophic defeat at the hands of the international coalition after the invasion of Kuwait and in the face of the uprisings by the Shia Muslims in southern Iraq and the Kurds in northern Iraq. Meanwhile, Luxembourg expects the US secretary of State, James Baker, to stop by for talks on his way back to the Middle East, where he intends to pursue his peace efforts. EC Ministers will be seeking a place at any international conference on the future of relations between Israel and the Palestinians—a move to which the Israeli Government is opposed. The EC Foreign Ministers also agreed to step up urgent humanitarian aid to help Kurdish refugees on Iraq's borders with Turkey and Iran beyond the package of funds 100 millions decided at last week's EC summit. A German diplomat said that there was a need for "hundreds of millions" of pounds of increased aid and announced that Bonn was sending 18 helicopters to Turkey and Iran to help distribute aid to the refugees.[8]

The British proposal for a UN mandated safe haven for the forcibly displaced Kurds in northern Iraq cannot but pose a classic dilemma for the international community at large. For, the proposal pits the sacrosanct idea of sovereignty against the ethical issue of human rights. After all creating an Kurdish enclave, "by force if necessary" within the Iraqi territory clearly violates the sovereignty of Iraq, which even the US and its allies have pledged to uphold all long. At the same time, given the savage repression of a defenseless people and their diaspora into inhospitable terrains and inhuman suffering, brings to force the issue of humanitarian obligation of the world community. Not surprisingly, major powers of the North are divided over the proposal. While the European Community has backed it, the US and the Soviet Union have cautiously rejected the same. The skepticism of the superpowers is understandable, as the British proposal can open up the pandora's box of ethnic questions in West Asia and beyond, and throw as under the already tenuous world order. The seemingly benging idea of an Kurdish enclave can tantamount to a de-facto state encompassing the entire region historically inhabited by the Kurds that spans across Turkey, Iran, Syria and even the Soviet Union. Neither antagonising its allies not alterning the power and territorial configuration of the region in any way serve the US strategic or economic interests.

It has been fairly obvious from the very outset that in order to avert precisely such an eventuality, the US President had abruptly halted the war efforts against Iraq, over and above the protestations of his commander on the field. Washington's latest warning to Iraq not to hinder relief work, beyond the 36th parallel is merely to allary the European pressure as also the domestic opinion which has already branded the White House's inertia as "Bush's Bay of Pigs". In this context, the deafening silence of the Non-aligned Movement is self-defeating and only exposes its diminishing role in world affairs. For, any western move to resolve the Kurdish crisis by browbeating Iraq can set a dangerous precedent. In fact, the western nations may use the Kurdish crisis to arm themselves with interventionist powers. France has already proposed an amendment to the UN charter to include the UN's "duty of interference in areas of particularly outrageous abuse of human and minority rights". The ominous implications of such a clause are obvious.[9] In the interests of the developing countries, therefore, it is imperative that the non-aligned apply pressure on President Saddam Hussein to find a humane and democratic solution to the Kurdish problem.

The British Prime Minister, speaking on a television interview here, said that the use of force was not ruled out by the nations involved in protecting the hundreds of thousands of Kurdish refugees in northern and southern Iraq. "I am neither ruling it in, nor ruling it out", said the Prime Minister on being questioned on countering Iraqi aggression towards the fleeing Kurds.

John Major, however, said that the refugee problem was to be solved by diplomatic means. So far Baghdad has indicated that it will not interfere with the UN aid operations.

On the issue of his proposed idea of a "safe haven" for the Kurdish population, Mr. Major said that the idea was not a short-term solution.

Meanwhile, Britain is continuing to urge the United Nations to establish a semi-permanent humanitarian mission in northern Iraq to oversee the international aid effort for the Kurdish refugees.

Britain's Ambassador to the UN, Sir David Hannay, told the United Nations Secretary-General, Javier Peres de Cuellar, yesterday that a few dozen aid workers should be set-up on Iraqi soil monitor operations and co-ordinate the work of various Governments and relief agencies.

Under continued strong attack at home allegedly exhorting the Kurds to revolt and letting them face the consequences when the revolt failed, president Bush on Saturday continued to express his desire to see Saddam fall but this time he did not urge the Iraqis to revolt.

He told an enthusiastic and respectful audience of 2,500 students and guests at the Maxwell Air Force Base War College: "With Saddam in power, Iraq will remain a Parish nation, its people denied moral contacts with most of the outside world", and he stopped there.

He also advanced a new argument for non-interference in internal affairs, though he also argued that in drawing a line above the 36th Parallel for the Iraqi armed forces and in creating "safe enclaves" he is not violating Iraqi sovereignty but acting out of humanitarian concerns.

Internal conflicts, said George Bush, "have been raging in Iraq for many years, and we're helping out, and we're going to continue to help these refugees," thus washing this hands clean of any responsibility for the uprising.

The new Washington line is that it was a spontaneous uprising of the kind that occurs in my "empire" with different ethic groups living there and which feel oppressed by the majority, when the centre is weakened.

In this case the Kurdish minority and Shiite majority saw a golden opportunity to assert themselves when they saw most of Saddam's troops in Kuwait and southern Iraq destroyed and they decide to raise against central authority.

For some reason, the plight of the Shiites is drawing less attention than that of the Kurds because of the past history of the Kurdish uprising and the alleged use of poison gas by Saddam Hussein the last time they challenged him.

The European Economic Community (EEC) heads of governments meeting in Luxembourg on April 8, 1991 has endorsed the British proposal to have a sanctuary created in the Kurdish area of Iraq in which the Kurds will come under the protection of the United Nations and be secure from the repression of the Iraqi government. The leader of Kurdish Democratic party, Masoud Barzani, has welcomed the proposal. The modalities of the new scheme are yet to be worked out. The British Prime Minister, who sponsored the proposal, has made it clear that the unity and integrity of Iraq would be guaranteed and the Saddam Hussein regime in Baghdad would be asked to keep off the area of sanctuary. It is expected. That under the present circumstances it would cooperate. If it does not then the UN may be asked to authorise use of force, to enforce the security of the sanctuary. Coming as it does in the wake of a controversy on how much can UN be permitted to intervene in internal affairs of nations it may also cause considerable concern among developing nations which face problems of insurgency. Some though will however reveal that there are already precedents of sorts though there is no identical case of a UN authorised sanctuary. The Turks have sent their army into the Turkish area of Cyprus and a Turkish Cypriot administration is functioning in that part of the island and defies the jurisdiction of the Cyprus government. Israelis have declared a security zone in southern Lebanon which is virtually under Israeli military control. The Syrains have their army in Labanon and many parts of that country are under the control of the Syrain Army. A west Africa peace-keeping force has intervened in the Liberian civil war and has interposed itself between two rival fighting factions. India, in pursuance of a Sri Lankan request sent its army into Tamil areas of Sri Lankan to disarm the LTTE.[10]

Therefore, the idea of a foreign military force creating a security cordon in a country is not new. In some cases it has happened with the consent of the country concerned and in other cases countries have been coerced to tolerate it.

However this will be the first occasion when the UN will be attempting to create such a security zone in a country under civil war. This no doubt constitutes a violation of the sovereignty of Iraq and an intervention in its internal affairs. Such an intervention should be considered totally impermissible in a country which has a legitimate, elected representative government. Prima facie when there is a conflict between a state where the government is democratically elected and a dissident group it should be left to be dealt with by the state itself.[11]

In Sri Lanka we have a case of a democratically elected government facing an insurgency with a minority which feels that its rights are not recognised. Even while in India we sympathies with the demand of the Tamils in Sri Lanka for their legitimate rights the Indian army was in Sri Lanka only as long as the Sri Lankan Government was prepared to accept it. Once they asked India to withdraw there was no alternative but to comply with the demand. This is in respect of a government whose legitimacy is beyond all doubt. Unfortunately in a majority of cases governments do not command that kind of legitimacy. Increases when there is an insurgency it becomes difficult to take a stand on the respective claims of the regime in power and dissidents. Nor do most of such undemocratic government exercise restraint in the use of force in countering insurgencies. Such genocides of population have occurred in Kampuchea, Syria in 1982 and Rwanda and in other cases large scale decimations of population have occurred because food was withheld from them by either government or insurgent forces in civil war situations. This has happened in Ethiopia and southern Sudan. A world which has adopted the declaration of human rights will have to give thought to this issue and cannot just brush aside the idea of UN sanctuary protection because it comes from western nations. Understandably enough, the proposal has created unease in China and the

Soviet Union. But the US reservation is interesting. It tends to confirm the suspicion that the US is more worried about the Iranian influence in Iraq then about Saddam Hussein's atrocities. The Iranians have already asked for a sanctuary for Iraqi Shias to be created along with for the Kurds.[12]

Strangely enough, it is in Iraq that the Kurds have enjoyed the greatest political rights. Kurdish political organisations have been active, Kurdish language and culture flourish, and the distinctive identity of the people recognised. It is only in Iraq that the Kurds have been offered autonomy and have enjoyed the same political rights as the others. Of course, the Baathist regime is repressive. Like most West Asian regimes, it is not known for its tolerance of dissidence. But if the Kurds have suffered more than others in Iraq. It is because they have been in state of almost permanent rebellion. All those who opposed the regime have suffered the same fate; the ranks of the Communist Party have been decimated and the Shias, when they finally rose up in revolt are being suppressed with the same ruthless savagery. Bombing rebels is nothing new in West Asia. Bomber Harris, who was later to acquire fame for this bombing of Germany, won his spurs by bombing the Kurds and Winston Chruchill. Colonial Secretary in the early twenties, advocated the use of mustard gas against the rebels in northern Iraq. Saddam Hussein is following excellent Anglo-Saxon precedents and it hardly behaves men who gloated over the "turkey shoot", the brutal bombing of a routed army retreating pell-mell, to criticise the Iraqi government for using its air power, or what remains of it, against the rebels. The Baathist regime did face a grave threat following its defeat. Incited by the Americans, including President Bush, who repeatedly called upon the Iraqi people to overthrow the government of Saddam Hussein, the Shias in the South and the Kurds in the North revolted, hoping that the United states would help them. However, Mr. Bush preferred to go fishing and left the Iraqi rebels to their fate. Faced with a threat to its very existence, the Baathist government used all the force at its disposal to crush the rebellion, it was certainly brutal, but wheather the Iraqi bombing of rebellious subjects was more brutal than the American bombing of civilian population in the cities of Iraq is open to question. To talk of genocide is certainly an exaggeration. Perhaps more people were killed by American bombs, but that, of course, was part of the design to teach the Third World countries a lesson.[13]

What is significant is the Western reaction. At first, it refused to intervene when it appeared that the Kurds might triumph, but as the tide turned and the refugees started moving towards the frontiers, Turkey, which till recently denied the Kurds even minimum human rights, closed the border and demanded an enclave in Iraq for them. This was taken up by John Major, who after demanding an enclave, switched over to more neutral term, safe haven. This sudden expression of concern for the Kurds is truly amazing coming as it does from people who have be friended Pol Pot and his murderous Khmer Rouge, who did nothing when their proteges in Africa, like Emperor Bokassa, Marshal Mobutu and Master Sergeant Doe of Liberia systematically murdered their subjects. Israel, of course, is a special case. It is above the law, this action in the occupied territories and Lebanon is, of course, part of the war against terrorism. If there were protests against the South African recist regime's war against the blacks in South Africa and its aggression against the people of Angola and Mazambique, it was extremely muted; John Major's predecessor was not even willing to impose sanctions. No, it is not humanitarian consideration that lies behind the Western move. After all, their embargo did affeçt baby food and medicines and there is nothing to prevent them providing humanitarian aid. The idea was to establish the right to intervene in Third World countries; accusation of human right violations and genocide are easily made. Of course, the West will be able to protect its friends by exercising the veto, but others not so lucky would be punished by establishing UN protected enclaves in their territories. This along with the bombing to extinction as demonstrated in Iraq is part of the New World Order which America is trying to impose. For the moment the idea of the enclave has been given up, but it is bound to be revived sooner than later.[14]

The European Community has approved more that $ 180 million in aid for hundreds of thousands of Kurdish and other refugees fleeing Iraqi forces after a failed rebellion.

The aid worth 150 million European currency units (about & $ 183 million) was approved at a meeting of the leaders of the twelve EC nations in Luxembourg, on April 9, 1991.

A spokesman, said the EC leaders denounced Iraqi president Saddam Hussein for the brutal suppression of a Kurdish rebellion that has sent hundreds of thousands of refugees fleeing to Iran and Turkey.

He said the EC leaders also endorsed curbing arms sales to Iraq and discussed the creation, in Iraq of a protected area under United Nations supervision as a safe haven for Iraqi refugees.

Officials said France, Germany, Belgium and Spain were among the countries supporting a plea by British Prime Minister John Major for an enclave under U.N. protection which would provide shelter and housing to Kurds until it is safe for them to return to their own homes.

In a related development the German government has provided Kurdish refugees with aid to the tune of DM 25 million ($ 16 million), that is $ six million more than initially planned, government spokesman Dieter Vogel announced on April 18.

Some 40 tonnes of blankets, medicaments and food was dispatched this weekend by military plane to Diyarbakir (south eastern Rurkey, near the Iraqi border) and 10 tonnes were sent on April 9.

Two Bundeswehr Transall planes left on April 9 to take 40 tonnes of additional aid dispatched by the German Red Cross.

On April 6 Vogel had announced the German government would provide the Kurdish refugees with aid to the tune of $ 10 million.

A report emanating from Turkey says chewing gum, coffee, cream and sugar and toilet paper are among the goods – initially packed for US troops – being parachuted to Kurdish refugees along the Turkish-Iraqi border.

US personnel said on Monday during a flight that the eight packages dropped to the refugees on the Iraqi side of the border each contained 576 rations designed for US troops for use during the war to free Kuwait.

The packages were pushed out of the rear of the C-130 Hercules transport planned on the Iraqi side of the border near the Turkish village of Cukurea, where 30,000 refugees have assembled.

The flight of several Hercules was escorted by F-15 and F-16 fighter jets and an A-10 reconnaissance aircraft that pinpointed the exact target location for the droop.

There are between 200,000 and 300,000 refugees in the immediate vicinity of the border, US and Turkish officials say, and the number is expected to double in the next few days. Reports add 426,500 had taken refuge in Bakhtaran province, 243,200 in West Azarbaijan, 31,500 in Kurdistan, 2,500 in Ilam and 68,150 in Khuzestan.

The British Premier John Major has called for the establishment of a 'safe haven' for the Kurdish refugees inside Iraq, as part of a programme to stem the growing refugee problem on the borders of Iran and Turkey.

Announcing this on April 9,1991 in Luxembourg, the British Ambassador said that the area designated for returning Kurds will be policed and administered by forces of the United Nations.

John Major spelt out two immediate needs in regards to preventing the refugee problem into becoming a human catastrophe. First, was to get the hundreds thousands of Kurdish people down from the mountains in northern Iraq, where many face death due to exposure and starvation. The second step was to ensure their safe passage back to Iraq.

John Major ruled out the suggestion that the West was trying to partition Iraq into two particular halfs and that it had always remained the Allies intention to keep Iraqi sovereignty intact.

However, the plan for ensuring a safe haven for the fleeing Kurdish population is not without political and military risk, as the West may be faced with a Palestinian type of situation in the region inregards to a demand for a Turkish homeland.

A proposal by Western nations to create a United Nations administered 'safe haven' inside Iraq along its borders with Iran and Turkey for Kurds fleeing Baghdad's 'repression' has raked up a major controversy with several diplomats saying that the action could set a dangerous precedent for the future.

Through the proposal of Britain is being vehemently opposed in the Council by several member states, diplomats said a resolution incorporating the idea would surely be carried as Western nations could easily muster nine votes needed in the 15-member council for such a resolution to be adopted.

China, the only member who could veto the proposal, is unlikely to vote against and may only abstain.

Coming out of the consultations, diplomats refused to commit themselves saying they were awaiting instructions from their capitals.

In recent days, the United States has been lobbying in capitals before presenting a proposal in the council.

Several questions remained unanswered including how the area would be administered and how long. Fears are, however, being expressed that if the proposal is accepted, it might in effect mean carving out of a separate territory. For, Kurds once they get settled there are likely to resist any attempt to hand it back to Iraq.

Though it was being explained that the area would be administered by the civilian force, senior diplomat speaking on the condition of anonymity said that it is mostly likely to be a police force. After all some agency would be needed to maintain order in the area.

Things would become clear as a concrete proposal is presented and if usual procedure is followed the five permanent members may finalize the details before formally presenting it to the Security Council.

The Security Council had met to discuss, among other things, humanitarian aid to Kurdish people as Iran said around 772,000 Iraqis have crossed over its border areas and more are coming. Besides, hundreds of thousands have fled into Turkey creating a major humanitarian problem in the region. Hundreds of fleeing refugees, including women and children, are reported to have died while trekking to the border.

Iraq's crushing of the Kurdish rebellion while the world looks on should spur the UN to rething its of "non-interference", says French foreign minister Roland Dumas.

He said on April 4, 1991 that international law had evolved after World War-II when the new concept of "crimes against humanity" was added, and he hoped it would do so again in light of the Kurdish, tragedy.

"I believe the Kurdish crisis could act as a detonator", he told reporters after testifying before the senate foreign affairs committee in private.

"When new crimes exist, why shouldn't rules of law be planned to respond to these crimes?"

Dumas was commenting on a widespread impression that the international community, in particular the US and its Gulf allies, was paralysed by the long-standing UN ban on interference in a member-state's internal affairs.

France has urged the UN to warn Iraq that persecution of the Kurds must stop. It decided unilaterally on Wednesday to send emergency aid to Kurdish refugees. On April 4, Britain joined the appeal and called on the US cooperate.

However, none of the Gulf allies was prepared to give the Kurds weapons or to even the military odds by restricting Iraq's use of helicopters and artillery against them.

The west European press on April 4, decried what was widely termed a betrayal of rebels who had acted on President George Bush's call on Iraqis to overthrow the regime of President Saddam Hussein.

French commentators said France's UN initiative came late in the day and was of doubtful practical value.

Kurds have asked if the devastation wreaked by allied bombing of Iraq was not interference, and whether a government has the right to slaughter its citizens.

The French have suggested a rethink of the concept of non-interference several times in the past few years, urging that at the international community claim the right to undertake emergency humanitarian action inside sovereign states.

In 1987, President Francois Mitterrand said: "No state can be considered the proprietor of the sufferings it causes or permits".

Next year, humanitarian affairs minister Bernard Kouchner, now on a mission to Turkey and Iran to assess the need of Kurdish refugees, upheld what he called the "right to humanitarian assistance" in natural catastrophes and similar situations. Meanwhile, the UN Security Council has condemned the repression of Kurdish civilians and demanded an immediate end to it.

The 15-nation Council on April 4 night voted 10-3, with Yemen, Cuba and Zimbabwe opposing, and India and China abstaining on a fresh move for an open dialogue within Iraq to ensure respect for Iraqi citizens' human and political rights. The vote came after a long debate in which many delegates pointed out that under the UN charter the council is forbidden to interfere in the internal affairs of member states. It should not prescribe what should be done, India's UN envoy Chinmaya Gharekhan said. That would impinge on the internal affairs of states, he argued. The USSR, Austria, the US, Romania, Zaire, Ivory Coast and Ecuador supported the draft, while the UK and Belgium cosponsored it.

Germany and France are two prominent members of the European Community (EC) to protest vigorously against the repression of the Kurds by the Iraqi regime. In contrast the reaction of the rest of Europe has been muted with cautious criticism. Bonn on April 5, 1991 has formally conveyed its strong reaction to the Iraqi Ambassador, protesting the treatment given to the Kurds as also urging Baghdad to observe human rights. The German government has gone to the extent of asking Iraq to recognise the right of autonomy for the Kurdish people.[15]

For his part, a significant move made by the German Foreign Minister, Hans Dietrich Gfenscher was his appeal to five permanent members of the Security Council urging them to include unlimited protection for the minority rights of the Kurds in the ceasefire resolution.

The German opposition has gone a step further. The social democrats want the Kurdish question to be included in a future peace arrangement for the region. The party wants a guarantee to ensure the Kurds are given the right of self-determination.

There has been stronger sympathy for the Kurds in France. The France government has been in the forefront in sending humanitarian aid for the Kurds. President Mitterrand has told his Cabinet that he recognised "the right of the Kurds wherever they are to their own identity, language and culture, while respecting states". The French Foreign Minister Roland Dumas, said his government was trying to awaken the conscience of the world to ease the plight of the repressed minority.

"The Kurdish tragedy starts to move us", wrote Lal Libre Belgique. The Irish Times compared the West's inaction to the Soviet Union's failure to intervene in the Vistula when the Nazis crushed the

Warasaw uprising in 1944. Spain's leading newspaper El Pais supported the French stand that the UN was facing a test of its credibility and attacked pacifists who opposed the United States for waging war against Iraq. The paper wondered why they had become silent over the Kurdish plight. The German paper Bild also wondered what had happened to peace protestors who had taken to the streets before the Gulf war. "Who is demonstrating for the Kurds?" it asked.

Meanwhile, Britian has announced donation of 20 million pounds towards the UN appeal for Kurdish refugees. It is also funding an airlift or blankets and tents for the refugees.

British Prime Minister John Major has discussed the Kurdish plight with President Bush on telephone. But he has ruled any intervention in the Kurdish rebellion. He denied that the west had incited the Kurds to rise in rebellion.

"What is happening in Iraq is very distressing and is malignant, but it is also within the borders or Iraq and we have no international authority to interfere with that", he said.

President Saddam Hussein's decisive defeat in the Gulf war must, theoretically, have spelt an advance, if not an imminent victory, for Iraq's permanently embattled Kurds. Their long-time adversary, who had ruthlessly suppressed their past revolts, had been humbled over his Kuwait misadventure and the triumphant Allies seemed to be bent on ousting him from power. The conditions appeared favourable for a fresh attempt by the ethnic minority to liberate itself. So the leadership of the mountain people thought, and the miscalculation has proved horribly costly. The offensive launched by them in north Iraq in concernt with the Shi'ite rebels of the south has ended in a phenomenally tragic failure. The Kurds have been betrayed again, by the regional powers that egged them on to stage yet another rebellion only to watch Baghdad putting it down with brutal ferocity. The US-led West, which rejoiced initially over the anti-Saddam uprisings in the vanquished land soon saw reason for caution in supporting the Kurdish cause because of the advantage that Iran was apparently seeking to derive from the unsettled situation. Turkey and Iran, with sizeable populations of West Asia's most unwanted minority, has been at one with iraq in their refusal to countenance the idea of a Kurdistan. And, they have hardly been ready to receive and rehabilitate the tens of thousands of Kurd refugees pushed out of Iraq.

It was to stem the tide and to carry the Iraq-breaking exercise further that Ankara mooted the proposal for a Kurdish "enclave" inside Iraq. Britain's Mr. John Major hastened to back the plan, but has been constrained to retreat in the face of opposition from the US as well as the Soviet Union with its own Kurdish pockets. The whole sordid affair has run true to the sorry, familiar pattern of the Kurds of the entire region – some 25 million dispersed into the peripheral regions of Iran, Iraq, Turkey and Syria – serving as pawns in the cruel power games played across the West Asia board.[16] The focus is clearly on relief for and rehabilitation of the victims of the Gulf war aftermath. Having lost yet another unequal battle, they are now waiting for minimum humanitarian aid form the outside world in "buffer zones" within striking range of the Saddam Hussein force restrained only by fear of an Allied reprisal. Uprooted from their homes and unwelcome elsewhere, starving and sick, the 700,000 men, women and children depend on the supplies of food and medicine that are, by all accounts, woefully inadequate. Ahead is a challenging task for the United Nations agencies, due to take over charge of the displaced from the US towards the month-end. Before the international community remains the even more important responsibility of finding an answer to the Kurdish problem that has caused recurring human tragedies of a heart-rending scale.

A million Kurdish refugees have gathered to cross over into Turkey and another million Kurds are on the Iranian border. If they all finally become refugees then a new refugee problem bigger than the original Palestinian problem will be created in the Islamic world. The confrontation between Iraq and Iran has once again flared up with the former accusing the latter of not only instigating Shias of Iraq to revolt against the Saddam Hussein regime but of sending armed personnel into Iraq and entertaining territorial ambitions. Sporadic clashes between the Iraq army and Iranian revolutionary guards are also reported.

According to some diplomats the Arabs now feel that the US war aim was to destroy Iraqi military power, reassert control over oil and keep a weakened Saddam Hussein in office as a countervailing factor to other Arab countries and perhaps Iran too. This is President Bush's new international disorder. In one of the Father Brown's Stories the question is asked where does one hide a pebble, a leaf and a dead body. The answer is in a beach, a forest and a battle-field respectively. Bearing that in mind one is tempted to wonder whether a larger refugee problem of Kurds is now intended to obfuscate the Palestinian problem. So long as Saddam Hussein continues in office the attention of surrounding Arab states is likely to be focused on him. The new Kurdish refugee problem is bound to absorb international attention. The PLO leadership has alienated itself from the major Arab states – Egypt, Syria Saudi Arabia and the Gulf states. In these circumstances Israeli Housing Minister General Ariel Sharon is pushing ahead with his programme of settling the immigrant Soviet Jews in the West Bank ignoring the feeble protests of US and USSR made just for record.[17]

In the coming days there are likely to be a lot of analyses some of which may come out with deep conspiracy theories about the dark US plots which deliberately inveigled Saddam Hussein into war but also subsequently used him to create the Kurdish refugee problem. Some other may prefer to attribute the diabolical designs to the Zionists manipulating the United States. Perhaps the simpler, more straight forward and possibly more accurate explanation could be the Americans failed to assess Saddam Hussein, his ambitions, effectiveness of his state apparatus and the ethnic animosities in the area and have committed one costly mistake after another. Further instead of learning from their mistakes they became over-confident following the high technology military victory and proceeded to create additional disorder, in the name of a new international order without consulting other nations. No other nation could have suffered the kind of utterly disastrous defeat that Iraq did and yet continue to keep the leadership responsible for it in power. The earlier calls of President Bush to Iraqi forces to replace Saddam Hussein were presumably based on certain assessment of the capabilities and willingness of the Iraqi generals to act, individually or collectively. Even now there seems to be an expectation that sooner or later this would happen. President Bush now claims that he did not call on Iraqi people to overthrow Saddam Hussein and in the process suffer his butchery and hence he has no moral responsibility for the current sorry state of affairs. This defence is somewhat on the lines of Ambassador Glaspie's plea that she did not give an impression to Saddam Hussein that he could annex Kuwait without worrying about US intervention. Incidentally following Ms Glaspie's interview with Saddam Hussein there was a message from president Bush to the Iraqi leader in the last days of July, 1990. The impact of that message on Saddam Hussein has not attracted any public attention.[18]

Permitting the Iraqi leadership to keep and, use its armour, artillery and helicopter gun ships must surely have been based on an assessment of the situation likely to prevail in Iraq following the ceasefire and the manner in which the Iraqi leader would use his remnant military capability. That, following the military defeat the Shias and the Kurds would attempt to assert their long suppressed rights should have been an elementarily logical conclusion. It would be interesting to know on what basis Saddam Hussein was allowed the freedom to put down the Shias and the Kurds with such savagery. The world has to brace itself for more international disorders to be contributed by the US so long at that country persists in its arrogance of power, the long forgotten term of Senator Fulbright, and its inbred and consequently deeply flawed assessments.[19]

REFERENCES

1. K. Subrahmanyam. Kurds. *The Business and Political Observer*, 6 April, 1991.
2. *Ibid.*
3. *Patriot*, 15 April, 1991.
4. K.M. Panikkar. Western generosity is Suspect. *Patriot*, 27 April, 1991.
5. *Ibid.*
6. *Ibid.*
7. *The Hindustan Times*, 17 April, 1991.
8. *Ibid.*
9. *The Business and Political Observer*, 15 April, 1991.
10. K. Subrahmanyam. A Sanctuary for the Kurds *The Business and Political Observer*, 12 April, 1991.
11. *Ibid.*
12. *Ibid.*
13. K.M. Panikkar. Kurds. *Patriot*, 13 April, 1991.
14. *Ibid.*
15. *The Hindustan Times*, 6 April, 1991.
16. *The Hindustan Times*, 15 April, 1991.
17. K. Subrahmanyam. The New International. *The Business and Political Observer*, 11 April, 1991.
18. *Ibid.*
19. *Ibid.*

7

THE AUTONOMY

The Kurdish question has been one of the oldest festering problems in the Middle East subregion. The Kurds, a Muslim ethnic group numbering some 18 million people, inhabit several Middle Eastern countries, as well as some Soviet Republics. The bulk of the Kurds, however, reside in Turkey, Iran, and Iraq. Although there are no reliable estimates of the size of the Kurdish population, there are probably 8 million Kurds in Turkey, where they are officially referred to as the mountain Turks', 5 million in Iran, and 3 million in Iraq. The origin of the Kurds has also created controversy among scholars. Many, including the Kurds themselves, trace their origin to the Medes, a tribal group which moved into the Iranian Plateau from Central Asia at the end of the second millennium and ruled over the area from 614 BC to 550 BC. However, there has never been an Independent country of Kurdistan (the land of the Kurds), nor has there ever been a self-governing political entity exercising exclusive jurisdiction over all the Kurds.[1]

From the time of the Arab conquest in the mid-seventh century, the name 'Kurd' has been applied to the Western Iranians and other socio-culturally related peoples 'established astride the mountain system of the Zagros and the easter extension of Taurus'[2]. The Kurds, is a group, played an important role in the history of Western Asia until 1258, when the Arab caliphate of Baghdad was destroyed by the Mongol invation. Individual leaders of Kurdish origin also became prominent leaders in the Islamic World. One such leader was Salah-ed-din (Saladin) Ayubbi, who was born a Kurd in 1137 at Tikrit on the Tigris, Saladin, however, fought as an Muslim, and not as a Kurd, against the Crusaders and Richard the Lion-hearted, and eventually reclaimed Jerusalem for the Muslims. It is important to note that Saladin never emphasised his Kurdish extraction, nor did he rule or control the major part of the Kurdish-inhabited lands.

The Kurds have long contended that as a distinct ethnic group and as a nation, they are entitled to the universally recognized right of self-determination. The Kurds, like many other ethnic groups, have adhered to a set of shared principles which have shaped the course of their ethnic awareness. Scholars of ethnicity have differed on what differentiates an ethnic group from the dominant group(s) in the larger society. Nevertheless, most students of ethnicity have attributed the development of ethnonationalism to the existence, actual or perceived, of a common language, race, religion and historical experience. The development of ethnic consciousness would give an ethnic group (or nation) a sense of distinctiveness from that of the larger national within which it lives.

In most multiethnic Third World societies, ethnonationalism has been suspect in the eyes of the dominant elite. They view this phenomenon as a hindrance to unity and the process of nation-building. Although not totally rejecting the appeal of ethnic identity, the Third World has remained suspicious of the disintegrative potential of ethnonationalism in societies too fragile to withstand the barrage of demands from their ethnic groups with often contradictory or opposing objectives. Consequently, multiethnic Third World nations have endeavoured to amekiorate ethnic consciousness among their ethnic groups by accentuating their commonalities with the dominant sub-group(s) and integrating largely through the processes of acculturation, amalgamation, and identification. Acculturation refers to a process by which an ethnic group gradually absorb the cultural ethos of the dominant societal group. The Kurdish acculturation in Iran and Iraq has taken several forms. In pre-revolutionary Iran, the principal vehicle of acculturation was the institution of monarchy, Glorification of the ancient Persian empires and the contributions of the Kurds to achievements made by those empires in various fields was to serve as a reminder of Kurdish affinity and unity with the dominant group in Iranian society – the Persians.

Following the overthrow of the Iranian monarchy in 1979 and the establishment of the Islamic Republic, the concept of Islamic unity was to serve as the channel of acculturation. For the Iranian leader, Ayatollah Khomeini, ethnonationalism and conflicts arising out of ethnic distinctiveness are secondary issues which will wither away after the greater goal of Muslim unity is achieved. In other words, unity of the Islamic community will, in time, overcome ethnic conflict.

In Iran, neither monarchial institutions nor the illusive concept of Islamic unity succeeded in overcoming Kurdish ethnonationalism.

Unlike Iranian Kurds, the Kurds in Iraq have been able to gain recognition of their ethnic separateness from the Arab majority. However, successive Iraqi governments, through glorification of Arabism and Arab nationalism as interpreted by the ruling Ba'ath party, have sought, albeit unsuccessfully, to acculturate their Kurdish population by suppressing Kurdish cultural, educational and political institutions. As we shall discuss later, none of the attempts made to date have dampened the Kurdish desire to maintain its socio-cultural identity in the country. The second vehicle of ethnic integration is amalgamation. Amalgamation occurs mostly through the process of miscegenation among two or more ethnic groups in society. Since intermarrying rarely occurs between a Kurd and a non-Kurd, the Kurds are a long way from assimilation into the dominant groups in Iran and Iraq. The third assimilative variable is identification, either on individual or group levels, of ethnic elements with a larger and more pluralistic society. In both Iran and Iraq. Kurdish identification has been minimal and generally limited to individual levels of assimilation. That is, while some prominent Kurds have attained high-level positions in the Iranian and Iraqi governments and have been co-opted into the dominant groups of their respective countries, the Kurdish nation has left outside the social mainstream and has remained marginal to it. In short, the assimilative variables of acculturation, amalgamation and identification have been outweighed by the potentially disintegrative factors of cultural distinctiveness exhibited by the Kurds. Among the principal factors contributing to Kurdish ethnic nationalism, as alluded to earlier, are a shared language, religion, race and territoriality. The degree of shared experience in language and religion has long been recognised as a major contributor to the development of ethnic consciousness. The Kurdish language is composed of three major dialects and a number of sub-dialects. The three major dialects of Kermanji, Kurdi and Zaza are to some extent, mutually exclusive, and in the case of Zara, not intelligible to the speakers of the other two dialects. Despite this apparent lack of homogeneity, the perception of a common language as an integral part of the Kurdish nation is very strong among Kurdish nationalists. With respect to the existance of a common religion, the Kurds are overwhelmingly Sunni (orthodox) Muslims, in the Kermanshah (Bakhraran) region of Iran, most Kurds, like their Persian counterparts, are adherents of the minority Sh'a sect of Islam. The Sunni-Shi'a shism, which from time to time has erupted into Muslim communal conflicts elsewhere, has been remarkably absent among the Kurds. If there have been conflicts between Kurdish Sunni and Shia'a leaders, they have generally occurred not over religious and doctrinal disputes, but over political matters affecting the Kurdish nation. Prominent Kurdish religious leaders have traditionally been able to use their prestige and social status to transcend religious sectarianism and act on behalf of the Kurdish nation as a unified whole. Radically, the Kurds have retained their distinctiveness more than most other Muslim ethnic groups in the Middle East. Because the phenomenon of miscegenation has not significantly affected the Kurdish population, they have tended to pride themselves on belonging to a pure racial stock and, hence, being distinct from other ethnic groups in the region. As Aryans, however, the Kurds share similar traits with the Persians, but are certainly distinct from the semitic Arabs and the Turks. The importance of race, however, should not be overemphasised in the development of Kurdish ethnic consciousness, but we should recognise that it has given an added dimension to the Kurdish claim of ethnic distinctiveness. Finally, the notion of territoriality refers to the geographic concentration of an ethnic community and the concomitant sense of belonging to a relatively well-defined territory. The overwhelming majority of the Kurds have always resided in the territory of Kurdistan encompassing areas in Iran, Iraq, Turkey and Syria (see the map). This fact of continuous habitation in Kurdistan, albeit without recognised boundaries, has provided the Kurds with an emotive force to demand autonomy and/or independence for their homeland. Modern Kurdish nationalist movements, which started in the late nineteenth century, were not successful in achieving the goal of statehood for the Kurds (the following chart illustrates the highlight of major Kurdish nationalistic events). However, in the first half of the twentieth century, two watershed events augured the dawn of a new era for the Kurds. The first event occurred after the conclusion of World War I and the defeat of the Ottoman Empire which had controlled Kurdish areas in modern-day Turkey and Iraq. Among the treaties signed between the victorious Allied powers and the defeated Ottoman Sultan, the Treaty of Sevres beyond the hope of Kurdish nationalists as it called,*inter alia*, for the establishment of an independent Kurdish state. However, due to the emergence of Mustafa Kamal as an important stabilising force in Turkey opposing further dismemberment of his country, and because of the rise of British economic interests in Iraq, the provisions of the Treaty of Sevres were not fully implemented. After several ill-fated attempts to resolve the Kurdish question, the Council of the League of Nations, in December 1925, voted in favour of maintaining the *status quo* and allowing Turkey and the newly independent Iraq to control their Kurdish areas on the vague condition that minority rights be guaranteed for the Kurds. The second major event was the establishment in December 1945 of an independent Kurdish state in the city of Mahabad, Iran. The new state, the Kurdish Republic of Mahabad, received material and moral support from the Soviet Union whose forces, occupying northern Iran part of the Allied occupation forces in the latter stages of World War II, helped set up the new Kurdish state. The Kurdish Republic of Mahabad was short-lived as it disintegrated in December 1946 in the face of Iranian armed forces and after the Soviet Union's withdrawal from Iran.[3] Despite its brief existence, it remained the only independent Kurdish state to date and is still a source of reference and inspiration for Kurdish nationalists.

The Kurdish setbacks, both in terms of non-implementation of the provisions of the Treaty of Sevres and the defeat of the Kurdish Republic of Mahabad, placed them in a precarious bargaining position vis-a-vis the Pahlavi monarchy in Iran and the Hashemite Kingdom in Iraq. Because of non-recognition and military suppression of Kurdish ethnic demands by those two regimes, the Kurds became active supporters of movements that overthrew the two monarchies. However, as we shall see in the following discussion, neither the Iraqi revolution of 1958 nor the Iranian revolution of 1979 resulted in the realisation of long-standing Kurdish aspirations.

In 1958, a group of military officers under the titular leadership of Abdul Karim Qussem, overthrew the Hashemite family and declared the establishment of a new republican political system in Iraq. The new regime promised to bring about a drastic transformation in the condition of the Kurds. A provisional constitution was promulgated which, for the first time, acknowledged the Kurds as a legitimate ethnic group with national right. The 1958 constitution, after reaffirming Iraq's place as an integral and inseparable part of the Arab nation, Stated that 'Arabs and Kurds are considered partners in this nation.'[4]

Qussem, himself, was intent on improving the lot of the Kurds. His mother was purportedly a Shi'a Kurd, and several Kurds were appointed to prominent positions after Qussem's accession to power. Most importantly, the exiled Kurdish leader. Mullah Mustafa Barzani, was allowed to return to Iraq and was given a hero's welcome.

In the early years of the Qussem regime, a symbiotic relationship developed between the government and the Kurds. While allowing Kurdish political and cultural activities to flourish, Qussem used the Kurds to keep his enemies (the monarchists, the Ba'athists and other Arab nationalists) at bay. Furthermore, Barzani's political ascendancy and *new alliance with* Baghdad allowed him to settle 'old scores' with other Kurdish tribes, 'especially the Bardosts, who had helped the Iraqi government in the 1930s and 1940s against Barzani'.[5] Similarly, Mullah Mustafa used his newfound power to gain control of the Kurdish Democratic Party of Iraq which he had lost during his exile years in the Soviet Union.

As Mullah Mustafa's power increased and as he solidified his control over the Kurdish movement, his relations with Qussem began to deteriorate Barzani's requests that the Kurds be given virtual autonomy was deemed unacceptable by Qussem. As a result, fighting erupted with the Iraqi forces and Barzani's peshmergas in the Autumn of 1961; it continued until January 1963 when a ceasefire agreement was signed.[6]

A month after the ceasefire, Qussem was overthrown by his Ba'athist enemies. The new regime was in turn overthrown in November 1963 by Abdul Salam Arif. Barzani's initial reaction to this dizzying pace of governmental change was to offer a truce, which halted the fighting between the two sides. However, the 1964 Iraqi Constitution undermined the skaky true as it did not specifically recognise the equality of the Kurds and the Arabs in their partnership endeavour to build a new Iraq.

The Kurdish position vis-a-vis iraqi government was weakened as a major split occurred within the leadership of the KDP. The younger and intellectual elements of the KDP politburo, particularly Jalal Talabani and Ibrahim Ahmad, challenged Barzani's handling of ceasefire negotiations with the government. Undeterred, Barzani continued to negotiate a ceasefire with the Iraqi regime while simultaneously fighting the Iraqi troops and his opposition within the KDP.

President Arif died in a place crash in April 1966 and was replaced by his brother, General Abdul Rahman Arif. Barzani seized this opportunity to offer a truce to the new government and to gain a breathing spell from the fighting'.[7] A major breakthrough appears to have occurred in the Kurdish-Iraqi stalemate in July 1966 when Prime Minister Adbul Rahman al-Bazzar offered his 'Twelve-Point Programme' for Kurdish self-rule. Although this did not satisfy all of Barzani's demands, it nevertheless did represent the first genuine government commitment since 1958 towards accommodating Kurdish autonomy requests. Moreover, Bazzaz's reputation for integrity compelled Barzani to accept the government's proposal as the basis for Kurdish-Iraqi negotiations. Prime Minister Bazzaz, however, was unable to implement his programme as he was replaced by Naji Talib, who unlike Bazzaz, was of the opinion that Barzani was not the presentative of all the Iraqi Kurds and that acceding to Barzani's autonomy demands would result in the de facto partition of the country. Talib's rejection of Kurdish demands resulted in intensification of Kurdish-Iraqi clashes which persisted throughout Abdul Rahman Arif's regime. Arif was overthrown in July 1968 and the second Ba'ath government since the Iraqi Revolution came to power. After twenty months of bloody fighting with the Kurds, the Ba'athist regime in March 1970 issued a directive the government's new policy towards the Kurdish movement. The document, known as the March Manifesto, was the most extensive programme which the Iraqi government had hitherto adopted to accommodate Kurdish national desires. Its major parts included the recognition of Kurdish as the official language in areas where a Kurdish majority was in existence, appointment of a Kurdish vice-president, self-rule and the creation of national administrative units in the Kurdish region, and the constitutional recognition of the equality of the Kurdish nation in bi-national Iraq.[8]

Other provisions of the March Manifesto included the establishment of a Kurdish academy of letters and a Kurdish university at Sulaymanieh, the appointment of various ministers and governors of Kurdish origin, the formation of the Duhok governorate encompassing the Kurdish province of Mosul, and implementation of a major land reform programme in Kurdistan. In return, the Kurds would relinquish their heavy arms to the government and dissolve their clandestine broadcasting station. Although efforts were made to implement the provisions of the March Manifesto, problems began to hinder the full realisation of the Kurdish autonomy demands. The question of a Kurdish vice- president was never resolved as the Iraqi government refused to accept the nomination of KDP's Secretary, Habib Mohammad Karim, ostensibly because of Karim's Iranian origin. The Kurds could not agree on an alternate candidate acceptable to the Iraqi regime. The major drawback of the March Manifesto, however was its failure to define the geographic area to be covered by the autonomy provisions of the Manifesto. The latter proved to be the stumbling block to instituting self-rule in Kurdistan. Bazzani was adamant in his demand that Kirkuk and other oil-producing areas be part of the Kurdish autonomous area. The Ba'athist government, on the other hand, insisted that only in areas with a proven Kurdish majority should the provisions of self-rule apply. Barzani was well aware of the fact that, due to the removal of the Kurds from the north to other parts of Iraq in previous years, the census might confirm the government's contention that Kirkuk did not contain a Kurdish majority, hence it would not be part of the Kurdish autonomous region. As Barzani stated, 'Kirkuk is part of Kurdistan. If the population census shows that the majority of its inhabitants are not Kurds, I will not recognise this. I will not bear, before the Kurds, the responsibility for relinquishing Kirkuk. May be this can take place after me'.[9] With the deadlock in implementing the March Manifesto, another full- scale war erupted between the Kurds and the Iraqi armed forces. With the support of the Shah of Iran. Israel and the United States, Barzani's *peshmergas* engaged the Iraqi troops for four years in protracted guerrilla warfare and inflicted heavy casualities of them.

Faced with the protracted war it could not win, on 12 December 1973 the Iraqi government offered a new plan for Kurdish autonomy, but it fell short of demands made by the KDP. The chief objection of the KDP revolved around the government's insistence that the 1957 census be used to demarcate the boundaries of the Kurdish autonomous region—a point which had previously been rejected by Mullah Mustafa and the KDP. The Ba'athist government once again reformulated its autonomy plans for the Kurds. On 11 March 1974 Iraqi President Hassan al-Bakr passed an extensive new law of self-rule in the Kurdish area and related constitutional amendments. In addition to provisions for Kurdish cultural autonomy, the law provided for the establishment of a Kurdish legislature and an executive council as governing organs of the autonomous region.

The Iraqi government gave the Kurds 15 days to accept the 11 March 1974 autonomy law of forfeit any chance of gaining self- rule. The Kurdish leadership, after along period of indecision, rejected the government's latest offer. This was mainly due to the KDP's demand that Kirkuk be designated the administrative centre of the Kurdish autonomous region, whereas the government insisted on maintaining the city of Irbil as the administrative heart of the area. Another, and perhaps more serious reason for Barzani's rejection of the autonomy law of 1974 was the promise of aid he had received from the Shah of Iran, the United States and Israel. As Barzani later contended: 'Without American promises, we would not have acted the way we did, were it not for American promises, we would never have become trapped and involved to such an extent.[10]

Indeed, early indications pointed to the United States' commitment to Barzani's cause. In Spring 1974, a US Army operations headquarters was established in the Iranian city of Rezayieh (now Urumiyeb), near the Iraqi border, to advise the Kurdish peshmergas. Furthermore, CIA Station was reportedly established in the border village of Haj Umran, not far from Barzani's headquarters. High-level Kurdish personalities and KDP officials have acknowledged the presence of American, Iranian and Israeli advisers amongst their forces.[11]

Barzani's initial optimism regarding an unending supply of American weapons for his forces proved to be premature. Henry Kissinger, the chief architect of the US assistance programme to Barzani, became obsessed with implementing the Sinai disengagement agreement between Egypt and Israel which Syria opposed. In order to put pressure on Syria to ameliorate its opposition, Kissinger found it prudent to lessen pressure on Syria's Ba'athist rival, Iraq. Consequently, American commitment to the Kurds began to weaken.

The Shah of Iran was also beginning to re-evaluate his policy of allowing his country to be used as a conduit for weapons destined for Barzani and as a staging ground for Kurdish military operations against the Iraqi forces. After years of confrontation with many Arab states, the Shah had decided to pursue a policy of accommodation towards major Arab countries and 'did not want to alienate them by waging a direct war with his Arab neighbour'.[12]

In early Spring 1975, the Shah officially terminated Iran's support for the Kurds. At an OPEC meeting in Algiers in March 1975, the Shah and Saddam Hussein, the Vice-President of the Iraqi Revolutionary Command Council (RCC – the governing body of Iraq) signed an agreement which 'completely eliminated the conflict between the two brotherly countries.[13] The Algiers agreement obligated Iran to withdraw its support for the Kurds in return for Iraq's abandonment of its claim of absolute sovereignty over a lot of the Shatt-al Arab river (which formed the southernmost border between the two countries), and some minor adjustments over land boundaries between Iran and Iraq.

With its supply route closed, the Kurdish rebellion seemed to have reached a dead end. The Iraqi government subsequently offered an amnestry to Kurdish peshmergas who would surrender by 1 April 1975. Similarly, the Iranian government informed Kurdish refugees that the border between Iran and Iraq would soon be sealed along the Kurdish regions, and those willing to return to Iraq should do so before the 1 April deadline. The Shah also offered to allow Barzani and some of his fighters to reside in Iran. After fleeing to Iran, Barzani and his peshmergas were housed in camps away from Kurdistan and in areas where they could be closely supervised.[14]

The Algiers agreement, however, did not bring about a permanent cessation of Iraqi-Kurdish hostilities. The Kurdish peshmergas regrouped themselves under the banner of the Kurdish Democratic Party-Provisional Leadership. This group, under the leadership of Mullah Mustafa's sons, Massoud and Idris, continued to fight the Iraqi government with little success. Still, other allies and associates of Mullah Mustafa accepted the Iraqi regime's limited autonomy. They, under the leadership of Hassam Aqrawi, the current head of the Iraqi Kurdish Democratic Party, they have supported the Ba'athist government against the KDP-Provisional Leadership. Still another split in the ranks of the Iraqi Kurds occurred in November 1975 when a few KDP members, who had been ousted by Mullah Mustafa, accused him of betraying the Kurdish cause and held him responsible for the defeat of the Kurdish resistance. These dissidents, led by Jalal Talabani, formed a group called the patriotic Union of Kurdistan (PUK). All these groups have continued to fight each other, thereby debilitating the strength of the Kurdish movement in Iraq.

Of all the post-Barzani Kurdish groups, only the official KDP (Aqrawi's group) has participated in the autonomy scheme for the Kurdish region, which now includes Dahuk, Irbil, and Sulaymanieh but not Kirkuk. As alluded to earlier, the governing structure of the Kurdish autonomous region is composed of the Executive Council and the Legislative Assembly located in Irbil. The latter organ acts as an advisory body to the former, which wields both executive and legislative power. The Legislative Assembly's eighty members are principally large landowners or traditional tribal chiefs and are appointed by the Iraqi government and are, hence subservient to Baghdad. The Executive Council is headed by a cabinet and includes up to twelve members appointed from the deputies of the Legislative Assembly. The powers of the local government in the Kurdish autonomous region are severely limited and the majority of the Kurds consider the local governmental organs as puppets of the Baghdad government.

In December 1983, Jalal Talabani's PUK, in a dramatic turnaround, announced its decision to accept a ceasefire with the Iraqi government and begin negotiations over a new autonomy scheme with Saddam Hussein's regime. The PUK, which had been fighting the Iraqi army, the Iranian forces, and the KDP-Provisional Leadership, apparently found it debilitating to take on three forces simultaneously. As one PUK official contended: 'At least we can talk to Saddam Hussain . . . Khomeini has killed 20,000 Iranian Kurds and sees all minorities as agents of Satan.[15]

In addition to extracting a pledge for further cultural autonomy, Talabani was able to obtain promises from Baghdad to allow all previously deported Kurds to return to their homes, and that PUK peshmergas be allowed to carry arms for the purpose of defending the Kurdish region. The new agreement was given the PUK an opportunity to lessen its dependence on Syria. In the words of a PUK official: 'We know the agreement will not last, but at least it has proved that we are independent from Damascus or any other regime . . . It has given us a breathing space which we will use to prepare for the next onslaught.[16]

A high-level delegation of Kurds concluded an agreement with the Iraqi government representatives in Baghdad on Kurdish autonomy within the Iraqi republic. Terms of the agreement have been roused of an end to the tragic events of the past ten weeks, in which thousands of Kurds perished and over a million became destitutes and refugees in the neighbouring territories of Turkey and Iran. The third and the bloodiest of the three major Kurd uprisings in the post-world war second period has once again proved that the none of the super or smaller powers is prepared to do anything more than use the fiercely independent minded Kurds for their own immediate end and then forget about them. The one difference between the earlier uprisings and the recent one is that the US President, who used all the rhetoric in his script writers arsenal to incite the Kurds to rebel against Saddam Hussein, has gradually owned the moral responsibility for the tragic plight of those who trusted his words. The US has rushed food, medicine, blankets and tents to provide much needed help without making any pre-condition of Saddam Hussein's overthrow for refugees to return home. The exact number of Kurds killed in the Iraqi military operation is still a matter of conjecture but the number of Kurds and other uprooted, mainly Shiite fundamentalists, is estimated between one to two millions. The 20 million Kurds inhabit a vast mountainous area spread over Iran, Iraq, Turkey and Syria. A tiny part of the Kurdish population lives in a corner of the Soviet Union as well. The Kurds belong to the Indo-European racial stock. Before embracing the Sunni sect of Islam they practiced animist forms of Buddhism. The present day Mosul was once a seat of Baddhist learning and had intimate contacts with India. They trace their origins to Meda, in ancient Persoa, some even to the Greek mythology of Mede or Medes.

Shepherds and warriors, organised into tight tribal structures, they grouped together into principalities in the Middle Ages but ended up falling under Ottoman rule, against which they revolted several times.

In 1914, northern Kurdistan was among the many gifts offered by Britain and France to Tsar Nicolas Second for his entering the war on their side, France kept for itself the southern part along with Mosul's oil which finally ended up in British hands. The Allies took advantage of the October Revolution to renege on their commitments to Russia, and so it was without it that on August 20, 1920, at the Treaty of Sevres they divided up the Sultan's possessions among themselves, leaving him only Anatolia, Shora of Smyrne and Aremenia. The treaty provided for a French, British and Italian commission to prepare within six months a plan for local autonomy for the largely Kurdish regions situated east of the Euphrates to the south of Armenia's southern border. . and to the north of Turkey's border with Syria and Mesopotamia*, Mesopotamia is now Iraq. Turkey understood to implement a possible 'recommendation' of the Kurdish people if within a year they were to show that a majority of them wanted independence. Today, Kurdish leaders frequently refer to the provision, but the least one could say of it is that, unlike the treaty's other provisions, clarity is not its strongest point. In any casé, this particular provision has never been applied, for its extreme severity towards the Turks touched off a revolt which was to lead to the proclamation of the Turkish republic and the expulsion of the Greeks.[18]

Given the clauses of the Treaty of Sevres, the Kurds sided with the Sultan. However, the future Ataturk succeeded in getting them to join his crusade to free Asia Minor of Greek occupation. But once the Treaty of Lausanne was signed normalising relations between the infant Turkish republic and the West, Ataturk turned against the Kurds. He quite simply denied that there was any such thing as a Kurdish nation, wiped out all the educated Kurds and crushed three successive insurrection without compuction. For a long time Ankara pretended that the Kurds were "mountain Turks". It is only recently that President Turgut Ozal has began talking of what he calls a "Basque solution" to a problem which for years has sustained a state of violence in eastern Turkey. Iran holds a similar attitude to the Kurds. It considers its Kurds to be Persians like the rest of its population. After all, don't they speak the same language? Yet it was on Kurdish territory that, right after the second World War, the only independent Kurdish republic was ever was proclaimed. Though strongly supported by Stalin, who gave its president Mullah Mustafa al-Barzani his general's starts and got the Soviet Union's own Kurds – about 100,000 strong – to go to work on its neighbours, the Kurdish republic failed to survive the first test of the Cold War which force the USSR to evacuate Iranian Azerbaijan on March 25, 1946. The legendary Mullah's son is now one of the most respected leaders of Kurds. Later the Shah of Iran took an interest in the Kurds, though mostly those in Iraq whose honey-moon with the Ba'athist regime after the 1958 revolution, following the recognition of their autonomy, did not last long. In his struggle with Baghdad for control of the Shatt Al-Arab, the Shah was only too happy to have Barzani on his side this time. But the alliance was dictated by expediency. The Shah of Iran feared that if the Iraqi Kurds won autonomy it would be bound to affect the attitudes of their fellow Kurds in Iran. Consequently he was seen going to Algiers a few months later where he reached a compromise settlement with Saddam Hussein on all the bilateral issues. At this juncture the Kurds once again felt they had been betrayed. A few years later Mullah Barzani went into exile, in the United States, where he died. This was less true on the Turkish border where large numbers of Kurds apparently crossed into Iraq after Saddam Hussein's defeat in the Gulf war, believing that the hour of their liberation had at last come. Today, tens of thousands of refugees with nothing but the clothes on their backs are massed at the cold, wind-swept border having lost their illusions, and there are even more on the Iranian border. The UN is also sending aid to refugees but has declined to go to the areas where US military-protected camps are located. The Kurds are as bitter with George Bush as with Saddam Hussein. But for Bush's promises of aid, they would not have gambled with the lives of their people. Neither Iran nor Turkey are prepared to accept the Kurdish demand for a homeland of their own. They would be more than happy if Kurds return to Iraq with a sense of *security*.[19]

The rugged, undulating plains of Anatolia give way to mountains from the east bank of the Tigris river. This is also the beginning of rebel country. Here the writ of Turkish government extends only to any hamlets sheltering the Gendarmerie, the para- military responsible for internal security. For decades, this Kurdish dominated eastern corner of Turkey has been in a state of insurrection. In the high mountains, some of them snow capped even in early summer, and in the deep gorges, armed Kurdish guerillas still reign supreme. They, like their compatriots in parts of Syria, Iraq and Iran, believe they have been chealed out of a homeland and till this day remain determined to reverse the historical wrong. The Kurds' perception of history and nationalism has not endeared them to the Governments of the countries they inhabi. And for decades they have been persecuted some thousands gassed, shot and hanged. The Kurdish cause has rarely hit the headlines in the past. Mainly because their demand embarrasses even the West, which believes that the fragile equilibrium in the Middle East would be further disturbed if the Kurds were to get Kurdistan: a separate nation carved out of portions of Turkey, Syria, Iraq and Iran. The Kurds would have in all probability remained a forgotten race struggling mutely in their mountains had it not been for Saddam Hussein and the extraordinary chain of events be set off in the Middle East. By early summer this year, the whole world was suddenly talking about the Kurds. The current bugbear of the world, Saddam Hussein, after being humiliated by Western Armies for trying to annex Kuwait on the unfortunate Kurds. American President Bush's call for an internal[20] revolt against Saddam Hussein had been taken most seriously by Iraq's Kurdish population which saw in Iraq's military defeat a heaven sent opportunity to finally free themselves. They revolted, and violently too. Kurdish guerillas inside Iraq captured several towns, including the oil rich city of Mosul, and were on the verge of proclaiming independence when Saddam Hussein counter-attacked. This time, the Iraqi leader's forces, many of them made up of Sudanese and Palestinian mercenaries, attempted a final solution to their Kurdish problem. Instead of merely fighting the armed guerillas, they attacked towns and villages inhabited by Kurds. Entire families were wiped out and their properties gutted. This led to the infamous exodus, the pictures of which were generously flashed across newspaper frontpages and television screens. The world had suddenly woken up to the Kurdish tragedy. While these extraordinary events were unfolding, I was in the Turkish capital Ankara trying to get hold of someone who would drive me 1,500 kilometers across the breadth of Turkey to the borders. The local airlines, Turkish Hava Yollari, was on strike and a chartered plane was out of the question. Finally, two days after arriving in Ankara I managed to pack my crew, one interpreter, a hundred kilos of equipment, and myself into a Toyota and left while a freezing drizzle came down over Ankara. We drove through the nigh, stopped for 12 hours at the Anatolian dam project site and arrived on the morning of the day after at the ancient town of Cizre. It was Ramadan and the grey streets, guarded by silent minareted buildings, were deserted. Most of the shops were closed. Business had come to a grinding halt ever since Saddam Hussein invaded Kuwait and the once busy international highway that ran from Baghdad through this town onwards to Istanbul and Europe was closed at the border. On our way, we had seen giant trailers parked by deserted petrol pumps. Even the restaurants in the conce busy

'Service Stations' were abandoned. The only food to be had on the highway was goats cheese, Turkish bread and bitter lemons. Our interpreter made enquiries at the sole hotel still open and was told that something was happening at the borders, 'May be, there will be a war,' the interpreter said. "Our President Torgut Ozal had warned Saddam that if the Kurdish refugees keep coming then he would be forced to attack. 'But war on this warm Anatolian morming seemed so utterly remote a possibility that we decided to go ahead to the border town of Habur some 46 km away.[21]

Kurdish autonomy in Iraq would be a constant challenge to Kurds in other countries to attain autonomy and would encourage their aspirations for the creation of a unified Kurdish state.

In the event of a positive outcome of the ongoing Iraqi Kurdish negotiations in Baghdad, he said, the creation of a Kurdish enclave within Iraq would encourage in future similar demands by the Kurdish population living in neighbouring Turkey, Iran, Syria and the Soviet Union.

In such a case, declaration of Kurdish autonomy in northern Iraq could be Iraq's revenge on Turkey and Iran because of their support to the Kurds and Shi'ites.

Diplomatic sources here said that after the ongoing autonomy talks between the Iraqi government and Kurdish rebel leaders nothing would be the same as before.

The main obstacle for the Kurds in achieving their goals is demand put forward by their leaders that the international community guarantee their agreement with Baghdad.

This, Iraq says, is not acceptable to it as it would mean the direct interference of other countries in its internal affairs.

Analysts in Baghdad felt the basis for the setting up of Kurdish autonomy in northern Iraq would be an agreement between the two sides from March 11, 1970. This document was signed by the legendary Kurdish leader Mustafa Al-Barazani and Saddam Hussein, then number two in the ruling Arab Baath Co-Socialist Party.

The agreement recognised the Kurds' rights to take part in state bodies, to hold the post of vice-president of the republic, and the right to use the Kurdish language officially along with Arabic. It also envisaged carrying out agrarian reforms in the region occupied by Kurds.

However, the agreement collapsed only a year' later and conflict was renewed and has lasted up to the present.

And now, Iraqi-Kurdish relations are back where they were two decades ago. The next few days will show if the stalemate between Iraqi-Kurdish leaders will finally end.

Kurds and Iraqi officials agreed on July 19, 1991 to end fighting in northern Iraq reported to have caused hundreds of casualities.

They agreed to stop fighting, Kemal Kirkukli, a senior official of the Kurdistan Democratic Party (KDP), said.

Kirkukli said tension had spilled into the former allied security zone from which western troops withdrew on Monday, but there had been no actual fighting there.

Kirkukli said he had no accurate casualty figures on clashes in the northern Iraqi towns of Irbil and Sulaimaniya this week. But he said 2,500 Iraqis, including 70 officers, had been taken prisoner and six Iraqi tanks had been destroyed and 11 captured. The prisoners were being held in Sulaimaniya.

Kirkukli said KDP leader Masoud Barzani, engaged in autonomy talks with Iraqi officials in Baghdad, had ordered factions grouped in the Kurdistan front to send delegation to Sulaimaniya.

Meanwhile, Turkey has officially confirmed that it has approved the stationing of "mobile allied forces" numbering around 3,000 troops in the southeastern city of Silopi, Tanjug-Poll adds from Ankara.

The task of the forces will be to protect the population of northern Iraq from possible attacks by the Iraqi army, the Turkish Premier Mesut Ilmaz as saying on Friday.

He said the forces will be "under Turkish control" and added that "the details of their stationing are being discussed by military officials."

According to Ilmaz's statement, Turkey will participate with around 1,000 men in the "mobile forces" which are made up troops from the United States, Great Britain, the Netherlands, Belgium. France and Italy.

Monitoring of northern Iraq from Turkey will also be carried out from the NATO base in Incirlik, where the airforce is stationed, and from the Mediterranean, near the Turkish border, where the US aircraft carrier is located.

A feather was added to cap of Iraqi President Saddam Hussein when he won open support on July 20, 1991 from the Kurdish leader Massound Barzani.

Barzani declared in Baghdad that all issues between the government of Iraq and the Kurdish people were resolved and a comprehensive agreement had been agreed upon by the two sides.

For the first time since the trouble started in the two Kurdish-dominated towns of Suleimaniyeh and Arbil, the foremost spokesman for the Kurdish people accused the foreign powers for fomenting trouble in the areas for their vested interests.

Without naming the countries, Barzani said it was the handiwork' of the evil forces that created obstacles in the way of the government of Iraq by spreading concocted stories through the western media and also incited the Kurdish people.

Barzani said the situation in the two provinces was stable and the law would take its own course to punish the mischief-makers.

He said the government and the Kurdish people were now working as one group and expressed full confidence that the matter would be resolved for the good.

He said the details of the agreement would be announced soon.

This new development in the region has created tremendous public opinion in favour of the Iraqi president and has disappointed the western powers led by the USA seeking a pound of flesh from the heart of President Saddam Hussein, said a Senior leader of the Iraq's Baath party.

In another development, Iraqi information minister Hamid Yous if Hummadi has publicly attacked Iran in a statement for abetting and financing the infiltrators from across the border in the northern procines.

This is the first attack by the Iraqi government against Iran since the Gulf war broke out in January 1991.

Political circles feel some change in the Iraqi-Iran relations in near future was imminent.

Iran has not yet reacted to the allegation.

Meanwhile, in Geneva the International Committee of the Red Cross has visited several hundred Iraqi soldiers taken prisoner by Kurdish rebels in recent fighting in northern Iraq.

The ICRC said its workers also helped evacuate dozens of people wounded in fighting on July 17 and 18, 1991 around the town of Suleimaniyey, some across the border to the Iranian town paveh.

The all-Swiss humanitarian agency said it was bringing medical supplies to the area from Tehran, Iran and preparing more for shipment from Baghdad, if needed.

In New York, diplomats said on July 19 1991 that Iraq had admitted it had been making a supergun, just as suspected by the western intelligence agencies.

A western diplomate showed reporters a document Iraq had filed with the UN special commission in charge of destroying Iraq's weapons of mass destruction.

In the document Iraq admitted having a gun barrel that was more than 150 feet (52.5 metres) long.

A special commission official said the gun would have been too inaccurate to be used as a conventional armament.

"The conclusion we drew from seeing the document was that if could only had been used for one of three purposes: chemical, biological or nuclear", said the official, who spoke on condition of anonymity.

Iraq also admitted having other steel tubes for advanced artillery, including one intended to be used as part of the 1,000 calibre supergun, the official said. It was not known whether the gun was close to completion.

It was not listed in earlier Iraqi documents of arms destroyed during the war. Western countries in 1990 claimed that Iraq had been trying to build a supergun that would increase its artillery fire in the region.

The success of the American and their allies in returning so many Kurds to Iraq from the Turkish border may have given the impression that the Kurdish refugee problem has been solved. It has not. The commander of the British force, General Robin Ross, calls the international effort in Kurdistan "a blueprint for future disaster relief". But the plain fact is that most of the 1.6 million or so Kurds who fled from the Iraqi army in March 12, 1991 are still homeless.

Of the half a million Kurds who bolted towards Turkey, all but 10,000 (most of them Christians who are trying to emigrate) have gone back to Iraq. About 30,000 remain in big camps at zakho and Amadiyah and tens of thousands more are living in tents or makeshift shelters throughout the sanctuary created for them. These people are either to afraid to return to their own homes, because they live in parts of Kurdistan controlled by the Iraqi army, or cannot return, because the Iraqis have destroyed their home. Iraqi demolition squads have been especially busy in the Kurdish quarters of Mosul and Kirkuk. The refugees from the Turkish-border are at least getting medicine and food from the United Nations, which assumed "humanitarian" responsibility for the safe haven in early June. The one million Kurds who fled to Iran have fared less well. More than half are still in Iran, which says it is finding it difficult, given international miserlines, to provide for them. Most or the refugees who have crossed back have not dared go further than the 50-kilometre (30-mile) mountain strip inside Iraq under the control of the Kurdish peshmerga guerillas. In this strip, tens or possibly hundreds of thousands are camping in the rubble of what used to be their home villages. The Iraqis started destroying these places 16 years ago, ostensibly to secure the frontiers region and give the Kurds easier access to education and services. The policy entailed destroying 4,000 Kurdish villages and a score of towns, and deporting their inhabitants. Much of Kurdistan still looks as though it has been hit by an earthquake. In village after village every building has been razed. Here and there returning refugees are bringing these desolate places to life. In the Hiran valley hundreds of families have returned to villages destroyed in 1988. They are rebuilding irrigation channels to revive parched orchards and vineyards. "Nazinin used to be famous for its pomegranates", said one returning refugees of his ruined hamlet, "God willing it will be again." The devastated main street of Qala Diza, once a town of 60,000 people, is bustling. Shops built out of blocks of rubble sell everything from potatoes to Kalashnikovs. Other towns such as Halabja and Penjwin are also coming back to life.[22]

Water is plentiful: under the rubble many waterpipes are intact and can be tapped. But food is scarce and expensive. At six dinars a kilo rice is 25 times its-pre-war price. With Iraq still under sanctions, few goods arrive from the south. Most of the trade is across the border with Iran; the Kurds exchange television sets and cars for food and essentials. Little foreign aid reaches this area, although it is possible to encounter a handful of UN officials and Europeans from charities.

Equilibre, a French-based organisation, trucks in a little flour, rice, cheese and powdered milk from Zakho. Medicins sans Frontieres and Medicins du Monde run clinics, which treat, among other things, injuries from landmines. All the aid workers give warning that more help is needed before the autumn rains begin. The biggest worry is that the mass migration will start again – either because of an Iraqi attack or because a political agreement lures back all the Kurds sheltering in Iran (a new round of talks between the Iraqi government and the Kurdish guerilla leadership began on July 6th). Equilibre has only five tents in its depleted warehouse.[23]

In the middle of the dual carriage way where six hot and tired US Marines wave returning Kurdish refugees through their wire chicane, there stands a sign". To the east, a battery of Marine 105 mm howitzers nestle under camouflage netting. Summer is coming to northern Iraq a warm breeze rippling the hundreds of square miles of wheat fields around Dihok. Anticipating United Nations sanctions in 1990. Saddam Hussein ordered the Iraqis to plant wheat on all available arable land. Thus the American humanitarin groups, the US military and the UN are now encouraging the Kurds – who are, after all, *Iraqi citizens* – to harvest the crop that was sown to beat the UN sanctions. The allied presence in northern Iraq is rich in such ironies. In Zakho, for example, the US military are adhering strictly to the theory that they are merely protecting and assisting the resettlement of Kurdish refugees, that they have no argument with the Iraqi authorities. But the Kurds – despite their talks with President Saddam in Baghdad – do have a very bloody agrument with the Iraqis; thus three Humvee military vehicles manned by armed US Marines are posted outside the Zakho police station to protect the Iraqi police from their own people. Allied negotiations with the Iraqi police and army are held daily, adding a modicum of new legitimacy to President Saddam's regime. And while the Iraqi government continues to denounce the allies' presence in norther Iraq as a flagrant violation of its sovereignty, US and British technicians have cheerfully touring Dihok in the company of Iraqi officials in order to restore power lines, hospitals, water and sewage systems damaged during the abortive Kurdish uprising two months ago. North of that line on the highway, the allies have real though not legal power. South of the line, they have no power at all, merely an understanding with the Iraqis that they will send military and civilian personnel to help reconstruct Dihok. When

Kurds attacked the police station there at the weekened, a US Army coloneal watched but did not intervene.

American troops here are not blind to the implications of their persence. Some suspect that Kurdish leaders, particularly those in the KDP, are using the allied military power as a cover to prepare for a continuation of their war against Iraq if—or when—the talks in Baghdad are finally acknowledged to have broken down. The allies are reconstituting the towns of northern Iraqi Kurdistan, resettling the refugees and taking a humanitarian burden from the Kurdish leadership—thus allowing the latter a free hand to plan their own future as an autonomous or free Kurdish state.[24]

The World's conscience is being eased. The tragedy of the Kurdish retreat to the mountains—a logical result of the allied call to overthrow Saddam—has been ameliorated by return resettlement. Instead of dying babies and sick children, the fields around Zakho are now filled with thriving children. Convoys of trucks and cars carrying thousands of civilians through the allied checkpoints—up to 20,000 on Monday along. At night, a moving necklace of light down the mountains to the north tells of the return south. The Kurds are going home. But to what? South of that checkpoint on the Dihok road, the only security is provided by the peshmerga guerrillas who have, temporarily, agreed to keep their gunds out of sight. The UN's security guards make no secret of their own impotence. They are a symbol of the World's concern, not its shield. A magic date—15 June—is now circulating among allied trooops in the Western sector of the "Control Zone", a day upon which US and British forces may begin their withdrawal. The darkest scenario sees the Kurds leaving with them, the television cameras recording weeping families clinging to the retreating American vehicles in a seond flight to the mountains.[25]

Landmines are posing a serious threat to Kurdish refugees returning to abandoned villages in a border zone which was once *Iraq's frontline with* Iran.

German doctor Matthias Funk said on August 17, 1991 his team now treats a mine victim about every other day at a field hospital in northern Iraq's Choman valley.

"The people we see have lost a foot or sometimes an entire leg," he said "For them, it is too late. We need a mine awareness and demining programme".

Eight of the 13 Kurds currently under his care are mine victims.

Bloody, fly-covered bandages cover the stumps of their amputated limbs as they sprawl on cotton matresses in hospital tents 25 km from the *Iranian* border.

After an average of two weeks they are discharged without physiotherapy or artificial lims which no relief group in northern Iraq is equipped to provide.

"I'm sure such things are available in Baghdad," says Funk who works for the Komitee Cap Anamur, a private relief group.

"These people are too frightened to go there. So it might as well be the moon," he said.

The Choman valley, which stretches into Iran, is just one area along the border. Relief Officials further south in Penjwin and Halapca also report increasing numbers of mine injuries.

Hundreds of thousands of mines were planted by both sides during the 1980-88 Iran-Iraq war. Even before the Iraqi government had destroyed and mined many villages in an attempt to eradicate Kurdish rebel strong holds.

After theis year's war over Kuwait and the failed Kurdish revolt that followed in March 1991. US-led forces limited the deployment of Iraqi and aircraft in Kurdistan.

This encouraged tens of thousands of Kurdish refugees to return to villages emptied years before.

Officials of the Kurdish Democractic Party say they have asked both the United Nations and the European Community to establish mine programmes in Kurdistan but have received no reply so far.

Otto Hagenbuchle, director of the UN refugee office in the Choman area, acknowledges the need but says others are more pressing.

"The mines are assuming more and more importance as we encourage people to settle in their former villages. When it comes to the developmental reconstruction of Iraq we will have to deal with miens all along the border, not just in Kurdistan," he said.

REFERENCES

1. Nader Entessar. The Kurds in Past Revolutionary Iran and Iraq. *Third World quarterly*, October, 1984.

2. C.J. Edmonds. Kurdish Nationalism. *Journal of Contemporary History*, 6(1) 1971; p. 8.
3. Archic Roosevelt. The Kurdish Republic of Mahabad. In Gerard Chaliand, (ed). *People without a country*, London, 1980.
4. Richard F. Nyrop, *ed. Iraq*. Washington, 1979, p. 61.
5. E. Ghareeb. *The Kurdish Question in Iraq*. Syracuse, 1981; pp. 38-39.
6. Saad Jowad. *Iraq and the Kurdish Question*. London, 1981; p. 63.
7. Ghareeb. *op. cit*., p. 41.
8. *Settlement of the Kurdish Problem in Iraq*, Baghdad Ath- thawra Publications, nd, pp. 111-22.
9. *Ibid*. pp. 38-9.
10. Ghareeb. *The Kurdish Question* Syracuse, 1981; p. 159.
11. *Ibid.*, p. 180. See also *New York Times*, 30 September, 1980.
12. *Ibid*., p. 165.
13. R. Sim. Kurdistan. *Conflict Studies*, (124), November 1980, p. 14. See also. Fareq Y. Ismael. *Iraq and Iran*, Syracuse, 1982; pp. 60-68.
14. Suffering from cancer, Mullah Mustafa Barzani left Iran for the United States a few months after his arrival in the Iran. He died in 1979 in Washington and was buried in Oshnovich, Iran.
15. Quoted in *the Middle East*, (112), February 1984; p. 10.
16. *Ibid.*
17. Kurds. *New Wave*, 5 May, 1991.
18. *Ibid.*
19. *Ibid.*
20. Indranil Banerjee. Nobody's People, *The Hindustan Times*, 3 August, 1991.
21. *Ibid.*
22. *The Hindustan Times*, 22 July, 1991.
23. *Ibid.*
24. *The Hindustan Times*, 30 May, 1991.
25. *Ibid.*

8

THE IRANIAN MUSLIM MINORITY – THE KURDS

The Iranian Revolution of 1978-9 was supported enthusiastically by a broad spectrum of the Kurdish population of Iran. The Kurds participated actively in the revolutionary process from the outset. The memory of the Algiers agreement and what the Kurds considered the Shah's betrayal of them without 'the least bit of compunction'[1]: provided added incentives for the Kurds to join the revolutionary bandwagon in Iran. The only group which refrinaed from partaking in anti-Shah activities was composed of traditional tribal chiefs who had been co-opted into the monarchial system through a policy of financial and political rewards.

The Jaf tribal chiefs are a good case in point. The traditional power-holders in the tribe were given high-level positions in local and central governments, and their large landholdings were practically untouched by the Shah's land reform programme. Sardar Jaf became an influential tribal member of the majlis (the lower house of parliament) and his brother, Salar Jaf, was a high-level official in the Shah's palace. Similarly, the Aradalan tribe provided a large number of people who rose to prominence during the Shah's reign, and the Shah's last court minister was an Ardalan Kurd.[2] The Kurds also provided good soldiers whose loyalty catapulted them to the highest ranks in the armed forces of the monarchial Iran. One of the most loyal supporters of the Shah, even after the overthrow of the Pahlavi monarchy, was General Palizban, the Kurdish Governor General of Kermanshah. Using his knowledge of the region and his Kurdish connections, Palizban has continued to haunt the Islamic Republic from his base in Iraq. The initial Kurdish euphoria over the downfall of the Shah, however, gave way to the bitter realisation that the Kurdish autonomy demands would go unheeded by the new regime in

Tehran. It was evident that Khomeini's goal of creating a strong, centralised Islamic Republic would clash with that of the autonomy-seeking Kurds. As Sheikh Ezzedin Husseini, the influential religious leader of the Mahabad Kurds stated: 'We fought in the revolution not out of religious convictions but for political goals. We want autonomy – our own parliament, our own language, our own culture.[3] To this end, the Kurds held free elections in several cities and elected city councillors, many of whom were members or sympathisers of the newly-revived Kurdish Democratic Party of Iran (KDPI). Dr. Abdul Rahman Qassemlou, who had returned to Iran after several years of exile in Europe, assumed the leadership of the KDPI. Qassemlou's Marxist ideology coupled with Sheikh Husseini's socialist views couched in religious terms, compelled Ayatollah Khomeini to view the Kurdish demands as Marxist-inspired and conspiracy against the nascent Islamic Republic of Iran. Consequently, Khomeini declared the elections of Kurdish city councillors void and began to refer to both Qassemlou and Ezzedin Husseini as "Satanic" figures. Qassemlou, for his part, insisted that his goal was not to establish an independent Kurdish state, but his motto was 'democracy for Iran, autonomy for Kurdistan'. Which has now become a popular slogan for the KDPI. Qassemlou's autonomy scheme has, in fact, required the establishment of a Kurdish region in which only defence, foreign relations and finance would be controlled by Tehran. Religious factors also played an important role in exacerbating tensions between the Iranian Kurds (who are mostly Sunni) and the Shi'a religious leadership in Tehran and Qom. However, the Kermanshah Kurds, who are predominantly Shi'a, tended to support Khomeini. The Qom clerics, in return, promoted Ahmad Moftizadeh, a conservative Shi'a cleric, as the true representative of the Kurdish nation. Sheikh Ezzedin Husseini, on the other hand, continued to oppose Ayatollah Khomeini's theory of Islamic government with its emphasis on velayat-e-faqih (government of jurisprudence), which promotes the concentration of all power in the hands of an infallible faqih. Sheikh Husseini summarised his objections to Khomeini's notion of a just government thus:

Many governments in the past have claimed to act in the name of Islam, but in reality they were not Islamic. The Safavid and Ottomen governments were cases in point; more recently we have the case of Khomeini in Iran. They are queshri – backward and vulgar –

and have ruined Islam and is spirit. What we have is not religious government, but a dictatorship under the name of Islam. . . . In Sunni Islam there is no imam as political leader or na'ib (deputy) imam. The role of the clergy is to be morshed, or guide, in knowing God. You will also find some Shi'i clergy who reject Khomeini's concept of faqih. It is not an Islamic regime.[4]

The notion of clergy as guides and interpreters of Islamic laws collided with Khomeini's conception of clergy as active participants and perhaps the dominant force in society.

Notwithstanding tensions between the Kurds and the theocratic establishment in Iran, the first post-revolutionary cabinet included two Kurds in its ranks: Dr. Karim Sanjabi, the Veteran leader of the National Front, and Dariush Foruhar. Sanjabi was appointed Foreign Minister while Foruhar was given the Labour portfolio. Both of these men were respected nationalists with anti-Shah credentials.

On 14 February, 1979, Foruhar was sent to Mahabad as the head of a goodwill government delegation to discuss Kurdish autonomy demands. However, due to the multiplicity of power centres in Tehran and the weakness of Prime Minister Bazargan's government vis-a-vis the Revolutionary Council (the de facto government of Iran), the Foruhar delegation was unable to make any firm commitments to the Kurdish side. Compounding the problem was the ambiguity of the nature of Kurdish autonomy demands. It was assumed that the areas of defence, foreign policy, and economic planning and trade would be the exclusive domain of the central government. The powers and functions of the local government were not clearly stated.

Another vexing problem was the boundaries of the Kurdish homeland. The Kurds insisted that any future autonomy plans be implemented in the provinces of West Azarbaijan, Ilam, Kermanshah as well as Kurdistan. Although Kurds have resided in all of these for the inclusion of the concept of Kurdish autonomy in the national constitution, the recognition by the government of the provinces of West Azarbaijan, Ilam Kermanshah and Kurdistan as an autonomous region, the establishment of a freely-elected Kurdish national assembly with jurisdiction over all local affairs (including internal security functions), guarantee of the freedom of religion, speech and assembly throughout Iran, the inclusion of Kurdish representatives in the central government machinery, use of Kurdish (along with Farsi) as the primary language in official business and schools, and the allocation of a fixed amounts of the national budget to the development of the backward economy of kurdistan. The Kurdish plan also reiterated the supremacy of the central government in national defence, foreign policy and economic planning.

These demands, with minor modifications, were accepted by the Foruhar delegation. However, as it became known that the Islamic Republic's new constitution did not expressly recognise Kurdish minority rights, the eight-point plan unravelled. In an attempt to induce the Kurds, and other Muslim ethnic minorities in the country, to participate in the 1980 presidential election, Ayatollah Khomeini announced that he was prepared to guarantee Sunni minority rights, possibly in the form of an amendment to the new Islamic constitution. The amendment would allow the Sunnis to have their own religious courts in areas where they constituted the majority of the population. However, Sheikh Ezzedin Husseini, and other Kurdish leaders, rejected Khomeini's proposal as insufficient in meeting the Kurdish autonomy demands. By 1980, hopes of a negotiated settlement of the Kurdish issue had all but vanished. As the fighting between the Iranian forces and Kurds continued, the Kurdish strong-holds in major cities gradually fell to the government forces. The Kurdish Peshmergas were forced to retreat to the countryside and take up defensive positions there.

The tenacity and intensity of Kurdish guerrilla fighting against the forces of the Islamic Republic have masked to a great extent the intra-factional tensions and conflicts among Kurdish factions. Currently, the major groups fighting against the Khomeini regime in Kurdistan include:

(a) The Kurdish Democratic Party of Iran (KDPI). The largest and one of the most active Kurdish groups, the KDPI has embraced leftist slogans. Under the leadership of Abdul Rahman Qassemlou, the party has expanded its membership and has joined forces with other non-Kurdish groups opposing the Khomeini regime. This is particularly true in the case of military and political collaboration between the KDPI and the Mujahedin-e Khalq, an Islamic, non-Marxist leftist guerrilla organisation which, like the KDPI, is a member of the Paris-based National Council of Resistance (NCR). The NCR is a broad-based umbrella organisation comprising several leftist and nationalist opposition movements to the Khomeini regime.

The KDPI's programme is strikingly similar to that of the original Kurdish Democratic Party established in 1945, the exception being the KDPI's commitment to the integrity of Iran. The phrase 'Democracy for Iran, Autonomy for Kurdistan' is the essence of the KDPI's programme.[5] That is, for autonomy to be established in Kurdistan, democracy should first be achieved in all of Iran. It is only within this democratic framework, the KDPI contends, that Kurdish autonomy could be realised. Qassemlous on several occasions has accused foreign interests, especially the United States, of creating obstacles in the path of democracy in Iran, principally throught tacit support of the Khomeini regime. In Qassemlou's words, 'Imperialism, through Khomeini, is launching a massive attack on radical and revolutionary forces as to facilitate instituting an American alternative in Iran.[6] In addition to fighting the pasadarans and regular Iranian forces, the KDPI peshmergas have fought against the KDP-Provisional Leadership whose leaders, Massoud and Idris Barzani, have received aid from the Khomeini government and have on occasion supported and fought alongside the Iranian forces against the Iraqis as well as anti-Khomeini Kurds.

(b) The Revolutionary Organisation of the Kurdish Toilers of Iran (Komala). A Marxist-Leninist movement which ranks second to the KDPI in membership and influence among the Iranian Kurds. Komala's relations with the KDPI have vacillated from co-operative to conflictual. Occasionally, Komala has received the endorsement of Sheikh Ezzedin Husseini and, thus, it has claimed Husseini as the movement's spiritual leader. However, Sheikh Husseini has no official ties with Komala. Komala's platform calls for Kurdish autonomy via a Marxist revolution in Iran.[7]

In September 1983, Komala underwent structural transformations. It patterned itself after the hierarchical communist parties elsewhere with a central committee, secretariat and politburo as its core. At the same time, it renamed itself the Communist Party of Iran in Kurdistan – Komala. Under the leadership of its first Secretary-General, Abdullah Mohtadi, the new Komala has become more assertive in challenging the hitherto dominant position of the KDPI in Kurdish affairs and has staged some of the fiercest intra-Kurdish factional attacks against the KDPI peshmergas in recent history.

(c) Mujahedin-e Khalq. This leftist Islamic guerrilla organisation has, as mentioned earlier, joined forces with the KDPI to oppose the Khomeini regime. Both Kurdish and non-Kurdish Mujahedin have fought alongside regular KDPI peshmergas and have coordinated their politico-military activities with them. It was through the Mujahedin that the former Iranian President, Abul Hassan Bani-Sadr was given shelter by the Kurds while planning his escape from the country.[8] After the decimation of Mojahedin guerrillas by Khomeini's forces, the guerrilla organisation has found it necessary to concentrate its remaining military forces in Kurdistan where they will be less vulnerable and carry out their guerrilla attacks against the regime more effectively. For its part, the government has accused the Mujahedin, as well as other Kurdish groups, of being the tools of an 'international imperialist conspiracy' against the Islamic Republic.[9]

(d) Fadayan-e Khalq. This Marxist-Leninist guerrilla group has experienced tumultuous and devastating factional infighting since the advent of the Islamic Republic. After a year of tacit approval of the new regime, two contrasting tendencies developed within the leadership of the Fadayan. The majority was of the opinion that Khomeini as an 'anti-imperialist' leader should be supported, and that opposing his regime would inflict irreparable damage to the revolution. A minority view within the Fedayan leadership argued that it would be a tactical error to support the 'bourgeois' clerical regime.

The majority faction eventually allied itself with the pro-Moscow Tudeh Party and sought to bring about changes through working within the system. The minority faction, which ironically surpassed the majority faction in membership, continued its armed resistance against the Khomeini regime. In kurdistan, it joined forces with Komala and the Ashraf Dehqani group (a Fadayan faction named after its revolutionary leader) and fought the Iranian theocracy from its bases in that area.

In 1983 yet another tendency developed within the socalled minority faction of the Fadayan which further fractured opposition to Khomeini in Kurdistan. Reiterating the necessity for armed struggle, one sub-group argued for expansion of its organisation's military activities throughout Iran. The other sub-group, on the other hand, asserted the desirability of concentrating the organisation's military activities in Kurdisthan where the Khomeini forces were most vulnerable.

In addition to the aforemented groups, a number of smaller movements have sprung up to advance the Kurdish cause. For example, Jama'e-e Zanan-e Mobarez-e Saqqez (Society of Militant Women of Saqqez) as was formed in March 1979 in the Kurdish city of Saqqez with the broad objective of 'crushing the conspiracies of the reactionaries and continuing the struggle for the liberation of all toiling forces and the elimination of the exploitation of man by man...[10] More specifically, this organisation has endeavoured to provide what it has termed 'gender-specific' benefits to Kurdish women. These include improving welfare benefits and working conditions of working Kurdish women.[11]

The fractious nature of the Kurdish movement and internecine infighting has substantially weakened the Kurdish cause. The assortment of Peshmergas still conduct hit-and-run tactics against the Iranian government forces, but they have all but lost their strategic positions in the urban areas of Kurdistan. Moreover, by playing one faction against another, the Islamic Republic has succeeded in weakening the Kurdish movement. The regime, for example, has provided aid to Massoud and Idris Barzani's KDP-Provisional Leadership to fight the leftist KDPI forces. In return, the KDP-Provisional Leadership has hoped to receive material and logistical support in its fight against the Iraqi government. In July 1983, when the Iranian Army overran the mountain village of Haj Umran in Northern Iraq, the Barzani guerrillas were invited to take over their former strong-holds in the area.

The Iran-Iraq War, which could have provided an opportunity for the Kurds to exploit the conditions created by the preoccupation of the two Gulf countries with each other, exacerbated the tensions among major Kurdish groups. The pro-Baathist official KDP in Iraq called upon its members, supporters and 'the sons of the Kurdish people in the autonomous region to intensify their strikes against the Iranian enemy . . .[12]. Similarly, the Islamic Republic urged the Iraqi Kurds to 'rise up for the support of your religion, Islam, in order to establish an Islamic homeland as your brethren in the Islamic Republic of Iran did.[13] However, the shifting constellation of power and the fluidity of inter-Kurdish relations have prevented the two major protagonists in the Gulf war from using the Kurds against each other. By the same token, the Kurdish weakness has prevented them from exploiting politico-military situations opened to them' as the result of the Iran-Iraq conflict.

REFERENCES

1. Yosef Gotlieb, *Self-Determination in the Middle East*, New York, 1982, p. 100.
2. Nader Entessar. The Kurds in Post-Revolutionary Iran and Iraq. *Third World Quarterly, October, 1984.*
3. *New York Times*, 1 March, 1979.
4. *MERIP Reports*, No. 113, March-April 1983, pp. 9-10.
5. For details, see *Fourth Congress of the KDPI, 19-23 February 1980*, Mahabad, Iran.
6. *Iran Times*, 1 July, 1983.
7. *Junbish-e Moqavamet-e-Khalq-e Kurd va Komala*. Document Series 2, 1980.
8. See Bani Sadr's statement in the *New York Times*, 5 July, 1981.
9. Kurdistan:, Teheran: Political Bureau of the Islamic Revolutionary Guards, 1980, pp. 10-52.
10. As quoted in Azar Tabari and Nahid Yeganch (eds). In the Shadow of Islam: the women's movement in Iran, London: Zed Press, 1982, p. 222.
11. A smaller group of Kurdish women has established *Etehadieh-e Zanan-e Kurdistan* (Union of Kurdish Women), which is associated with the Komala party. Other minor Kurdish groups include Rastgari Corps and the III Corps. See Foreign Broadcast Information Service (FBIS), *Daily Report, South Asia*, 21 July, 1983, p. 13.
12. FBIS, *Daily Report, Middle East and Africa*, 26 July 1983, p. E3.
13. FBIS, *Daily Report, South Asia*, 26 July 1983, p. 13. For a brief analaysis of the Kurdish position in the Gulf War, see Edgar O'Ballance, 'The Kurdish Factor in the Gulf War', Military Review 61(6) June 1981, pp. 17-19.

9

THE AMERICAN INTERESTS

Whether the US-led efforts to extent relief to the Kurdish refugees are purely altruistic in nature will not be known for a while, but these certainly are setting precedents in a new world order whose controus are yet to be defined. It is arguable that the US felt impelled to aid the Kurds who have been dying by the thousand because of a situation in creating which the coalition forces have at least partly contributed. The Kurdish minority in Iraq has for long felt oppressed under the Baathist regime, But it is questionable whether it would have revolted against Iraqi President Saddam Hussein had he not suffered a humiliating defeat at the hands of the coalition forces. The savage suppression of that revolt could not be defended. But the US intervention on behalf of the Kurds does raise the serious question of a nation's sovereignty, even while Washington vows to hand over the refugee camps it is setting up in nother with the US plans, the issue of sovereignty does not become irrelevant. What is happening in Iraq is the imposition of a trans-border arrangement on a country which is patently being punished for the sins of its leader of day. The pernicious British doctrine of a "safe heaven" for the Kurds can easily be applied to much of the rest of the world. It is not difficult to spot countries where minoities of various descriptions rebel from time to time and are suppressed, sometimes ruthlessly. The pattern so far has been that these countries are delivered rebukes and lectures on human rights. But is tere a guarantee or a reasonable assurance that the Iraqi president would not be invoked infuture to deal with a government that looks like sinning? The only justification for the US-led moves in post-war Iraq seems to be the continuance of Mr. Saddam Hussein in office. If he could not be eliminated, politically or otherwise, his country must be torn into pieces so that his mischief potential is reduced. For, the safe heven idea appears to be the beginning of a process of vivisection of Iraq.[1] Saddam Hussein has south to contain this threat by his reported offer to discuss autonomy with the Kurds. Soon, he may be forced to consider a similar arrangement for the Shias in southern Iraq. Were that to happen, 70 per cent of Iraq's population would be autonomous of the rest of the 30 per cent of Sunni Arabs. That absurd situation could only end with a formal parting of ways. The US-led coalition may before long have to explain whether Kuwait's sovereignty must necessarily lead to the disintegration of Iraq. Is recasting of nations boundaries going to be a part of the New World Order?

Some fundamental issues have been raised by the American decision to intervene in Iraq. True, it is claimed that it is the fear that unless a haven is provided for the Kurds in northern Iraq, an extremly large number will leave that country creating a massive refugee problem overwhelming the economies of Iran and Turkey and unsettling these countries. It cannot be denied if food, shelter and medical assistance can be provided in Iraq itself. There will be considerable easing of political tensions in West Asia, and Baghdad has not stood in the way of relief being provided to Iraqis who have suffered from the consequences of the war. It appears that America, having incited the Kurds and Shias to revolt, after their failure to overthrow Saddam Hussein is now planning a direct intervention. The conditions. In large parts of Africa such situations had existed at some time or the other without eliciting active sympathy form the Western countries. Even Idi Amin's atrocities in Uganda or the attempt at genocide in Rwanda and Burundi at different times did not lead to any kind of intervention; indeed when Tanzania intervened to overthrow General Amin the Western countries which now claim the right to intervene were extremely irritated. Worse still, when Vietnam intervened in Cambodia to overthrow the murderous regime of Pol Pot which was really guilty of genocide the Western countries were infuriated. Vietnam had to be punshed for its insolence. Pol Pot still remains an ally of the West; his crimes are never mentioned, he is painted as a patriot who defended Cambodia against Vietnam. It is obvious that atrocities by America's friends do not count as crimes: it is only when it is in America's interest to highlight such incidents that the West notices them. More important is the fact that the Western countries have established a new principle – the right to intervene in the internal affairs of sovereign independent states. The basis for this intervention is not clear. The decision apparently has not been made by the UN what has to be clarified is under what conditions can intervention take place and who has the right to intervene. It is said that the US action is of a purely temporary nature, and once the safety of the Kurds is assured, the US troops will be withdrawn. But what happens if the Iraqi troops resist? Will the US get involved in Iraq's internal conflict? And what if after US troops are withdrawn the government in Baghdad tries to reestablish its authority over the Kurds and this leads to another wave of refugees?[2] If the US can intervene in northern Iraq to protect the Kurds, can Iran do the same in the South to protect the Shias? To many the intervention will be seen as a deliberate attempt to dismember Iraq; a heaven can turn into an aunomous region or an independent state and the Kurds will now be prepared to accept nothing less than that. What is sinister about this new doctrine of the right to intervene is that it places the Third World countries at the mercy of the US. On the slightest pretext it can intervene anywhere it likes. No Third World country will feel safe. If this is Mr. George Bush's New World Order, there is every reason for the world to be on the lookout.

'A dream come true. I wish form the roots of my hairs to kiss V.S. President George Bush. To kiss him, yes, to kiss him' creid the Dohuk man, the moment Gulf war eneded. UN just started preparing official ceasefire draft to recoup the wartime Iraqi damaged. But in this moment of crisis anti-Saddam Hussein slogan sparwled up in roars in the streets of Iraq by the Kurds. Kurdish people clustering notice boards covered were seen with blurred photo-copeed posters. The streets of much dreamt Kurdistan looked frail in tragic collapse, its abandonment by the west, and the trial of Saddam's Army inexorably crushing down the hopes and the aspirations of the Kurdish people. Kurds as an ethnic group, seriously stand for the establishment of Kurdistan. Pesh Merg is the Kurdish Nationalist Force harping on the dream of Iraqi Kurdistan for long. History of Kurdistan goes back to 1988 when the Iraqi President, Saddam Hussein's regime used chimical weapons to suppress the Kurdish uprising at the end of the Iran-Iraq war, killing thousands of civilians and driving manymore into exile in Turkey and Iran. The Kurds are politically organized under the Kurdish Democratic party (KDP) and a break-way faction based in Syria called the Kurdish Worker's party. A smaller resistance groups calls itself Patriotic Union of Kurdistan. Kurds were used at political pawns during 70s. It was by playing the Kurdish card that Shah of Iran compelled Saddam Hussein to sign the

Algiers Agreement of 1975 in which Iraq renounced the British claim for the entire waterspread of Shatt-Ai-Arab river and principle to democrate the boder. In 1980 Saddam Hussein launched his attack on Iran to reverse the agreement in favour Iraq. After the Algiers Agreement, the Kurds were let down by the Americans and the Shah.[3]

The Kurds have been agitating for autonomy since then. They were regularly bombed by the Royal Air Force based in Baghdad in the late twenties and early thirties. Subsequently, successive Iraqi regimes have been keeping down the Kurds who have been waging a long struggle first under the leadership of the Marist leader Mustafa Barzani ('the Red Mullah' as he was then known), and subsequently that of his son Masoud Barzani, the present leader of the Peshmergas. But US never interfered in Kurd issue and put a ban on talks with the Kurds possibly considering Turkish sensibilities Turkey, which is a NATO ally, has a Kurdish population considerably larger than that of Iraq, has been fighting a guerrilla war against Kurdish separatists for nearly seven years. Turkey accepted about 65,000 Kurdish refugees in 1988, overriding an earlier "hot pursuit" pact with Iraq. But it was firmly hostile too to the political game of the Iraqi Kurds, believing that they were helping their separatist counterpart in Turkey and thereby fearing that any success for them would act as a stimulus to greater unrest across the border which will straddle the territory of Turkey, Iraq, Iran and Syria. The European Economic Community is meeting to consider the problem. Iran is not placing and impediments for the refugees to cross over. These people are neither Arabs nor Iranians but a separate subnational groups. Their ambition to have a separate Kurdistan at the end of the World War I was thwarted by the British and the French with the arbitrary marking of the borders of Iraq, Syria and Turkey. But in the last few weeks, the Turkish President, Mr. Ozal had declared a readical revision of Turkish policy towards Iraq and the Kurds. Talabani, a leader of the Kurdish Pat Alliance said that Turkey is supporting the Kurdish rebellion in Northern Iraq to soup Saddam. In a summit reportedly held in Ankara on March 8, 1991.Talabani confirmed that the summit in Ankara had laid our the future organisation of Iraq without Saddam. Under the resolution, 2 million Kurds and Turkomans would have a federal unit within the framework of a new democratic Iraq. The Kurd demonstrators have already storned two Iraqi prisons releasing 4,000 political prisoners. One Turkish journalist Oungor

Mnegi has claimed that President Ozal has a four-stage plan, of which lifting the ban on the language and backing the Iraqi Kurds are the first two stages, to be followed by an alliance with moderate Kurdish group in Turkey against the separatist PKK (worker's party of Kurdistan), and finally the introduction of a federal system. But Iraqi Kurds have not accepted the further proposition for it goes against their working class brethren.[4]

The Iraqi Kurds fear that Saddam Hussein, if he remains in power in Baghdad, may succeed in crushing the Shia uprising in the South and then again in North on Kurdistan with chemical weapons after the allied forces have gone home. Germany and France are two prominent members of the European Community (EC) to protest vigorously against the repression of the Kurds. The German government had asked Iraq to recognise the right of autonomy for the Kurdish people. Hans Dietecich Gfenscher, the German Foreign Minister appealed to the five permanent members of the Security Council urging them to include unlimited protection for the minority rights of the Kurds in ceasefire resolution.[5]

French Foreign Minister Rol and Dumas is reported to have said that recent events in the Kurdistan area of Iraq should inspire the United Nations to rethink its code of "non-interference", US Secretary of state James Baker, while on a visit to Turkey, has also referred to the sensitivity of nations to the issue of intervention in their internal affairs. On the other hand, some academic experts in international law have pointed out that where a situation in a nation spills over its boundaries and threatens international peace, the UN has the necessary jurisdiction even under the present charter to intervene in the situation. India's intervention in Bangladesh in 1971 and air dropping of food supplies on Jaffan in 1987 were justified onsimilar grounds. So also Tanzanian military action to topple Idi Amin of Uganda and the UN intervention in Congo in the sixties. Such legal arguments in regard to permissibility of intervention in internal affairs of nations had never in the past inhibited major powers form intiating action against other nations or form supporting one side or the other in civil war situations. US ubterventions in Cuba, Dominican Republic, Greneda Nicaragua, Panama Lebanon, South Vietnam and Combodia insupport of one side in a civil war are well known. So are the Soviet interventions in East Germany, Hungary, Czechoslovakia and Afghanistan. The French have intervened in a number of Franco-phone African countries the most will known bring Chad. The lesser known ones were Gabon, Benin Central African republic Djitbouti and Comoros. The British, after decolonisation, responded to calls for help from Mauritius and Kenya. Such interventions have also been carried out by developing nations Syria (in Lebanon), Cuba (in Angola), Egypt (in Yemen), Iran (in Oman), Turkey (in Cyprus), Libya (in Chad), India (in Nepal in 1952, Srilanka in 1971 and Maldives in 1989) and South Africa in many of its neighbours. Many of these intervent ons were in favour of regimes in power and there have been occasions when the interventions have also been in support of urisings against the regmies in power. Israel intervenes almost like a major power without worrying about the UN or international opprobrium.[6]

The above only illustrates over interventions. There have been any number of covert interventions sometimes successful and on other occasions not. The welldocumented successful CIA exploits were toppling Mossadegn of Iran. Arbenz in Guatemala, Partrice Lumumba of Congo, Allende in Chile. Similar Soviet explotis not so publicly documented were in respect of Rubiya Ali Yemen and Sardar Daud in Afghanistan. Given this background it is difficult to judge whether the references to international inhibitions by James Baker and Mr. Dumas are an exercise in cynicism or a healthy new development in the post cold war international milieu when the US and its allies felt it expedient to cover their actions with UN endorsements. The international community has been demanding intervention in South Africa and brought about sanctions. At that stage some western countries sued to argue such sanctions were counter productive. When it comes to Israel, though the majority of the nations would like to get Israel out of West Bank and Gaza, the support of the US has facilitated Israeli defiance of all UN resolutions. In the case of Kashmir, Bangladesh, Vietnam or Cambodia the UN has not behaved in an impartial manner but has been influenced by cold war politics. Under these circumstances there are reasonable justifications of fear whether the UN can be trusted to act with impartialit in cases where there is an overlap between aspects of international security and domestic jurisdiction, especially if it involved developing nations. However, there has been considerable evolution in the concept of domestic jurisdiction since the UN charter was drafted. The adoption of the Declaration of Human Rights by the UN, issues of ecological pollution across borders, global ecological demage, narcotics, traffic, international terrorism and narcoterrorism, money laundering of drug proceeds evolution of concepts of women and children's rights, dealing with global epidemics, etc. are slowly extending the jurisdictions of the international community at the expense of exclusivity of the domestic jurisdiction of nations over their territories and populations and activities of this citizens and institutions. The issue is very complex. Hence India could not vote against the resolution condemning Iraq in regard to this suppression of Kurds. It is obvious that the subject needs to be debated and a fresh list of crimes against humanity, which would distinguish between tyrannical acts by authoritarian states and legitimate action by democratic governments to suppress terroristic activity, has to be drawn up.[7]

The national sovereignty and territorial integrity of states are meaningless ideals: outmoded concepts, hangovers from the age of nationalism and meaningless now that George Bush in on the way to establishing his New World Order? The British have been arguing that 'legal niceties' cannot be allowed to abstruct creating 'safe havens' for the Kurds in Iraq, and Turgut Ozal, who with his large Kurdish minority should have, at least, realised that discretion is the better part of valour, has been another staunch champion of ignoring national sovereignty and territorial integrity. This is not the first time that the faithful allies of America have launched a sustained campaign against national sovereignty. If I remember correctly, in 1965, during the height of the Dominican crisis, when ideological fervour had reached a feverish pitch, the Argentine dictator had come out with the doctrine of interdependence. The argument ran something like this. In a period of ideological conflict, it is not the wars between nation states that is really significant but the internal wars inside each state. It is an age of interpendence because no nation state could expect success in its internal war, in which the enemy was backed by the international communist movement and supported by a superpower, the Soviet Union. It is now necessary to point out that the primary objective of these formalities was to justify the intervention by the United States in the affairs of the Dominican Republic, communist penetration of that state was merely the bogey. After a long and desperate search a small number of communists were discovered, but communism did not pose any kind of threat. The Latin American dictators Ongania was not the only one to take this line – had of course, other ideas; they wanted American support for the dirty war they were waging on their own people. The violation of human rights in these countries was no such a massive scale that even their time, we were living under the old world order; human right violations became objectionable only when happening in countries which insisted on pursuing an independent policy. The right to intervene has now been raised to the level of a principle. France, which has now assumed the role of the champion of human rights, it is one of those countries, always in seach of a role, says the right to intervene in countries which violate human rights should be written not the UN Charter. This, I am prepared to agree, is an admirable proposal but it will prove difficult to implement.

We all know that the five permanent members of the Security Council, their protestations of virtue can be ignored, do not respect human rights when their national interests are under challenge; the American record in the Caribean and Central America is hardly encouraging. Equally important, no Western nation has raised its voice in any international fora* against the daily violation of human rights in Israel. Indeed, the United States never hesitated to exercise its veto to protect its faithful ally, Israel.[8]

Since Turgut Ozal has taken on the role of the protector of the Kurds, I will be prepared to take him seriously as a champion of human rights if he is willing to extend the same kind of rights which is being demanded for Iraqi Kurds for the Kurds who happen to be citizens of Turkey. After all, there are 14 million Kurds in Turkey as against a mere 4 million in Iraq and it is only proper that their rights as an ethnic group with a language and culture of their own should be recognised. Iraq can be accused of atrocities, but it cannot be denied that Baghdad has recognised that the Kurds are an ethnic group and given encouragement to Kurdish language and culture. Turkey, too, can be said to have committed atrocities but can it be seriously maintained that it allowed the Kurds to develop their culture and language. Indeed, if the truth is told it will have to be accepted that Ankara did everything in its power to suppress the enthnic identity of the Kurds. It dismissed them as mountain Turks. If there is a case for intervention surely Turkey cannot be ignored. In that case, there are, perhaps, other reason for Ozal's exuberance. He is most probably aware that as a member of the NATO, he, like Israel, is immune from intervention. Countries, which are the allies and friends of America, have always got away with muder; the right to intervene will, I am sure,

* fora means a forum

apply only if violations take place in third world countries. It is a new form of imperialism; it is West which will be prosecutor, judge and executioner, even if the UN is used to provide a cloak of respectability. In the war for Kuwait's liberation, the UN became an auxiliary of the United States, and in the New World Order, one can expect this to happen quite often. It is in this context that the Western intervention in Iraq has to be viewed. The intervention is not under UN aegis. It is an operation mounted by the United States, France and the United Kingdom and the aim is to provide safe havens in Iraq for Kurds, havens from which the authority of Baghdad has been removed. Since the Kurds say that they will not feel secure as long as Saddam Hussein remains in power, it appears to be an open ended commitment. If Western troops are to remain in northern Iraq for any length of time, it will only encourage Kurdish separation; the intervention in any case is to give the Pashmerga the freedom to operate against the government forces for they will not have to bother about their families. This is the real meaning of the safe havens. It has given the Kurdish guerrillas the freedom to manoeuvre and operate.[9]

The report that some Kurdish rebel groups have arrived at a settlement with Iraqi leader Saddam Hussein to provide greater autonomy to the Kurds has been received with scepticism in Washington.

A senior White House official has been quoted as saying that the Bush administration would welcome any accord that would facilitate the return of the more than 3.5 million refugees to their Iraqi homes but "in the longterm we are extremely sceptical. The problem, of course, is that Saddam Hussein has not had a good track record in fulfilling promises to the Kurds or in his treatment of the Kurdish civilian population."

The White House official also reiterated the US position on easing sanctions against Iraq, saying that unless there were stringent safeguards and more significant evidence of change on the part of the Iraqi Government, the sanctions would be in force.

Iraq and Allies have agreed that only 50 Iraqi policemen will remain in the northern town of Zakho, where the US Army is building a Kurdish refugee camp, the Iraqi ambassador has said, a report from United Nations says.

Iraqi Ambassador in the U.N. Abdul Amir Al-Anbari said after meeting with US Ambassador Thomas R. Pickering Yesterday that all

Iraqi soldiers had left the town, and that most police were leaving except for the contingent of 50.

US officials, speaking on condition of anonymity, said they had reported the Iraqi proposal to Washington to see if it meets with State Department approval, indicating that pickering had not raised any objection.

US officials have said the presence of Iraqi security forces in the Zakho area is deterring the Kurds from leaving their mountain refugees and going home.

"The Iraqi authorities will be more than willing to cooperate and pacify, in the proper sense of the word, the town and accelerate the humanitarian assistance given to the Kurds in the area, Amri Al-Anbari said.

US President George Bush hoped it was true that Iraq has had removed most of its forces from the border town in reponse to the ultimatum from Washington and its Gulf War allies to leave.

"I hope that's all very true," Bush told reporters as he walked through a hallway in the White House "and it's very important that they do get out."

Anbari told reporters that the soldiers had already left Zakho, the bulk of the police force was leaving and "only 50 policemen remain in town and that is to the satisfaction of both sides."

The United States, Britain and France late on Wednesday ordered Iraqi security forces out of the northern Iraqi town at the weekened to make the area safe for Kurdish refugees.

In a follow-up, US Secretary Dick Cheney on Thursday warned Iraq to withdraw its forces from the town by the weekend of face force, if necessary.

All there three nations are building camps in the Zakho region for hundreds of thousands of Kurds who fled in remote mountains along Iraq's border with Turkey after their rebellion was crushed.

Anbari later spoke to Secretary-General Javier Perez de Cuellar on UN humanitarian aid in Iraq.

Both the allies and Iraq want the world body to take over the running of the US camps. However, some UN officials are questioning whether they can do this while allied troops are on the scene without violating a separate agreement with Iraq on humanitarian aid.

Consequently, Perez de Cuellar would review all the various proposals with Mr. Anbari.

He also said he had no further knowledge of the talks between Kurdish leaders and Iraqi President Saddam Hussein which both sides say have resulted in an agreement that would allow more than a million refugees to return home.

In a related development, Prince Sadruddin Aga Khan of the United Nations Gulf programme coordination said the organisation does not have sufficient resources to turn the run the Kurdish refugee camps in northern Iraq, a London dispatch says.

President George Bush has said that US troops will stay in northern Iraq until the safety of Kurds is assured.

Bush said US forces "will stay there as long as it takes to ensure these refugees are taken care of, and not a minute longer . . . I want these kids home and so do the American people."

He added the United States "will do what's necessary to see that this refugee aid gets to the people who need if it and gets to the people who need it and gets there so that they can have it in safety."

Bush said in Washington on April 27, 1991 during a brief question-and-answer session on the White House grounds that he believes Iraq will make good on its promise to pull security forces out of the area the United States has declared a haven for Kurds.

"They don't want to tangle with the US again", he said. Asked if Iraq's word was good, Bush said, "our forces are there to make sure that it's good."

But he said, "we're not looking for any fight" and added that he does not expect a confrontation with Iraqi forces.

UN Secretary General Javier Perez de Cuellar has said that he is taking steps to ensure that United Nations assumes responsibility for the refugee camps established by United States and its Allies in the Zakhau region of northern Iraq.

In a report to the Security Council, De Cuellar said the executive delegate Prince Sadruddin Aga Khan, who is coordinating the relief effort, would hold discussions with senior officials over the weak-end to work out a time-table for establishment of UN humanitarian centres with appropriate arrangements for adequate safety and protection of the people returning to their homes and villages.

The Security Council briefly considered the report during which members supported the United Nations taking charge of the camps.

The principal aim, De Cuellar said, is to be in a position to assume responsibility for both the humanitarian centres and refugee camps as soon as possible.

"We are discussing modalities by which we can achieve this purpose, beginning with the most effective integration at the operational level," he said.

The actual time-table, he added, would depend on agreements reached with US, British and French authorities and "our ability to meet all necessary conditions."

After the meeting, the diplomat said the United State, Britain and France too seemed to be interested in handing over the camps to UN officials. But the process could take several days as the hundreds of officials needed to man them is assembled. The exact strength of the manpower needed was not immediately known.

Giving the latest available figures of Kurdish refugees, De Cuellar said there were 1,020,000 refugees, with 416,000 at the Turkish border and inside Turkey and another 200,000 to 400,000 on the Iraqi side.

There are around 25 million Kurds in Iraq and spread over the border areas of Turkey, Syria, Iran and the Soviet Union.

Giving details, De Cuellar said under the direction of the United Nations High Commissioner for Refugees (UNHCR), a convoy of relief supplies accompanied by UN staff would cross from Turkey into Iraq on Monday.

It would travel to areas where the largest concentration of "Iraqi displaced persons" is located. Another convoy would leave Baghdad the same day and together they would set up facilities for distribution and storage of relief commodities.

The two teams would also discuss modalities for the take over "in due course" of camps at present being run by American, British and French forces in northern Iraq.

"On that basis, a plan of action would be prepared for my approval and immediate action," De Cuellar said.

Belatedly, unwillingly and without directly acknowledging the fact, the United States has taken on the role of protector of hundreds of thousands of Kurdish refugees. But the Bush Administration does not yet appear to have fully grasped the implications of its decision to set up refugee centres for Kurdish refugees on Iraqi territory protected by US troops, political analysts say. By placing our military in northern Iraq, we have implicitly established, a situation of protecting Kurds, said David Sheffer, an international legal analyst with the Carnegie Endowment. Bush Administration spokesman insists that Washington wants its troops to hand the camps over the United Nations.

The United States, at odds with UN Secretary General Javier Perez de Cuellar over the legality of the latest US actions, propose to set up refugee camps for Kurds inside Iraqi territory not only on the Turkish border as originally stated but deep inside Iraq – as much as 96 kms deep – for 700,000 refugees.

With the British and French joining in the plan is being described as a "combined operation".

Disclosing the scheme Marines Ltd. Gen. Martin Brandtuner, the new Operations Director for the Joint Chiefs of Staff, said the nearby Iraqi forces had been warned "to just cease and assist to evacuate that area" – a brad swath of Iraq's Tigris river valley, from the town of Zakhu south as far perhaps as Mosul.

"If we see Iraqi forces, obviously that's going to be a decision point, and I'm not prepared to say what we are going to decide to do. But we are telling Iraq to stay out of these areas," Gen. Brandtner added.

Later, with the administration realising that Iraqi forces cannot be asked to leave a wide area of Iraqi territory without a UN resolution which is now impossible to obtain. Gen. Brandtner said the Iraqi troops in the region need not actually evacuate their positions but must not interfere with the establishment of the camps.

Earlier, the administration had said that troops could not enter northern Iraq from Turkey to help the refugees without a UN resolution. Now that the US had decided to go along with the British and French and do exactly that, the administration is simply brushing aside all questions about Iraqi sovereignty. The groundwork for such action had been laid a few days ago under the rubric of "peace and stability" included in one of the Security Council resolutions passed during the ground war.

Small survey teams of army doctors, engineers and projected US force to upto 10,000 arrived uninvited by helicopter inside northern Iraq on April 18, 1991 to begin site selection in a plains region away from the rugged Turkish-Iraqi border zones where 700,00 Kurdish refugees have massed. Administration officials said the reversal of the earlier US position came in response to reprated appeals to the Bush Administration from Britain, France and Turkey.

President George Bush did pronounce on a number of occasions that the military operation that the military operation he initiated in the Persian Gulf constituted a just and moral war. But with Saddam Hussein's forces routed in utter ignominy, and with US forces occupying a fifth of Iraq and in total control of the skies, some uncomfortable questions of justice, morality and humanity are beginning to be raised about the White House policy of not intervening as Iraqi helicopter gunships are used to curb the activity of Shi'ite rebels in the south and their Kurdish counterparts in the north. Attempts are being made to show that White House policy towards the rebels has changed drastically over time. The extent of the change is sought to be portrayed by juxtaposing two of President Bush's statements. March 13, 1991: "Iraq's use of helicopters to fight rebel groups has got to be resolved before we are going to have any permanence to any ceasefire." March 26: "There will be a ceasefire (even if Saddam Hussein continues to use helicopters against the rebels). That was not a requirement of the United Nations – it is not in the ceasefire resolution."[10]

The alleged incongruity in the two statements has troubled the socalled conscience of a few media heavyweights, including a few in positions of power and influence. It was the United States that called on Iraqis to oust Saddam Hussein, they point out, and now that sizable sections of the Iraqi population are attempting to do just that, America has responsibility to ensure that they are not massacred for following the US advice. In other words, US forces should once again confront what is left of Saddam Hussein's army and help the rebels carve out independent territories for themselves.

What the critics conveniently forget is that President Bush never specifically suggested that the Shi'ites or the Kurds should try to wrest freedom for their respective areas of Iraq. President Bush has been on record from the very beginning that he was for maintaining the territorial integrity of Iraq. In fact, he even issued a statement of warning that he would not tolerate any attempt by any nation to grab a piece of Iraq. The pronouncement was prompted by fears that in the confusion after the war and in Iraqi's weakened state, Iran, Syria and Turkey might decide to press their longstanding territorial claims against Iraq. True, George Bush did suggest that the best way to end the bloodshed would be for the Iraqi people to force Saddam Hussein to step down. That was intended to step down. That was intended for the people of Iraq as a whole, and never directed at any particular ethnic group. The most recent criticism came from none other than New York Times columnist William Safire. "Why wobble now?" asked Safire. "If we are too timid to impose democracy, we owe it to our sense of right and wrong to atleast level the playing field." Levelling the playing field, of course, refers to the need to give the rebels better odds in a battle that Safire feels has so far been terribly one-sided. But sectoral rebellions are supposed to be one-sided. Instances where selfless freedom fighters come marching into the acclaim of the local populace and bring peace and order and stability only occur when there are revolutions. And true revolutions are very rare. No one with a sense of history can claim that the sporadic stirrings of the Kurds or the Shi'ites can rate as revolutions. Thus, although it took coalition forces just 100 hours to crush Saddam Hussein's massive army and his carefully assembled arsenal, Baghdad still has enough artillery and armour for its troops to roll over the lightly armed rebels. But what has been really hurting the rebels – and terrorising their civilian supporters – is Baghdad's use of helicopter gunships. These terrible weapons, which the Russians used so effectively against the Mujaheddin in Afghanistan until the rebels started using Stinger missiles, wrought great havoc among the Shi'ites in the south and the Kurds in the north. They just had no defence against the deadly choppers. Terrible as the affect of deploying the gunships might be, no Government can be expected not to use all the means at its command to put down rebellions. It would be remiss of the rebels, particularly the Kurds, to feel that they have been used and then discarded – in other words exploited for temporary and selfish gains. Many of them refer to Mr. Bush's statement calling on the Iraqi people to revolt and get rid of Saddam Hussein – many also refer to the Pentagon statement that the Iraqi army is finished – they also talk about Mr. Bush's statement suggesting that helicopter gunships would not be used against the rebels. The thousands of civilians who flee areas of conflict and arrive at US military camps as refugees in their own land have nowhere to go. The US troops have been giving them food and medical treatment. The greatest fear of the refugees, paradoxically, is that a permanent ceasefire would be signed: The troops would then depart, leaving them to the tender mercies of Saddam Hussein's regime or whatever dispensation is in place. But then, there is nothing new in such straumas: Every attempt to balkanise a nation inherently carries the risk of a bloddy and painful outcome for civilian supporters of the rebels. But disillusionment runs very deep among the Kurds. When they began their revolt, town after town fell under their control, apparently without much effort. The Kurdish fighters were exhilarated, ecstatic – and over-confident. Any American journalist visiting the areas held by the Kurds – it extended at one time all the way to the oil town of Kirkuk – was warmly welcomed and lionised. He was told to convey the greetings of the Kurds to "Haji Bush, father of the Kurds. What the hapless Kurds did not realise was that Saddam Hussein still had enough forces and arms to crush them with no trouble at all. His troops were busy "pacifying". His troops were busy "pacifying" the Shi'ites in the south, and as soon as that was achieve, they wheeled and marched north to crush the Kurds. Thousands upon thousands of Kurdish villagers and guerrilla fighters fled across the border to Iran, Syria and Turkey, where the gloomy prospect of refugee camp life awaited them. It is no wonder that within ten days of the commencement of their revolt, the attitude of the Kurds towards President Bush had turned from hail to hate. It is, however, difficult to see how George Bush can be bale blamed for impressions the rebels gained on their own. Their sense that the US would come to their rescue was not born out of any firm commitment. It was more a case of wish being father to the thought. The Bush administration is beginning to display a degree of sensitivity to potential reaction to the alleged flip-flop. Reacting rightly to the New York Times column by Safire, State Department spokesman Richard Boucher commented: " Our policy is decided on the basis of what we think is in the best interest of the United States and what the President decides to do, not on the basis of columnists. We don't think that we, or any others for that matter, should interfere in the internal affairs of

Iraq, nor should we try to choose what sort of government there should be in the future in Iraq. That is for the Iraqi people to decide".[11]

What are some of the considerations that made the U.S. President George Bush decide that US interests would be best served by not involving himself in Iraq's domestic strife? The President had really come across during the crisis in the Gulf as a moral crusader who sincerely believed that America, as the only superpower left, has an obligation to right a wrong. But he is now being attacked by vested interests on the same moral grounds. That he caused the deaths of thousands of innocent Shi'ite and Kurdish rebels and innocent civilians by reneging on his word. The President's critics do not seem to bother that he had never once pledged to come to the aid of the rebels. But such trifles do not count with opposition politicians in search of a cause. Bush's determination not to interfere in Iraq's internal affairs is reportedly further strengthened by a private meassage from Saddam Hussein, brought by Turkish President Turgut Ozal, beseeching the United States not to provide any arms or assistance to the Iraqi rebels. More to the point, President Ozal also argued persuasively that at least for the time being, a more or less stable Iraq under Saddam Hussein was preferable to a chaotic Iraq without him and on the brink of Lebanisation. Ozal, it is said, has made a deeply favourable impression on President Bush with his ideas for closer ties between their two countries that would make them guarantors of long range political stability in the Gulf. It is also significant that Ozal maintained his diplomatic mission in Baghdad until the last possible moment. Iraq, on its part, is anxious to restore full cooperation with Turkey. In fact, Baghdad never broke relations with Ankara, as it did with Washington.

Not that the Turkish President does not have his own angle to pursue. He is willing to support autonomy for the Kurds within Iraq's predent borders present Kurdish State. Quite naturally too, since that is bound to encourage his own Kurdish minority to become more than restive. Meanwhile, a legitimate apprehension in Washington is that the ascendency of the numerically superior Shi'ites would make Iraq pro-Iranian and anti-American. That, in turn, will only encourage the diehard Ayatollahs in Iran to pursue their campaign against the "Great Satan" with even more vigour. Besides, Saddam Hussein's cabinet has always had Shi'ite members. Even during the current revolts, there were many Shi'ites and even Kurds on the side of the Iraqi regime.[12]

The US is also apprehensive that a break of Iraq would leave a power vacuum and give undue weightage to Syria's Hafez Assad or Iran's Rafsanjani. The spread of fundamentalism, in the US view, is even a greater threat than anything that Saddam Hussein might pose. Moreover, Washington is fully aware that it cannot stay in the Gulf for ever and control the political order in Iraq. Israel tried that strategy with the much weaker Lebanon and had to withdraw in defeat. An involvement of that nature could indeed to the "morass" that critics of intervention keep talking about. Another problem is the indication that some coalition members would not be too happy if the US intervened in. Iraq and would consider it illegal, unwarranted and far beyond the scope of the United Nations mandate. It is a common saying that foreign policy is based on pragmatism. That is another way of saying that policy cannot be formulated on the basis of the whims and fancies of some individuals who are impervious to the national interest. Considered in that light, Washington does have good, practical reasons for not interfering in the internal affairs of Iraq. President Bush, who surprised many by his firm resolve to get Iraqi troops out of Kuwait, is again standing firm against unjust criticism. He is playing the role of a seasoned politician pursuing enlightened self-interest on behalf of his country.[13]

In the post-war era that attitude may change. Many in the Kurdish opposition believe that Saddam Hussein can only be toppled if an internal armed struggle is mounted against him. If the Baathists are toppled, the Kurds want are-establishment of autonomy under the terms of the 1970 agreement and Kurdish participation in the central government in Baghdad. In short, they want recognition of the reality that Iraq is a multinational rather than a purely Arab State.[14]

The Bush administration on April 11, 1991 expanded humanitarian aid to the thousands of Kurds fleeing Iraq and warned Baghdad against attacks on the refugees. The new moves were clearly aimed at blunting criticism of George Bush's Post-war policy.

Spokesmen for the White House and the State Department fended off charges that the administration was slow to help the refugees and warned Baghdad against using military helicopters or troops to stop the Kurds from reaching protected camps on the

Turkish border. An official confirmed that the warnings were passed on to Baghdad through diplomatic channels.[15]

"There should not be any air activity north of the 36th parallel," an official said. "It was just a blanket warning with respect to any air activity north of the 36th parallel. It was passed through diplomatic channels."

The 36th parallel cuts across the northernmost corner of Iraq. The line is about 20 miles south of Mosul and takes in most of Iraq's Kurdish area. According to officials here, the Iraqi military has not operated near the refugee camps for the past week.

"We want to make it clear that the world expects that humanitarian assistance to be carried out without threat," said White House spokesman Marlin Fitzwater. He said Washington warned Iraq through diplomatic channels last weekend "not to interfere with humanitarian relief efforts underway in Iraq."

The latest Bush policy essentially sets up sanctuaries for the Kurds, a move that gives the US military authority in northern Iraq for the first time time since the informal ceasefire with Baghdad.

Meanwhile, Teheran Radio quoted Foreign Minister Ali Akbar Velayati as saying that the idea of havens could gain more support if the United Nations took the lead. "We believe Iraq should remain as a sovereign state," it quoted Velayati as saying in an interview. "At the same time, a safe environment should be created for Kurdish refugees in the north and one for the Shi'ites in the south."

The Iranian news agency said the total number of Iraqis taking refuge in Iran had reached 900,000 and was expected to rise to two million.

White House and State Department spokesmen said the US would send enough food to feed 300,000 persons for 30 days. The US was also sending medicine, tents, shoes, sleeping bags, balnkets and plastic sheeting to the Kurds.

The US has sent 30 medium and heavy lift helicopters to Turkey to shuttle the supplies from NATO's Incirik air base in Turkey. Some 52 air drops had been made by late last night. The administration has authorised 11 million dollars for the effort and expects to seek another 100 million dollars from Congress.

It is true that the Americans have a special responsibility to the Kurds. It is Henry Kissinger and his friend, the Shah of Iran, who persuaded the Kurds to rise in revolt in 1974. In 1970, the Kurds had reached an agreement with Baghdad on autonomy. The Americans promised them more, but were not willing to provide sufficient arms because the purpose was not to overthrow the Baathist regime but to exert sufficient pressure on Saddam Hussein to force him to negotiate with the Shah. In 1974 this was achieved and Henry Kissinger and the Shah abandoned the Kurds and Baghdad dealt with them savagely. In 1990 once again Washington incited them to revolt and created the problem which they now propose to resolve by dismembering Iraq.[16]

The US, which is providing relief to Kurdish refugees, and expanding it military presence there despite Iraq's protests that this is a job for the United Nations, may present Iraq a bill for $ 320 million for the aid.

Pentagon spokesman Bob Hall said, "Our objective is to provide secruity, provide humanitarian relief. Our overall objective is to set up conditions where they can move back to their homes. We're playing it by the ear to a certain extent. We're trying to get the Kurds out of the mountain. Our ability to do that is based on their perception of how secure they are."

Key congressional subcommittees have voted to appropriate $ 556.5 million to cover military and relief expenses for Kurdish refugees including $ 321 million for military expenses. The US has said that it hopes to recover all this money eventually from Iraq.

Meanwhile, in Iraq the US army, preparing to pull out of occupied southern Iraq, airlifted 1,700 more refugees to Saudi Arabia on May 5, 1991 and started domolishing their camp.

The commander of the 1,440 strong United Nations Iraq-Kuwait Observation Mission (UNIKOM) said he expected troops of the US-led coalition and Iraq to withdraw, soon.

REFERENCES

1. *The Hindustan Times*, 25 April, 1991.
2. *Patriot*, 19 April, 1991.
3. Sreerupa Mitra. Chaudhury Gulf Kurdistan. *Democratic World, 14 April, 1991.*
4. *Ibid.*
5. *Ibid.*

6. K. Subrahmanyam Intervention in Internal Affairs of Nations. *The Business and Political Observer*, 9 April, 1991.
7. *Ibid.*
8. K.M. Panikkar. Human Rights and US Double-Speak. *Patriot*, 4 May, 1991.
9. *Ibid.*
10. N.C. Menon. Picking on the President. *The Hindustan Times*, 6 April, 1991.
11. *Ibid.*
12. N.C. Menon. Picking on the President. *The Hindustan Times*, 2 May, 1991.
13. *Ibid.*
14. Harvey Morris. Kurds. *The Independent*, (Bombay), 6 March, 1991.
15. *The Hindustan Times*, 12 April, 1991.
16. K.M. Panikkar. Human Rights and US Double-Speak. *Patriot*, 4 May, 1991.

10

KURDS AND KASHMIR PROBLEM

The pressure is slowly being applied on India over Kashmir and it is very much on the lines of what we faced in 1948 when the ceasefire was announced and the issue placed before the United Nations in the hope that the world body would condemn the Pakistani aggression. Then too with the help of the US Britain. Pakistan's covert aggression was given the veneer of an uprising in Kashmir in favour of Islamabad. If Jawaharlal Nehru's trust in the World body's sense of justice and fair-play is considered to have been a mistake, then recent event once again underscore the fact that Pakistan and its allies would prefer to ensure that the status quo in Kashmir is maintained till the rest of it is ripe to fall to Pakistan. It has been India's folly to believe otherwise. Recently, we have had the Organisation of Islamic Countries. US Ambassador in Pakistan Robert Oakley and the British "shadow foreign minister" Gerald Kauffman accentuating the international dimension, a dimension that has been a subterranean factor throughout the history of the Kashmir crisis. In particular the Briton's assertion that Kashmir is an international issue evokes a vision of Iraq where the Kurdish minority is being used by all and sundry to ravish Iraqi sovereignty and territorial integrity not the least of which is the Turkish incurssion meant to destroy the movement among its own Kurdish population for a separate homeland. "Hot pursuit" has been quoted as legitimate in the protection of Turkish territorial integrity. Similar was the case whenever Israel made raids into the territories of is neighbours. The activities of these two have also sought to lend legitimacy to the bastard concept of "security zones". In the light of these international events in which Britain and the US have participated in full measure, it is not surprising that they should be in the forefront to raise fears of an impending Indian attack on Pakistan for fomenting insurgency through the use of terrorists trained in "Azad Kashmir" and in camps in Pakistan. This is because they both know that India would be well within international law to launch a punitive attack for the harassment that has been wreaked on the Indian people through Punjab and Kashmir for more than a decade now. That is the reason why they, and many others who are part of the US coterie, have insisted that India must adhere to the Simla Agreement even while allowing full play to all the international factors that militate against its very spirit. On our own part we have perfected the art of self-delusion. Even in the face of the vast body of evidence of Pakistani involvement in the training and provisioning of the terrorists, we have been pursuing a policy of "confidence building" which has nothing to do with the realities of geopolitics. Rajiv Gandhi, in a state of permanent siege from the threat of assassination, was pressured by Washington to maintain a dialogue with Pakistan which became a talk-trap for giving legitimacy to the Line of Actual Control in Jammu and Kashmir. The talks on the demilitarisation of the Siachen Glacier made a mockery of what the architect of the Simla Agreement, Indira Gandhi, had envisaged for the future of the subcontinent. And can anybody deny that she did not make adequate investment for peace, for achieving it through peaceful dialogue? It was when the cup brimmed over with false protestations of good-will and amity that she ordered the deployment of the highest battlefield in the world because, once again, cartographic aggression was being made the forerunner of a falt accompli. It was heartening to read that Indian Ambassador to Pakistan, in retort to US Ambassador Oakley's assertion that his country does not accept India's claims to Kashmir, said: "Washington can take any position it chooses but Kashmir is an integral part of the Republic of India . . . it is non-negotiable". Yet the fact remains that the dialogue that we have maintained with Pakistan has tended to give the impression that this country is willing to accept the partition of Kashmir along the Line of Actual Control in the hope of buying peace (some have been maintained that the proposition formed part of a secret agreement between Zulfikar Ali Bhutto and Indira Gandhi.[1]

The result is a strong surge of foreign-inspired and aided ethnic secessionist revolts in Kashmir, Punjab and Assam and a strengthening of the ethnic sentiment throughout the country. The way to tackle such problems, of course, is to ensure justice to all the ethnic communities, but this justice has to be ensured to all their people, not only the lumpen and petty bourgeois elements making mischief in their names. Such an approach would require just the kind of leadership this nation had in 1947, a leadership vision and courage. But just at a time this nation needs a strong secular and democratic centrist political nucleus, its centrist parties are at logger-heads within and without. The Congress has not only been reduced to a minority status in Parliament but is showing little capacity to draw fresh cadres to its ranks. Its leadership appears fossilised and incapable of rising above narrow selfish interests. The Janata Dal plight is worse. With the Left apparently confused after the Soviet collapse, the communal right has the field free to itself and is making the most of it.

The nation is at a crucial crossroads of history. It is difficult to see how it can get over its ethnic problems unless it can throw up a leadership committed to secularism and egalitarianism that reaches out to the rural masses and ensures economic growth with social justice. Any other course is fraught with the danger of losing whatever we gained 44 years ago – our freedom, our unity, our elan. We gained that after decades of hard-fought struggle by all our people; we could lose it all for just a few years of consumerist bonanza for a few that may end up either in balkanising the country or throwing up a lumpen supremo in the mould of a Mussolini.[2]

It was most inappropriate for the Organisation of Islamic Conference – (OIC) to pass the resolution they did on Kashmir. As the world knows the OIC is one of the most ineffective forums, for it never has had any influence or impact on any substantive problems that continue to besiege the so-called Islamic countries or peoples of the world. Where was the OIC when Iraq and Iran were fighting each other? Or, for that matter, when the Kurds were being systematically massacred reminding of the notorious genocide perpetrated on Jews by Hitler during the Second World War? Then, again, the OIC has been unable to do anything insofar as the Afghan occupation by the Soviet troops is concerned; or to amicably settle the Afghan problem. And, why does the OIC think of intervening between India and Pakistan to resolve the Kashmir crisis when it is quite well known that Pakistan, having failed to establish a regime of its liking in Afghanistan, is now diverting all its energies through armed inflitration of trained youth both in Kashmir and in Punjab. In fact, the OIC is not a representative organisation of Muslims: How could it be when India, a country containing more than 125 million Muslims is not represented on it, even as an observer. India has more Muslims than Pakistan but is not a member of OIC simply because it is a secular, democratic republic. Pakistan's agrument for annexing Kashmir is ostensibly because it has a basically Muslim population; but, then, India has more Muslims than Pakistan, and as Justice Chhagla once said, "the Muslims of India are not a minority; they are the second majority of India". And Kashmir is the crowning glory of a secular, democratic India.[3]

While the Kurdish leader have a great deal to gain from the 20-point agreement that the Baghdad authorities, memories of the autonomy accords of 1970 argue in favour of caution. The tragedy – as with all non-European peoples whose fate had to be adjusted to imperial requirements – is that the Kurds have always been the plaything of history; and there is no reason to suppose that, even now, the West is interest in them per se rather than in further humiliating President Saddam Hussein of Iraq. The victors of World War-I would probably have honoured their commitment to an independent Kurdish homeland, as promised in the never to be ratified Treaty of Sevres, if it had not suited the British better to retain control of the region's oil deposists through a puppet Hashemite monarchy in Iraq. A tacit US promise to the Kurds, followed up with considerable supplied of arms and ammunition routed through the Shah of Iran, turned, out to be only a ploy to irritate Baghdad until the Shah and the Baathist regime had composed their differences. Nor was the West quite so outraged by Hussein's atrocities (including chemical warfare) against the Kurds until Iraq had to be cut down to size for a totally different set of reasons. Now, however, the regional autonomy provided for in the 20-point agreement may show the way out of the 70-year impasse, providing there is a genuine desire on both sides to make the arrangement work. But when Mr. Jalal Talabani of the Patriotic Union of Kurdistan claims to be fighting for "autonomy for Kurdistan and democracy for Iraq" he is setting himself a wider political objective that cannot but lead to reneweds conflict with Baghdad. The "Bushistan" appellation – which, Iraqis must inevitably find repugnant – may fode out once UN troops have replaced all the 8,000 allied forces, about 50 per cent of whom are American, but no permanent political settlement can really depend on the presence of any foreign troops at all. The main task of the UN forces will be protect UN personnel and supervise such action as destruction of Iraq's chemical and biological weapons; but they are also expected to give the Kurds a sense of security. It is not difficult to understand, therefore, why Iraqis might look on the UN presence with some degree of suspicion and hositlity.[4]

What even those Iraqis who do not support the Baathist authorities must find most bewildering is the implied discrimination in the West's attitude to Kurds in Iraq, and to Kurds in Turkey and Iran. Iraq has only about four million Kurds but they constitute 23 per cent of the country's population, whereas the 12 million in Turkey and the five million in Iran account for 20 and 10 percent respectively of the national population figures of those countries. No one complained when the Shah ruthlessly liquidated the Kurdish republic that the Soviets had set up in northern Iran – admittedly to extend Moscow's influence rather than to help the Kurds – or against the Ayatollah regime's fundamentalist persecution. Nor did anyone object that use of the Kurdish language was altogether forbidden in Turkey while it was recognized as a "national language" in Iraq and used as the medium of instruction in schools and universities. Like many other of the world's forgotten minorities – the Basques, Armenians, Bhutias, Lepchas and Chakmas, Karens or Ibas – the Kurds have had a raw deal from history and deserve better. But if the outlook seems a little brighter for them now, if is only because the allied powers have found in them an instrument that can be used to continue the Gulf war by other means.[5]

Four months after Kurdish leaders first voiced optimism for reaching an agreement with Baghdad on autonomy for their mountainous region, negotiations have bogged down and there are suspicious Saddam Hussein may be stalling. Kurdish leaders Masoud Barzani and Jalal Talabani have little option but to seek a compromise with Saddam since they cannot be sure any future Iraqi leadership would grant the country's 3.5 million Kurds autonomy. But on the other hand, there remains the niggling fear that if UN sanctions are lifted and Saddam cements his grip once more, he will tear up any agreement, as he has in the past.

Saddam appears to be consolidating his power base within his sect, as evidenced by his recent military recruits of Sunnis rather than Shiites. He also is making progress in getting the United Nations to at least ease the year-old sanctions strangling Iraq.[6]

Western troops have withdrawn from the Kurdish protective zone established in north-western Iraq, leaving the Kurds facing an uncertain future, and Turkish forces have attacked Kurdish guerrillas in Iraq under a 1983 hot-pursuit accord with Baghdad. These developments have put pressure on the Kurds as they try to break the dead-lock over democratic reforms and territory that have been the major stumbling blocks since the talks began in April following an ill-fated rebellion. Saddam's aim was to split the Iraqi opposition. In addition, Kurdish sources and travellers from the north report a major military build up in Kirkuk, a strategic oil-producing centre, long in dispute between Baghdad and the Kurds.

The sources say up to five Republican Guard divisions possibly 100,000 soldiers – have been deployed in the region. If true, the reports demonstrate that Saddam is determined not to give around in Kirkuk or allow the Kurds to take control as they did last month in the northern cities of Erbil and Suleimaniya. Kurdish guerrillas moved in after July riots over high food prices triggered fighting with the Iraqi army in which hundreds of people were killed or wounded.

The Turkish military strike in northern Iraq in the first week of August 1991 in "hot pursuit" against "rebel" Turkish Kurds alleged to be sheltering there coincided with the visit to Delhi and Srinagar of the British Labour Party's shadow foreign minister Gerald Kaufamn; and came on more or less the eve of Pakistan foreign secretary Shaharyar Khan's visit India as special envoy of Nawaz Sharief – who is repeatedly reported in the media as being keen to "mend relations" with India. Turkey's Prime Minister Mesut Yilmaz said the operation against the Kurdish "rebels" proceeded "according to a plan", and added that whatever needed to be done to "maintain peace and security for our people" would be done "resolutely". The situation in Turkey's Kurdish area is in many respects remarkably similar to that which prevails in Punjab and Jammu and Kashmir. The militants in these two States are, according to not only repeated accusations by the Indian Government but now also the statements of some leaders and others in the United States and elsewhere, actually provided sanctuary and assistance in Pakistan. The "rebel" Turkish Kurds, on the other hand, may not actually be provided sanctuary in northern Iraq: the Baghdad-Kurdish relationship is, it may be recalled, not too friendly. But in effect the situation is familiar enough in Delhi. The results of Kaufman's visit depend on how genuine he is about peace and a resolution of the "militants problem". His constituents at home inculde a large number of Muslim Kashmiris and Sikh Panjabis. Being a good democart, he has naturally to think of ensuring a fat balance in his vote bank. But meaningul hints might be dropped in Indain conversations with Shaharyar Khan, who should be here again some time in mid-September for the scheduled meeting of Indain and Pakistani foreign secretaries. If Kaufamn is genuinely concerned he too will hint at need for caution in militant as well as Pakistani official circles. Being, presumably, a sharp observer of international developments he must have considered the merits or otherwise, and implications as example and precedent, of the Turkish Government's action. It would be tragic if 'hot pursuit' sanctioned by precedent and example in international relations, were to be undertaken and lead to a situation or war – which could only take South Asia backward into grievous damage, poverty and desperation.[7] One of the dangerous hurdles in the way of such hints and suggestions ever going home to Pakistan administrations and to the militants is the impression of helpless dithering that the Indian Government leaves and has left for so many years. The Turkish Prime Minister used the word "resolutely" for his Government's efforts to maintain peace and security. Resoluteness is the one thing which various Indain Governments and leaders have not given an impression of possessing or being able to convey. To be resolute is not to be bombastic and blustering speech. Indeed, real power speaks in public sparingly with immense restraint and modestry: the Indain habit is loquaciously to exhaust superlatives almost before beginning.

This might be kept in mind if and when Shaharyar Khan is apprised of the possibilities, results and precedents relating to 'hot pursuit'. With the options placed before him, resolutely, he might be send back with a message to Pakistan's real powers-that-be, to the effect that cooperation in restoring peace and economic as well as political stability in Kashmir and Panjab would be of prime advantage to both countries and to the region generally, and that the alternative could be ruinous. Real powers-that-be, because there has been a series of reports and rumours about designs and efforts to "topple" Nawaz Sharief's Government. It may be pointed out that 'hot pursuit' has sanction in practice, on the ground, whatever big-powder precepts may say. In the 1960s the United States sent its bombers into North Vietnam because South Vietnam's Vietcong guerrillas were provided sanctuary there. Subsequently, US forces also entered Cambodia in 'hot pursuit'. An American admiral was reported saying, "what is the use of continuing to swat the flies if you don't remove the dirt heap?" – or words to that effect. More recently, South African forces are reported to have frequently invaded neighbouring territories in 'hot pursuit' of dissidents and militants. Isreal bombed Lebanon and sent in its armed forces because militants of the Palestine Liberation Organisation took shelter and launched their actions from there. Other precedents could be summoned. But what has to be conveyed to Shaharyar Khan is that compelled actions such as 'hot putsuit' by Indain forces must be avoided because economic and political setback at this fragile stage could be alomst fatally injurious for both countries. What might also be conveyed, as forcefully as bluntly as possibly, is the suspicion aroused in New Delhi by the curious statements and actions of Pakistani leaders in relation to Afghanistan, and by the activity of Pakistan-based Afghan 'mujaheedin' in relation to the situation on the Indain side of the Kashmir, evidently to assist Pakistan inspired miliants. However, Delhi's resoluteness in cautioning Pakistan on the tragic implications of 'hot putsuit' inherent in Islamabad's aid and abetment of militants in Panjab and Kashmir would be futile without equal resoluteness in pushing domestic measures to meet the genuine grievances of the militants in the two States. What India cannot any longer afford, at home and abroad, is to continue to drift.[8]

The road followed the Tigiris river for a while and on our left was the Syrian marked by barbed wire fences and watch towers. The fence and the border guards, our interpreter, explained was not meant so much for the Syrian Army as for the Kurdish rebels. Syrian President Hafez Assad, the Turks believe, had encouraged and sustained Kurdish secessionists for years. The leaders of the Kurdish guerrillas that operated in Eastern Turkey were based in Damascus and purported to be communists. And it was this same group that had led the attacks on Mosul and other towns in north Iraq. There was substance in the belief that Syria sustained Kurdish guerrillas but the barbed wire was evidently quite inadequate against Kurdish nationalism. A convey of Turkish battle tanks, painted black, trundled past us. Our driver was clearly worried and kept muttering someting about the 'Gendarmerie' . Sure enough, at the town of silopi, just 15 km short of the border we were stopped and told to get out of our car. We are under arrest. Screaming and gesticulating in English resulted in us being taken to the local area commander. After a half-an hour wait, the commander saw us and said there were no Kurdish refugees in the region. He apologised politely and told us there was no way he could allow us to get to the border. Try Hakkari, he suggested with a wink to the interpreter. Without a word we get back to the car, turned it around and sped off. The tanks had halted at Silopi and the place was crawling with soldiers. Something evidently was up. Later, I learnt, it was an exercise aimed at intimidating the Iraqis. An hour later, we had backtracted to Cizre and turned towards the high mountains of Hakkari. At the point where the road began to climb into the mountains, we came across the first of the innumerable Gendarmerie checkposts we were to encounter. In normal times we could not have got past the first one. But now the Gendarmerie had got instructions to allow selected foreigners to proceed till Hakkari. The Turkish government was playing up the Kurdish exodus and wanted to give the international media an upfront view of what was happening. Rebeal country was temporarily transformed into a centre of media tourism. After a body search and a cursory inspection of our equipment we were waved through.[9]

We were finally on the trail and expected the Kurdish hordes after every bend of the road. Instead, for the next few hours we only got more checkposts every few killometers. The Genarmerie were relaying the names of all foreigners crossing their checkposts to the next one. All of us had to keep fishing out our identity cards at every stop. It was frustrating because the hours were ticking away and the shadows lengthening across the valleys. The view was spectacular; towering mountains, picture book valleys and a forlorn landscape of eroded ravines. It was ideal guerrilla country. But there wasn't single armed Kurd in sight not any camp. In the villages we passed, the local Kurds avoided our gaze while the Gendarmerie tended to keep us waiting longer than necessary. The driver said that the soldiers, most of them in their late teens, seemed highly stung and delighted to talk to Turks. The local Kurdish population apparently avoided them like poison and soldiers got ambushed regularly in these parts. It reminded me of Kashmir and made me feel that perhaps things were not so bad in our part of the world – at least not as much as we made it out to be. In fact many people in Turkey told me that they felt the Indian government was weak and indecisive: that we should have carved out Eelam for the Tamils of Sri Lanka just as the Turks divided Cyprus. Turks also generally favoured the idea of strong military action in our Panjab and Kashmir. Their views would have made even the most hardline Indain bureaucrat blanch. I could understand now why the Turks felt so strongly about rebellious ethnic minorities.[10]

If law and law-enforcing agencies were all a nation-needed to keep its house in order, India need have no worries. It has plenty of both and can easily have more of them; its legislators have seldom shown any gualms about amending the constitution or enacting fresh laws "to save the nation"; its unemployed can supply any number of healthy youth for paramilitary forces. Why, then, the secessionist problems in Panjab, Kashmir and Assam? How come that even the armed forces have failed to either contain the "handfuls" of "our very own misguided youth" or wean them away from the path of terrorism? And, how come elections cannot be held in Panjab without barring the process to those demanding secessions, as the ruling Congress wants, or, putting the state under the armed forces, as the Bharatiya Janata Party often demands.

Is one to believe that the state can be retained as a part of India by force of law and armed strength? Does India's claim to Panjab rest only on the law of sucession, as successor to British India, and its capacity to enforce this claim, or in the will of the people of Panjab. Whatever the position in terms of legal history, the Indian Constitution takes care to take base India's sovereignty in the will of the people and proclaims in its Preamble that it is "we, the people of India" that have given it unto "ourselves". The only title India, thus, has to any of its parts lies in the will of its people, and if the people of Panjab, or any other part of India, will otherwise, India ceases to have any claim to that territory. No law or armed force can deprive the people of this inalienable right of theirs. Nor is there any need to. For, India's claim to Panjab is not so tenuous as to depend on this or that law, or this or that security force. Panjab is a part of India because its people want it to be so. It is not, and cannot be, otherwise. Those who doubt this, in fact, suffer from the grand delusion that it is they who consitute India. The chief motivation for the present poll postponement in Panjab, for example, is not so much to keep the secessionists at bay as to enable the Congress to contest the polls To sell this limited objective as a move to save the nation is neither fair nor politica. The nation is not synonymous with the Congress. As for the supposed threat from secessionism after "even the Akalis" have adopted Khalistan as their objective, one may recall that even during the 1989 Lok Sabha election, the Akali Dal (Mann) polled only 29.2 percent votes although it had the full support of various militant groups and enjoyed the advantages of the charisma associated with Mr. Simranjit Singh Mann's long incarceration and the sentimental appeal of such candidates as Mr. Bimal Khalsa. No great deal that when even the poorly organised and demoralised Congress could get 26.5 per cent votes and the combined vote of the parties committed firmly to India's territotial integrity totalled some 50 per cent, or nearly double that of the Akali Dal (M)! Why then the fear that the poll could give some kind of a legitimacy to the secessionists if they manage to win it through communal blackmail and physical threats and intimidation? The fear is grossly unfounded and merely shows the government's lack of faith in both the masses as also its security forces to ensure a free and fair poll. There is nothing to suggest that the militant-backed Akalis will fare any better now than did the Akali Dal (M) in 1989. On the other hand, there is reason to believe that they might fare a lot worse by losing a big part of the Akali Dal (M)'s 1989 vote that was people's reward for its participation in the democratic process. The reason for the Akalis falling for the militants' political objective, therefore, has to be seen not in the Akali Dal (M)'s "success" in 1989, or the capacity of terror to influence the vote, but to the tendency among many national leaders, including former prime minister V.P. Singh and Chandrashekhar, to view the militants as the real party to do business with. Assam Chief Minister Hiteshwar Saikia's soft line towards ULFA terrorists has also sent wrong signals.[11]

It is such wrong signals that have contributed to converting many a manageable problem into deep crisis. Panjab already has seen the havoc played by them. Irrespective of whether the military operations in 1984 were at all necessary, it needs must be conceded that the then government failed to estimate the damage these could do the states body social and the tragic signals these would send. True that Indira Gandhi's plans went away after her assassination and the anti-Sikh riots of 1984, and necessitated a fresh initiative by Rajiv Gandhi. But his accord with Sant Harchand Singh Longowal again sent out wrong signals as did its non-implementation later. The interests of the state and the nation were sacrificed again at the altar of Congress-Akali rivalry.

This rivalry was also the cause of the subsequent attempts to make the "moderate Akalis" irrelevant by seeking a modus vivendi now with a Bhai Jasbir Singh Rode, then with a Simranjit Singh Mann: The V.P.Singh and Chandrashekhar governments, particularly the latter, did worse by conveying that they were willing to talk to anybody without insisting on his giving up violence. It is good that the Narasimha Rao government has restored the perspective by making it categorically clear that it will not help legitimise terrorism, whatever the cost. One only hopes there will be no right-about-turns again. But if succumbing to terrorism is bad, creating breeding grounds for terrorism is worse. And the Congress cannot shrug away its responsibility for having created such a ground for terrorism and secessionism in Panjab. It was the Congress under Indira Gandhi that legitimised Sikh communalism when it first conceded a Panjabi suba that kept many Panjabi-speaking areas out of it to give it a Sikh majority, and then tried to outflank the Akalis by pursuing the Zail Singh line of creating a parallel centre of Sikh political power. This not only compromised the Congress commitment to secularism but also promoted Sikh fundamentalism that degenerated later into secessionist terrorism. If the Congress under Mr. Narasimha Rao means business, it must resist the temptation to fall in the same trap again. The Congress owed its greatness in the post-Independence India to the modernistic role it sought to play under Nehru. Its compromises with onscurantis forces to perpetuate the status quo have only made it incredible. It can regain relevance only as a vehicle of change.[12]

A population primarily derived its identity and unity from its language, ethnicity and culture. While in the case of homogeneous populations this identity alone would define its nationhood, in the case of composite nations unifying factors transcending the divisions of languages and ethnicities will have to prove stronger if the different populations are to be held together in one polity and consider themselves to be a nation. Fortunately the concept of India as a civilisational and cultural unity has been in the memory of our people for well over three millenia. In the last one century we have developed a common law and common market and shared memories of the struggle for freedom. The continuance of English, and officers of President, Chief Justice of India, and chiefs of staff being held by members of minority communities, the union Cabinet generelly getting representation from most of the states, and different parties holding power in the states have all conributed to sustaining the Indian polity without too much of greivance of domination by any linguistic or ethic group. Yet there are warning signals arising out of developments in Panjab, Kashmir and North East. There are negative trends in terms of ethnic and linguistic parochialisms.The political innovativeness of the fifties and sixties appears to have run out of steam. Now the international development compel us to take necessary steps to reinforce the Indian unity and sense nationalism. Fast economic growth, integration of markets and labour mobility tend to unite. So do decentralisation and increased autonomy in political activity. The giant states lead to inward looking politics and parochialism. Those who oppose break up of our mega-stages are in fact subliminally preferring the unity of the state to the unity of the nation. Today our nationalism cannot be sustained by invoking credible external threats to our sovereignty and territorial integrity. With satellite television, our culture and civilisation values are likely to be overwhelmed. That is a greater threat at our nationalism. The resurgent Indian nationalism has to be based on the Indian culture and civilisation, its unifying effect on the Indian polity and its potential contribution to further integration of humanity. Nationalism is derived from specfic identity and pride. The latter originates from a sense of achievement of forbearance and fortitute in suffering. Unfortunately this country has been preoccupied in the last three decades with parochial politics and medicore economic development where rapaciousness has been hidden behind dishonest rhetoric about social justice. This strategy has prevented the full exploitation of our R & D potential and entrepreneurial capabilities and inhibited possible achievements in all fields, including sports, and the arts sciences. Composite nations can preserve their composite identity and sense of nationalism only if the unity of the constituent units results in a synergistic effect in terms of achievement orientation. The break up of the Soviet Union and Yugoslavia illustrates that without achievements to boast of and with all innovations and creativity mothered by mediocrity in the name of dishonest egalitarianism (the Communist leaders lived like Princes) the constituent units neither had a sense of pride in belonging to the Union nor tangible benefits. Hence the rush of the former COMECON nations to get membership of EEC. Indian nationalism needs to be rejuvented on the basis of our millenia old culture and civilisational values, by freeing our entrepreneurial skills to maximise our economic growth, nurturing and promoting our arts, literature, science, sports and making Indians to feel proud to belong to this composite civilisational community.[13]

REFERENCES

1. Cecil Victor. Kashmir. *Patriot*, 16 August, 1991.
2. Devendra Chintan. The Nation at Crossroads. *The Business and Political Observer*, 14 August, 1991.
3. Abu Nadeem. Kashmir. *The Hindustan Times*, 20 August, 1991.
4. *The Statesman*, 1 June, 1991.
5. *Ibid.*
6. *The Business and Political Observer*, 14 August, 1991.
7. Rakshat Puri. Turkish Example. *The Hindustan Times*, 13 August, 1991.
8. *Ibid.*
9. Indrarvil Banerjee. Nobody's People. *The Hindustan Times*, 3 August, 1991.
10. *Ibid.*
11. Devendra Chintan. The Nationality Question. *The Business and Political Observer*, 11 September, 1991.
12. *Ibid.*
13. K. Subrahmanyam. Indian Nationalism. *The Business and Political Observer*, 16 September, 1991.

APPENDICES

Appendix—I

KURDISH NATIONALISM, 1880-1946

1880 Revolt of Sheikh Ubaydollah of the Hakari province of the Ottoman Empire. This was the first major Kurdish uprising with nationalistic, as opposed to feudalistic and tribal, overtones.

1897 Founding of the first Kurdish newspaper, *Kurdistan*, by the prominent Badr Khan family. It served as a conduit for the dissemination of Kurdish culture and nationalistic activities.

1919 Sheihk Mahmud of Suleymanieh declared his independence from British control, resulting in British military attacks on his stronghold and Sheikh Mahmud's eventual defeat.

1919-22 Ismail Agha Simitqo (or Simko) managed to create a semi-autonomous Kurdish entity along the northwest frontiers areas of Iran and Turkey.

1920 Treaty of Sevres was signed by the representatives of the victorious Allied Powers and the defeated Ottoman sultan. It called for the establishment of an independent Kurdistan in Kurdish-inhibited regions previously under the sovereignty of the Ottoman Empire.

1923 Sheikh Ahmad, and his younger brother, Mullah Mustafa, of the Barzan tribe initiated their long campaign for Kurdish autonomy.

1942 Komala, the first Kurdish nationalist political party, was created by a group of Kurdish activists in Mahabad, Iran.

1945 The Kurdish Democratic Party is founded, incorporating all Kurdish nationalist movements (including Komala) under its umbrella.

1945 The Kurdish Republic of Mahabad, with its own president, cabinet can legislature is established. The Mahabad Republic was the first and the only independent Kurdish state in history.

1946 The Imperial Iranian army retakes Mahabad and abolishes the Mahabad Republic. Many of its leaders, including President Qazi Mohammad, were subsequently executed.

1946 The Iraqi Kurdish Democratic Party is founded by a group of Iraqi Kurdish intellectuals. Mullah Mustafa Barzani accepts the leadership of the party.

Appendix—II

DISPLACED IRAQIS

The greatest migration in history is being witnessed in our region. Hundred of thousands of Northern Iraqis are fleeing to Turkey and Iran in order to be able to save themselves from the oppression of the despotic regime in their homeland. More than half a million of these people, the majority of which are the aged, women and children are on our borders. For these victims, who are being sheltered temporarily on and out of Turkish territory, the Turkish Republic, has mobilized its resources as a nation, government and state. She has extended a helping hand and shared her food and clothing with these people.

However, the countries who have not allowed even one of these dispaced Iraqis to be sheltered in their respective countries, and whose institutions and foundations have paid lip service to the championing of human rights and human dignity are now without conscience slandering Turkey and the Turkish people. What is most regrettable is that these accusations come from countries friendly to Turkey.

Ankara (DGPI)-Prime Minister Yildirim Akbulut conducted an inspection of the Turco-Iraqi border region on April 12, 1991.

Prime Minister Akbulut gave a briefing in the Isikveren accommodation centre in Uludere, Sirnak.

He later inspected the lodgings of the displaced Iraqis and listened to their problems and requests. Akbulut asked an Iraqi from Zaho if he wished to return to his country, upon which the Iraqi said that they did not want to go back because Saddam would kill them.

Upon this Prime Minister Akbulut said that they were expending all efforts to lodge and feed the people escaping from Iraq, however, it was their wish that these people could return to their own homes provided that they can do so in peace and security.

Akbulut said, "Of course an end should be made of this intolerable situation. We are in a position to do this However, I say this matter is not the concern of Turkey along. It is our hope that all countries will cooperate to end the intolerable situation and stop the suffering of these people. We are continuing our endeavours in this regard. But do not worry, in the shortest possible time we will save you from matters you are complaining about and we will make you attain your normal living conditions. You can be sure of this."

Prime Minister Akbulut said that he had given the necessary instructions to the authorities so that the people seeking refuge in Turkey could live under better conditions.

During his visit Prime Minister Akbulut also answered questions posed by some foreign television networks. He said that in 1988 some 100 thousand people from the same country has also sought refuge in Turkey and that she had lodged and fed these people on her own. However, some countries which just stood by doing nothing, saw fit to unjustly criticize and direct propaganda against Turkey. Akbulut went to share the full burden only on our own. This problem is not one of Turkey's along. At a time when human rights are in the fore, all countries should approach the problem from the humane angle and find the best possible solution. The solution should be found by the United Nations. All countries should find the solution, and whatever the dictates of this solution, it should be implemented.

Later Prime Minister Yildirim Akbulut organized a press conference at which he once again called upon all countries and organizations, especially those that give importance to human rights to help in the matter.

The Prime Minister criticized these countries and organizations for their stand in the face of the problem that had arisen in 1988, and now a general indifference was being exhibited and the requests of the displaced Iraqis who wished to go to other countries remained unanswered.

Prime Minister Akbulut said, "Would it not be better if these champions of human rights sheltered those people who wished to leave? When will these countries open their doors to people in such circumstances."

Hakkari, Van, Sirnak and Mardin provinces and in addition Yesilhisar (Kayseri), Kangal (Sivas) and Tatvan (Bitlis) have been designated accommodation centres for the Iraqis who have fled their country as a result of the Gulf Crisis.

Aid consisting to supplies and cash has been obtained from UN organizations for infrastructure services in the centres to be set up in the afore-mentioned regions.

The aid was sent through the intermediary of the General Chairmanship of the Red Crescent. Cash amounting to $ 317,000 has been obtained from the UN Office of High Commissioners for Refugees (UNHCR) and TL 1 billion and 50 million from UNICEF.

The aid received from UNHCR is to be spent for excavation work for infrastructure in the centres to be set up and the UNICEF aid is to be used for water and sewerage for infrastructure services.

Within the framework of the agreements made with UN organizations, of the aid received, TL 698 million have been sent to the Governorship of Kayseri, TL 670 million to the Governorship of Sivas, 400 million to Governorship of Hakkari and 350 million to the Governorship of Sirnak, totalling TL 2 billion and 128 million.

In addition, on April 9, 1991 TL 510 million and 720 thousand was obtained from UNICEF but has not as yet been sent to the respective governorships.

Work undertaken to set up tent camping areas in Kayseri and Sivas provinces is still continuing.

Other expenses are met by the Incentives Fund for Social Mutual Assistance and Solidarily and the Development Support Fund. Two temporary accommodation centres are in operation in Kayseri, one in Tatvan (Bitlis) and one in Kangal (Sivas).

Foreign Ministry Spokesman Murat Sungar said that many delegations have come to Turkey to make contacts concerning the displaced Iraqis.

In his weekly press conference on 24 April, Sungar stated that Swedish International Development Cooperation Minister Lena Hjelm-Wallen would observe the border region between 24-28 April.

Noting that Italian deputy Foreign Minister Claudio Lenaci had already visited the region, Sungar said that the Term-President Luxembourg State Secretary George Wollfart toured the region on behalf of the EC. Sungar also stated that Wollfart met Foreign Ministry Undersecretary Ambassador Tugay Özceri in Ankara.

DISTRIBUTION BY CAMPS

Site of camp	*Turkish territory*	*Iraqi territory*
Isikvöron (Uludere)	87.000	100.000
Yokmal (Uludere)	–	31.000
Andaç (Uludere)	–	13.000
Kayadibi (Uludere)	12.000	–
Ortaköy (Uludere)	–	4.000
Yildiz (Uludere)	–	5.000
Üzümlü (Çukurca)	50.000	–
No: 49 Border demarkation (Çuk)	–	65.000
Isikli (Çukurca)	3.000	–
Cayirli (Çukurca)	5.000	–
Karasu (Çukurca)	–	20.000
Pirinçakan (Çukurca)	12.000	–
Asagiköprü (Çukurca)	30.000	–
Yesilova (Hakkari)	15.000	–
Silopi (Sirnak)	15.641	–

AID FROM FOREIGN COUNTRIES

As of 22 April 1991

No.	*Country*	*Flights*	*Vehicles*	*Materials (Tons)*
1.	Germany	8	24	240
2.	USA	2	5	50
3.	Bulgaria	3	9	90
4.	Denmark	3	10	100
5.	France	2	1	10
6.	Holland	6	20	200
7.	Britain	5	19	190
8.	Spain	2	5	50
9.	Israel	1	1	10
10.	Sweden	6	27	270
11.	Italy	2	10	100
12.	Hungary	1	1	10
13.	Pakistan	4	20	40
Total	13 countries	45 planes	52 lorries	1520 tons

TURKEY'S RELIEF AID TO DISPLACED IRAQIS

As of 22 April 1991

Region	*Foodstuffs*	*Flour*	*Bread*	*Clothing*	*Blankets and bed dressing*	*Tent*	*Medicines and Medical supplies*	*Shoes*	*Total vehicles*	*Total (tons)*	*Water tanks*	*Mobile hospitals*
HAKKARI	488	26	26	8	11	5	17	13	594	5940	5	1
SIRNAK	377	32	140	118	34	23	60	8	792	7920	27	1
Total	865	58	166	126	45	28	77	21	1386	13,860	32	2

Spokesman Sungar also noted that a delegation from the U.S. Senate would visit Turkey on 27-28 April with the same purpose.

Saying that Japanese deputy Foregin Minister responsible for relations with the parliament Suzuki would come to Turkey to make contacts in the same region on 2 May, Sungar said that UN officials Sadrettin Aga Khan and Eric Sui would also pay a visit to Turkey but the date of their visit had not been set.

Sungar also stated that the aid Turkey has given to the displaced Iraqis was more than the total aid received from other countries. Sungar added that the person in charge of the situation was state Minister Vehbi Dincerler.

British Foreign Aid Minister Lynda Chalker stated that Turkey's efforts in supplying aid to the displaced Iraqis were appreciated. Chalker who came to Turkey last week and was met by Foreign Ministry Undersecretary Tugay Özceri at Esenboga airport said in a statement, "We would like the establishment of security zones for the dsiplaced Iraqis as soon as possible. Our aims are humanitarian and peaceful. We expect that the Iraqi administration will show cooperation in the implementation of all UN Security Council resolution."

NATO Secretary General Manfred Wöerner, speaking at a panel on Austrian Television had words of praise for Turkey.

Wöerner said that Turkey has done much more to lodge and feed Northern Iraqis, than those who persistently come up with requests. He said that those who criticize Turkey should first ascertain what they themselves have done in way of humane and material support.

Manfred Wöerner said that Turkey should not be left alone, share in the problem. Replying to a criticism on Turkey's stand in the matter, Wöerner said that as far as he knew, Turkey has been considerably generous in accepting the Kurds.

In this speech Wöerner said that he supported US President George Bush's policy in staying clear of the inner conflicts in Iraq.

Wöerner continued by saying that nobody could load the full responsibility for the problem on the US and the international community should comprise one whole. Europe should do her share by assisting in solving the Kurdish problem.

He added that all international pressure should be exercized in stopping the oppression practiced by Saddam Hussein on the northern Iraqis. These people should be allowed to return to their homes and to live in peace.

German Foreign Minister Hans Dietrich Genscher came to Ankara on April 19. He was met at Eseboga Airport by his Turkish counterpart Ahmet Kurtcebe Alptemocin, and a joint press Conference was held. Genscher left the same day for Antalya where he was received by President Turgut Özal. Present at the reception were Prime Minister Yildirim Akbulut, Foreign Minister Alptemocin and Germany's Ambassador to Ankara Ekkehard Eichoff.

After their discussions in Kemer, President Özal and German Foreign Minister Genscher, issued a joint communique.

Özal said that the plight of the displaced Iraquis was reviewed, and the visiting minister was told that the adverse climatic conditions on Turkey's southern border would disapper when he visited the region.The president said that Turkey has done all she could for the displaced Iraqis, and would continue her efforts.

The president said that the best solution would be if the Iraqis could return to their homeland. Both the UN agreement and President Bush's decision, he believed would facilitate in solving the matter. He said he also hoped that Iraq would show the necessary understanding. The sheer number of Iraqis has greatly complicated the matter. However, aid from Germany aside from the EC, would be highly beneficial in solving the problem. He thanked the visiting minister in this aspect and said that Germany's historical experience in those seeking asylum would also benefit Turkey.

German Foreign Minister Genscher in his turn said that it was necessary that aid to the displaced Iraqis be extended in the shortest possible time.

He went on to say, "In this respect we are of the same opinion. Our endeavors should advance simultaneously in two directions. First, urgent aid must be extended to these persons, and they must be sent to more suitable regions to live. Secondly, ways must be found whereby they can return to their homeland.

Saddam must not be permitted, under any circumstances, to force the people he does not approve of to flee the country and become a burden to two neighbouring countries."

Genscher also extended his thanks to President Özal for Turkey's permission for air passage of German aircraft and helicopters flying from Turkey to Iraq.

Genscher proceeded from Antalya to Diyarbakir and from thence to Batman. He was accompained on this trip by Foreign Minister Alptemocin.

The Belgain government has expressses their gratitude to Turkey for the support and help she has given to the Iraqis fleeing from the Saddam Hussein regime.

The Belgian Foreign Minister Marc Eysens received the Turkish Ambassador to Brussels Yildirim Keskin last week and conveyed the gratitude of his government.

Foreign Minister Eyskens told Ambassador Keskin that the matter was taken up in detail at the EC Foreign Ministers meetings held in Brussels and the help Turkey is extending to the people who were forced to to leave their lands was greatly appreciated.

The allegations regarding the confiscation, by Turkish soldiers, of a portion of the aid sent to the Northen Iraqis masses at the Turkish border and the firing upon some of the displaced Iraqis have been strongly refuted by EC commission officials.

Visiting Turkey and Iraq at the instruction of Commission Chairman Jacques Delors to coordinate aid and make an on-the-spot observation of the situation, special representative Juan Prat held a press conferences in Brussels week and expounded on the matter.

Stressing that all the news reported by the Western press, radio and televsion network directed against Turkey were all lies and fabrications, Prat said that they sent denials to the organisations reporting these news items.

Juan Prat stated that President Turgut Özal, Prime Minister Yildirim Akbulut and all officials were deeply concerned with the problem and helped him greatly, adding that he was surprised by the help, extended to him in Turkey were he was affected by unfavourable rumours.

Stating that he insisted on visiting Isikveren accommodation centre and the regions where there were rumours of imprompriety Juan Prat said, "I myself have observed the presence of the Turkish government in all these places." Prat also noted that the Turkish side of the border was not suited for settlement and it was very hard to reach people in these regions whereas in Iran due to geographic conditions aid could reach its destinations easier.

Prat pointed out that the lack of order seen in place near the Turkish border should be considered normal when considering geat numbers involved in the immigration and the difficult conditions that were encountered. (*Newspot, April 25,1991*)

Appendix—III

AUSTRALIA ON THE KURDISH CRISIS

Most of Iraq's three million Kurds (of a total Iraqi population of some 17 million) live in the north and north east of Iraq in an area bounded by the cities or towns of Suleimaniaya, Kirkuk, Arbil, Mosul and Zakho. In accordance with Iraq's 1968 Constitution and a 1970 agreement between the Iraqi Government and Kurdish representatives, most of this area is included in a Kurdish Autonomous Region, of which Arbil is the capital and the seat of a paliament to which Kurdish representatives are elected.

Following the start of the ground war in Kuwait on 24 February, Kurdish guerrillas mobilised against Iraqi troops in the north. Early successes encouraged uprisings in some of the major towns but, after suppressing the Shi'ite uprising in the south, Iraqi forces regrouped in the north, put down the uprisings in the towns and, in late March, began pushing the guerrillas back into the mountains. Kurdish families (as well as some other minorities) fled north to Turkey and east to Iran to escape the advancing Iraqi forces and the fighting.

While the general Iraqi offensive has halted and there is no large-scale fighting north of the 36th parallel, there are still occasional incidents between the Iraqi army and Kurdish guerrillas. Estimates of the casualties or the numbers of rebels involved since the beginning of the fighting in March are not available.

Although the numbers of people affected escalated quickly for early April, the total now appears to have stabilised. Of the more than 400,000 located in Turkey by the end of April, most are now reported to have returned to Iraq, though in the case of Iran the rate of border-crossing is about equal in both directions.

According to United Nations sources (refer to UN Sitrep No. 4)

- some 208,000 people are estimated to be on the Turkish border, with about another 62,000 receiving relief aid in the humanitarian camps set up in northern Iraq.
- on the eastern border, more than 1.4 million people are estimated to have crosses into iran, while another 150,000 are reportedly close to the border on the Iraqi sidd.

International relief efforts have involved UN agencies (especially UNHCR and UNDRO, as well as WHO, UNICEF, IOM and WFP) the ICRC (working with the League of Red Cross and Red Crescent Societies,) NGOs and individual governments. The UN relief system was stimulated and mandated by the adoption of SCR 688 on 5 April. Prince Sadruddin Aga Khan was appointed as the Secretary-General's Executive Delegate for the UN relief program, and on 15 May the UN announced a revised and coordinated appeal for $ US 415 million, superseding two earlier appeals and intended to meet ongoing costs and likely future expenditure.

President Bush announced on 16 April that following consultations with the UN Secretary General and the leaders of Britain, France, Germany and Turkey, he had directed the US armed forces to proceed with a major relief operation "Provide Comfort" which would include establishing encampments in northern Iraq from which relief supplies could be distributed to Kurds. This operation is intended as an interim measure only – to faciliate and encourage the Kurds' return to their homes – and not as a long-term solution to their plight. On the basis of SCR 688, forces from the UK, France, Spain, Canada, the Netherlands, Germany, Australia and other countries are also undertaking humanitarian work in Turkey and northern Iraq. The first three resettlement camps have now been established near Zakho in Iraq, and Kurds, have been set up in other locations.

Although Iraq has complained to the UN about the camps, it has done nothing to impede their construction. On 18 April, Iraq signed a Memorandum of Understanding with the United Nations, agreeing to cooperate with it in allowing a humanitarian presence in Iraq. The UN Secretary General has said that the UN will take over the camps was as soon as possible, and indeed the first of the Zakho camps taken over by the UN on 13 May. Security Council members have stressed their desire for the UN to assume this reponsibility, and an agreement has been reached between the UN and the Iraqi Government providing for 500 UN guards to be assigned to all the camps in northern Iraq. In addition, UN operations are being facilitated through the establishment of five UN sub-offices in Iraq, four of them in the north (at Suleimaniya, Arbil, Dohuk and Mosul), as well as nine field offices and 20 mobile teams.

On 13 April, President Saddam Hussein offered amnesty for refugees who were not "murderers, rapists and thieves". Since late April, Kurdish representatives including Patriotic Union of Kurdistan leader Jalal Talabani and Kurdish Democratic Party leader Massoud Barzani have been discussing with the Iraqi governments the question of greater autonomy and rights for the Kurds. While a formal agreement has yet to be signed, progress is reportedly being the control of Kirkuk and international guarantees about the security of the Iraqi Kurds are reportedly still being discussed. While some Kurds are returning to their homes from Turkey, the great majority (most of whom are in Iran) are apparently not yet convinced that their safety and well being will be assured.

Australia has for many years taken a strong position in UN and other forums about abuses of human rights affecting Kurds both in Iraq and elsewhere. For example, representations have been made by our embassies in Baghdad and Tehran about Kurdish concerns, we condemned the Iraqi Government's use on Human rights in Geneva this year we co-sponsored a resolution which condemned human rights abuses in Iraq, with particular reference to the Kurds.

Humanitarian Aid Response

On 9 April, Dr. Blewett announced a contribution of $A1 million to the relief effort, to be divided between the UN and the ICRC. On 13 April, an RAAF 707 aircraft left for Turkey with some 22 tonnes of relief supplies. On 22 April, the Government announced a further contribution of $A1.5 million to the relief efforts, earmarked specifically for use by UNICEF, UNHCR and the ICRC in Iran where the majority of the refugees are located. On 8 May, Mr. Howe announced that the Department of Community Services and Health contribute $500,000 to the Australian Red Cross to enable Australian medical personnel to join the ICRC relief operation in Iran. Two Australian doctors, a sanitary engineer and a relief administrator were already in the area and are expected to be joined shortly by about 14 others. These contributions are in addition to $A5 million in humanitarian assistance already provided for victims of the Gulf War.

On 6 May, Senator Ray announced Austalia's contribution of a contingent of 75 Australian Defence Force personnel to the multinational relief effort in northern Iraq. The contingent includes doctors, other medical personnel and terms with specialist skills in field hygiene, water purification and sanitation. The ADF contingent, which left Australia on 16 May, will make a valuable contribution by providing skilled humanitarian care to those who are most in need.

Resettlement

Most of the Kurdish refugees are understood to want to return to their homes in Iraq ànd this remains the primary objective of the international community and UN agencies. DILGEA is processing about 100 humanitarian and applications from Kurdish refugees who have been in Turkey since, 1988, and the first of these are expected to begin arriving in Australia next month. But, consistent with the approach of the international community and the UNHCR, DILGEA is not at this stage developing proposals for more extensive resettlement action.

Diplomatic Actioı.

Since the beginning of the crisis.

– our charged affaires in Tehran has visited the border area and reported in detail on the situation there, has had helpful and informative discussion which leaders of Iraqi Kurdish groups, and has assisted Australian NGOs and other visitors.

– our embassy in Ankara has been in close contact with the Turksih authoirities and other missions, including in the context of the despatch of the ADF contingent to Turkey and northern Iraq, and has also provided valuable reporting on the situation on the border.

– our mission in Geneva has been instrumental in encouraging action by UN relief agencies, for instance in chairing meetings between UN relief agencies and donor missions, most recently on 15 May

- the Iraqi charged affaires in Canberra has been told of Government's view that Iraq must cooperate with the UN and relief agencies, and that conditions must be created which will enable the Iraqi amnesty offer to be seen as a sincere one and the Kurds enabled to return to their homes.
- Mr. Hand visited Turkey and Iran from 6 to 11 May to see at first hand the situation facing the Kurds, and to be briefed in detail by UN officials and Ministers in Iran. He also visited refugee camps near Orumiyeh.
- Senator Evans and Dr. Blewett discussed with Iranian Foregin Minister Dr. Velayati on 16 May Iran's response to the crisis and its cooperation with international relief agencies.

In New York and Geneva, our missions to the UN continue to be very active in making known our political interests and concerns. In particular, our mission in New York has made known our whole hearted support for SCR 688 and our views in support of the safe haven concept, in which we are actively participating with other concerned governments.

Long Term Objectives

The longer term objectives continues to be to ensure the establishment of conditions which will enable the Kurdish people to return to their homes in Iraq and to enjoy the full range of civil and political rights as a minority in Iraq. UNSCR 687 appears to provide a framework for maintaining pressure on Iraq to this end

- through the possible use of the provisions of paragraph 21 which link the lifting of sanctions to Iraqi Government Policies and practices; and
- also in the sense that the resolution provides a means for the international community to maintain substantial general pressure on Iraq into the future.

What Australia Cannot Do?

International law and convention impose real constraints on what Australia, or the international community generally, can do to try to affect the situation in Iraq directly.

(a) UN-sanctioned military intervention to depose Saddam Hussein or restructure Iraq cannot be contemplated not only because such action would be contrary to the provisions of the UN Charter but also because of the reality that any such proposals are most unlikely to be adopted by the Security Council. While UN members have generally supported the actions being taken in accordance with SCR 688, there was opposition to its adoption.

(b) For reasons relating to the dismemberment of a UN member state we cannot support the creation of an independent Kurdish state.

The situation is not analogous to that the Palestinians in that the homeland or state we support for the Palestinians would be not in the sovereign territory of any UN member state, but rather in territories occupied by Israel to which no other country pursues a claim of sovereighnty

(c) Although the achievement of an independent state undoubtedly remains an aspiration for many Kurds, it is our understanding that for the most part they do accept the realities of the present international situation and do not demand an independent state or homeland in Iraq or elsewhere. (Australia Backgrounder 21 June, 1991)

Appendix—IV

ONLY INTEGRATION CAN ENSURE SECURITY FOR TURKEY'S *KURDS*

The Kurdish issue has suddenly erupted into the forefront of a multitude of chronic and complicated probelms in the Middle East, overshadowing even the perennial Palestinian issue. There is no doubt that Saddam Hussein is directly responsible for the tragic plight of more than a million Kurds, ethnic Turks and Shiite Iraqis who are trying to escape the wrath of his Republican Guard. But Turkey is receiving the brunt of this tragedy, and world public opinion seems eager to cast her in the role of the villain.

The international media conveniently forgets that Turkey is earnestly trying to cope with this human tragedy by sheltering and feeding thousands of refugees who have sought safe haven within her borders and thousands of others who are presently piling up in the mountainous terrain just outside Turkey. The media has also forgotten that Turkey gave haven to more than 60,000 Kurdish Pesh Merga, who fled the infamous chemical weapons massacre of two years ago. Thirty thousand of them are still in Turkey, and are being sheltered and fed at the expense of Turkey's own citizens.

Despite all this, the impression given by the media is that Turkey is callously closing its borders to thousands of suffering Kurdish men, women and children, and that Turkish soldiers are firing upon them and beating them with their riffle butts. Until the recent announcement by President George Bush that safe zones for sheltering and feeding the Iraqi refugees were being set up within Iraq. Turkey was left practically alone, stretching her economic and financial capacity in order to deal with the immense problem at her gates.

One wonders what Western countries would have done if a million refugees piled up on their borders or at their airports.

The Kurds have, at times, risen against the central government and have been subdued, not always by benevolent methods. The Kurdish insurgencies of 1926 and 1930 were instigated by foreign powers that wanted to check the growth of the young republic. These were not secessionist uprisings. Even the most ardent Kurdish intellectuals in Turkey did not aspire to autonomy or an independent Kurdistan. They wanted better conditions and to establish their ethnic identity. One of them, a descendant of an important Kurdish chieftain and a close friend of mine, told me, "We are not fools. Our past was closely linked with yours; our future is also linked. We can only survive and prosper within the general growth and economic prosperity of Turkey. But we do not want to be assimilated and lose our cultural and ethnic identity."

However, in recent years, and especially since the late 1970s, the Kurdish problem has become one of separatism and secessionism. There has emerged a Partia Karkaris Kurdistan (PKK) guerrilla organization: the Kurdish Independence Party, led by Abdullah Ocalan.

PKK bands are now terrorizing south-eastern Turkey to achieve autonomy or independence from Turkey. This organization was initially supported by the KGB. Until recently, it was supported, and perhaps armed, by Hafez Assad's regime in Syria, Syria allows Mr. Ocalan to camp and train his soldiers in the Bekaa valley of Lebanon.

While the PKK is a fringe movement and does not represent or appeal to the Kurdish Turks in general, it has been a murderous nuisance for Turkey because it ties down thousands of its security forces in the same regions where the Iraqi refugees are seeking haven in Turkey.

The implications for Turkey of the recent tragedy on her borders include more than just administrative, economic and financial diffi- culties. The very integrity and future of Turkey depends on resolution of the problem. If one million Iraqi Kurds settle in Turkey, its balance and security will be significantly upset.

The tragedy should have made clear that the Kurdish issue in Turkey is different from the Kurdish problem in Iraq or Iran. For one thing, while Kurds in those countries have always been considered an ethnic group that has been accorded minority status from time to time, Kurds in Turkey have always been a part of the Turkish national mosaic of different ethnic groups.

Therefore, any hint of Kurdish autonomy or Kurdish secession or even the possibility of a buffer region evolving into an independent Kurdistan, which might eventually incorporate parts of Turkey, is abhorrent to the Turkish government and to other Turks. This is the main reason why President Turgut Özal has been against both the dismembering of Iraq and the creation of an independent Kurdistan or Shiite state. Another, equally important, apprehension is that an independent Kurdistan would swallow some three million ethnic Turks of Iraq, who constitute the majority in the oil-rich Kirkuk region.

A Kurdish state has never existed in history, and its inception would bring to the region more complications and problems than it would solve. It must be clearly understood that no Turkish government nor any of the other Turks can relinquish an inch of their land to this adventure.

Indeed, the future the Turkish Kurds depends on the ability of Turkey as a whole, and especially south-eastern Turkey, to develop and prosper. Kurdish ethnicity can only be guaranteed within the framework of the whole of the Turkish nation. Just as the ethnic identities of the Scots and Welsh are tied to an economically integrated and prosperous United Kingdom, the maintenance of the cultural identity of the Kurds depends on a sound and stable Turkey.

By ALTEMUR KILIC